PRESIDENT FORD'S LETTER
ABOUT A CERTAIN CHAPTER
IN THIS BOOK.

Because it is highly unusual for a President of the United States to permit the use of his name and letter regarding a book, some explanation should be given how this came about. The explanation appears on page 75 with the chapter "If God spoke to the 38th President."

YOUR PERFECT PARTNERSHIP

(sequel to YOU ARE GREATER THAN YOU KNOW)

LOU AUSTIN

THE PARTNERSHIP FOUNDATION
CAPON SPRINGS, WEST VA.
26823

Contents

Foreword

By the time this book is published, the author will be well into his 84th year. He was past 40 when events in his business world persuaded him that of himself he was nothing, but by working with his Creator-Partner, almost anything was possible. He regarded this approach as practical, not religious.

He was guided to set down his experiences and beliefs in the book You Are Greater Than You Know, and later in three books for children:

The Little Me and the Great Me

My Secret Power

Why and How I Was Born

The response to these books about the Partnership of Man and Maker has been impressive indeed. Without advertising or sales effort, the books have spread from one person to another, so that more than a half million copies have been published.

The author has not accepted—and will not accept —one penny in royalties or any other form of payment. He knows he has been compensated every day in a way money can never equal. Thousands of people from every state in the union and from Europe, India, Australia, New Zealand, South Africa, and Israel have written to express their gratitude for help received from the concept of the partnership of Man and Maker.

If you are unhappy now and your future looks bleak, your outlook on life will undergo an almost unbelievable change, once you come to understand your perfect partnership with your Maker.

If, on the other hand, you are wealthy and/or hold a high position of prestige and power, and yet something is lacking in your life, you will come into a feeling of inner peace and truer happiness once you realize there is a Power within you infinitely greater than your own, and that this Power is in truth your Creator-Partner. Your health will be noticeably improved and your life span increased so that you have more years to enjoy your success. Better yet, you will be a more truly beloved person.

The author believes the failure of education to teach children about this potential power within them has contributed greatly to the signs of decay and disillusionment in our country today.

Had we, as children, been taught the simple truth that the Creative Spirit spends nine months in each of us building us a body and brain, this would be the beginning of understanding. Learning that the Creative Spirit never departs from us but remains as our Partner, doing things for us we cannot do ourselves, would ripen our understanding. Once understanding ourselves, we would better understand others, looking upon them not as competitors but as brothers, each having the same Creator-Partner. There would be more love where there is now hate. Instead of Self having its way, we would choose our Creator-Partner as "boss" of our Partnership.

Introduction

When a business man, so "irreligious" as not to belong to any church, projects upon others his positive conviction that the Creator made man for the sole purpose of living in partnership with Him, and thereupon challenges the church to recapture this conception —originally Christ's—he owes an explanation as to "how he gets that way."

The writer was born in poverty and raised in an orphan asylum. His parents had belonged to no church and could only be classed as agnostics. He himself had never thought much about God one way or the other until he was past forty.

He was brought face to face with the question, not by a crisis or tragedy as is often the case, but by a series of blessings for which he could find no reasonable explanation. At 32, in pursuit of the American standard of success—money, position, fame—he had gotten himself in a hopeless business tangle, which threatened him with ruin and disgrace. Ten years later, still holding the wildcat by the tail, he emerged owner of the property involved, as yet unproductive but offering great opportunity.

He paused long enough to analyze the factors that had snatched him from disaster and presented him with so wonderful a promise. What he saw in his mind's eye, was a huge jig-saw puzzle, put together, each piece of which was absolutely necessary to bring about the good fortune that had come his way.

Examining the pieces carefully, he discovered that not one of them had been laid by himself. They had all been put there by a Power greater than his own. Not only that, he had thrown some of the key pieces aside, in the belief they did not fit into his scheme of things. This greater power had quietly but with finality restored them to their place.

At the time, he had considered what happened to him as frustrations. Now, the force of events brought home the realization, for the first time in his life, that the Creative Spirit which had formed his frame and built his brain had not departed from him on birth. This great loving Spirit remained with him as his ever-present Partner. This discovery led to the realization that his Partner was dominant in his affairs and he capitulated before it.

"If it is in the Plan to entrust me with this responsibility," he covenanted with this Power, "I promise it will not be used for personal gain, but in accordance with Your guidance."

His realization that he was the beneficiary of the workings of a Higher Power caused him to read and re-read the words of Christ. To his amazement he discovered that the Partnership Life of man and Maker was what Christ was talking about. What Christ said made sense:

"I can of myself do nothing. It is the Father within me who does the work. He tells me what to say and what to do. The spirit of God is within you. The things I do, you, too, can do."

Christ spoke no gobbledegook. The early Christians who followed his Partnership Life got so much joy out of living, it makes some of the modern versions of Christianity look like counterfeit. What greater blessing could come to the church than to have Christ's Partnership Life restored as the guiding influence in our daily lives?

What does Partnership mean?

A definition of partnership is "union in business." In a successful partnership, the partners work in mutual trust and confidence.

Marriage is a higher form of partnership. The most successful marriages result when two fit their lives together.

Surely the highest form of partnership is the union of man and Maker. Until man finds this Partnership and endeavors to live as one with the great Creative Spirit, he "begins at no beginning and works to no end."

The highest revelation that can come to you is that God is your ever-present active Partner. Said Aristotle: "The realization of the Divine in man constitutes the most absolute and all-sufficient happiness."

From the writer's experience in the workaday world stems his unshakable faith in the Partnership Life of man and Maker. For the past 43 years, things have gravitated to him in a steady stream. Not merely material things, the accumulation of which often does the family more harm than good, but things with real value: love of friends, peace of mind, good health, a deeper, more satisfying life.

His business has been built for him by kind words from kind friends. Every frustration has, in his Partner's good time, turned out to be a blessing.

His own experiences have led him to Lincoln's belief:

"The purposes of the Almighty are perfect, and must prevail, though we weak mortals may fail to accurately perceive them in advance."

* * *

It will be observed that I make frequent references to Alcoholics Anonymous. While I have not had occasion to become a member of that splendid group, one of the two Co-Founders of A.A. was a warm friend of mine. I became indebted to Bill W- and to A.A. for many things, among them a new use for the word "KISS": *K*eep *I*t *S*imple, *S*tupid.

I am not a writer, as you may have already determined, but I have tried to keep this book simple.

The Author

Does God Speak to Humans?

If you believe in prayer, you believe you can speak to God. Would you deny that God can speak to you? Does not "Be still and know that I am God" mean that God will speak to us if we become quiet and listen? It is sad that prayer has become so misunderstood. Most always, prayer is used to ask God to do what we want. As if God doesn't know what we want before we ask! When Christ said "Ask and it shall be given unto you" was he not suggesting that we ask God to guide us in our every thought, word and deed? Surely, Christ did not intend that we ask God to do our will, as if we knew better than God what was best for us.

To the one suggesting "Let us pray", Jesus might say "When did you stop praying and why?". Jesus regarded prayer as constant communion with God—not necessarily with words but in quiet recognition of God's presence, listening for His guidance. *Pray without ceasing.*

What follows here in the chapters headed "If God Spoke" are thoughts I believe came from my Partner. As explained in the book YOU ARE GREATER THAN YOU KNOW, these 'conversations' were really only thoughts flowing thru me. They were not advanced (God forbid!) as God's words. I am sure you know what I am trying to say. You have had moments when inspiring thoughts came to you. You knew you didn't think

1

them up; they came *thru* you. Brother Lawrence, the layman whose 'Practice of the Presence of God' is a classic, wrote: "Everyone is capable of such familiar conversation with God, some more, some less." Lincoln put it: "Whenever God wants me to do or not to do a certain thing, He finds a way to tell it to me." Lincoln explained one such occurrence: "It was as though written out by pen and handed to me. Hereafter, thank your Heavenly Father, not me, for this." In those too seldom moments when I was able to get myself out of the picture, these waves of God would flow into me, conferring a sense of quiet strength and peace; these were indeed inspired moments. The conviction forced itself upon me that when man invites God to take over his mind, his Partner will inhabit, lead and speak thru it. For the time being, man lives with a divine unity, God guiding, man doing. Man is wiser than he knows. If he sincerely wants to know how he stands in God, the correct answer will flow thru him. That communication is an influx of God's mind into man's mind, every moment of which is memorable. God's light shines thru us, His wisdom breathes thru our intellect, giving us ordinary people an understanding denied to wise men who would be brilliant of themselves.

In the chapters which follow, in each of which "IF GOD SPOKE" to a particular group of people, please understand that no claim is made that God is really speaking thru the author to each of the groups. In each case, the author tried to place himself in the position of that group and then strove to hear God's message. The author can lay no claim to originating this approach. It has been used effectively by others. For example, that inspired group, Alcoholics Anonymous has published a leaflet, available free to all who ask for it, entitled "IF GOD SPOKE TO A.A. HE MIGHT HAVE SAID:" The author appreciates that you thru your prayers or meditations, may receive an entirely different message.

If God Spoke to the Author Might it be Something Like This:

> What you are about to read is simply the imagining of one who has learned when he sincerely strives to become "an agent and instrument of Divine Providence" (Lincoln's words) his Partner will guide him, speak thru him and work thru him. The author believes this holds true for you, too.

From our many conversations together, I know you constantly wonder why I have blessed you so bountifully: a devoted and helpful wife, a wonderful family, a beautiful and profitable resort, a host of friends who love your family, an unusual measure of good health and happiness. I know you constantly practice Lincoln's self-questioning: "What is God driving at?" And I know you are indeed aware that "to whom much hath been given, of him shall much be required."

As your Creator-Partner, I am now urging you to take all steps necessary before your time comes to make a final accounting to Me. I have granted you well beyond your three score and ten years, and you need not be concerned that I will call on you to relinquish your work before the time has come to do so.

On the other hand, I know you realize that what you

4

have done so far and what you are now working on are but groundwork for what will be done by your children and grandchildren, who have already demonstrated an unusual sense of responsibility and an earnest desire to take up the torch. Moreover, many friends will join in this work because I will move their spirit to this end.

With the knowledge and assurance that your work will not be in vain, you should not delay in simplifying for your brother-man and his children what I have made clear to you. The fact that you are being called on to challenge a way of life handed down from one generation to another may appear to many people as a futile effort, but from your own past experiences, you know that when you work with Me, nothing is impossible.

I know you are aware of this as you stated in your first book (p.18-20) that it was only My guidance and help that brought you out of your own-made disaster. You know you would have ended up as a run-of-the-mill clerk or perhaps even a complete failure, ruined and disgraced, had I not done what most business men would admit was the impossible. I do not say this to humble you but rather to remind you that I am ever with you in this difficult undertaking ahead of you.

From your own experiences with our Partnership, you know I do not ask you to take things on blind faith. There are ample and complete reasons for you to believe in Me, and that I am indeed in Partnership with you. I had to let you go thru some agonizing crises in order to get you to understand that there was a higher power at work in you than your own.

When you learned this truth, you capitulated before Me and you pledged fervently to serve as the junior member of our Partnership. You recall that things started to happen without much delay, and they have continued to happen, with temporary setbacks, aiming toward your highest happiness.

It has been more than forty years since I first forced the truth upon you, and because you strive to be honest with yourself, you do not hesitate to admit that the only time things have gone awry is when you took over control and insisted on occupying the number one spot. I allow this, as our Partnership arrangement permits you this freedom.

Later, you learned that every time you did this, it ended in trouble for you. Even now, when you believe so unshakably in our Partnership, there are times when you have to struggle to remind yourself that a higher power than your own is dominant in your affairs. Even though there is good reason to expect more from you, I have shown my forgiveness, knowing you live in a world where even people of greater intelligence leave Me out of their daily lives or at best shunt Me off into the field of religion.

Is it not strange that so few people ask themselves "What is man?" "What am I?" Many intelligent people avoid asking these questions, preferring to immerse themselves in vast details of specialized study and cease-less activity. They become so busy they lose all idea of where they should be trying to go. Jesus' mission was to answer these questions by living in Partnership with

Me. Most people seem to have ignored his way of life and even perverted his teachings.

Many centuries later, one of My prophets, Ralph Waldo Emerson, tried to remind people of Jesus's admonition: "Don't look here or there for God. The Spirit of God is within you." Emerson sought to give this statement the importance it deserved: "That which shows God in me fortifies me. That which shows God outside of me makes me a wart and a wen. There is no longer a necessary reason for my being." How many people—even those with noble aspirations—believe that My Spirit is within them and that we are actually Partners? There is a danger of being so confident in one's own unselfish motives that one comes to rely on his own judgment. Because I cannot get to these well-meaning people, they come to disregard the need for My kind of practicality.

You know you have been guilty of this yourself. Even after you had committed the inexcusably stupid business blunder of paying $50,000 for a contract to a man who was in the receiver's hands when he took your money, and after I let you operate for ten years with this sword hanging over your head, I finally rescued you. Indeed, I went much further. I handed you the property at issue as if on a silver platter. Nevertheless, like many other well-meaning people you took it unto yourself to make a decision without consulting Me.

You acted on blind faith, without looking into the practicality of such a decision, because you deemed it a generous thing to do and would prove helpful to many people. In a laudable desire to get to the most people the health-giving mineral water you were selling, you arbitrarily reduced the price of the water from $2.00 a gallon to 25¢ a gallon. Later, you admitted you "almost lost your shirt" in this deal. But again, I turned your stupidity to good purpose. By rescuing you once more, I made your belief in My Partnership with you so unshakable you became dedicated to inform others of their partnership with Me.

I want you and all My partners to realize that I work in all things in the most practical way. Everything I do is practical. Your scientists in their laboratories discover how uniformly practical are My operations. How dependable! Consider for a moment the sun which warms you and lightens your way and which you probably take for granted. I placed the sun some 93,000,000 miles from the earth, because this was the right place—the only place—for it to be.

If the sun were a little bit closer to the earth, you might burn to death. A little bit farther and you could freeze. Is this not practical planning? When you look at the things I cause to grow, you will find the same practical planning. Do people realize that My first purpose in causing food to grow is to sustain the life I gave you? I make things delicious to eat so that you will find them appealing. I create hunger in your bodies so that you find the things I grow irresistible. Is this not practical planning?

How many people know that I build them a new body each year? Your Atomic Energy Commission revealed this discovery in a recent published report, after tracing isotopes in the human body: "in a year approximately 98% of the atoms in you now will be replaced by other atoms that you take in your air, food and drink." I cause the rain to fall not only to make things grow, to fill your lakes, rivers and oceans, but also to seep into the ground to fill deep-seated springs in the interior of the earth which later bubble up and supply pure health-giving water. Is this not practical planning?

Then, there's that invisible thing you call Air. How many people give a thought to the contributions of air to their everyday living? You have gone into the blessings of air in some detail in your first book. Suffice it to say now that without air, the joy in life would be gone. You could not see to read, [or] hear music or speech. Indeed, there would be no life. Invisible air does things for you every moment of the day and night. Is this not practical planning? But there is something more than practicality in My plan to supply you with food and water and air to renew your body. I count on your intelligence gleaning something from the harmonious way everything works together to produce your food.

It took you personally many years to understand the significance of the way I cause the seed, the soil, the sun, the rain and the air to work together in harmony and love to produce the food necessary to sustain you. Now you know that I am not limited in my ways to do either spiritual works or practical works. There is LOVE in everything I do. Love is the necessary ingredient to everything good. It is the absence of love that makes for evil. Your mission is to help people to see with their eyes as well as with their understanding that I am the Creative Spirit of Love. Love is God. God is Love. It was Love that led to the creation of human beings. I longed for a higher form of intelligence than dumb animals. I yearned to give love and receive love from this higher form of intelligence. I realized this was fraught with danger as it meant giving this new animal a brain capable of almost unlimited development and also giving him freedom. It was this combination that gave Me pause. This accounts for the long interval between the creation of dumb animals and human beings. But in the end, the love I felt for this new creature—the desire to live in Partnership with him—transcended everything.

I created human beings out of love. And because of My love for infinite variety, I created them in different skin colors and in different ethnic groups and in various parts of the earth. I gave each group its own language. This meant more than 2000 different languages that I created. But the important thing holds true. My Creative Spirit of Love remains with each human I create. I am the Creator-Partner of each of them. It is My joy to express Myself through each one in a different way. It is to be each human's joy to work his individual Partnership with Me in a way to promote his highest happiness. The Partnership should work in simple fashion: God guiding, man doing. This would be Love in action. Any other way would prove disastrous. Without love, each person would be out for himself. To have your self-part guide you instead of your God-part would result in millions of little selves each demanding his own way. Why did I let the way open for such a possibility? Because I wanted My people to love Me voluntarily. I gave them freedom to disregard Me, because neither they nor I would be happy if I had created them puppets, compelled to do My bidding. You often hear talk of a calculated risk. There can be no more calculated risk than the one I took in creating humans.

Admittedly, there is much suffering because of the decision to create man, but this too shall pass, and man will learn the purpose for which he is here. You can repay some of My blessings by helping others gain that understanding. You know that everything that has happened to you—the good and the bad—has been for this one purpose, to prove the practicality of the Partnership of Man and Maker. Some will say this is an impossible task—but you and your family will have great joy in attempting it.

Then, under My guidance and prodding, you finally put your story in book form, stressing the personal, individual partnership existing between each person and his Maker. People by the thousands responded. They expressed gratitude for the six-second exercise I inspired you to practice: With every outgoing breath, breathe out ego. With every incoming breath, breathe in God. The earnest seeker knows that this practice never fails. Yet even the earnest seeker may be distracted and fail to practice steadily, but when he resumes, he becomes more convinced that this is My plan to keep him in remembrance of our Partnership.

This does not mean that one always gets the specific thing he hopes for. Too many people mistake prayer in that way. Getting what one wants may prove the worst thing that could happen to the seeker, as you personally know from the several occasions I frustrated you in what you were attempting to do, even though your motives may have been of the best. Christ made clear that the one thing to pray for is to be able to do My will, not one's own. This means getting your self-part out of My way so that I can work My will for your eventual highest happiness. When one prays to Me for a specific purpose, he may not realize he is trying to tell Me how to run My business. He is also trying to tell Me he knows better than I what is good for him. He does not seem to realize I know what he wants before he asks Me. What is more, he doesn't realize I know better than he if what he wants is really going to prove good for him.

Because you learned these truths the hard way, you tried to set them out in your first book. You know, as you have stated it often, you did not write that book. The book was written not *by* you but *thru* you. It is helping many people because you sincerely tried to follow My guidance. When it was clear the Partnership concept was helping people to understand their nature, you followed My guidance to put the Partnership way of life in simple language so that children could grasp it. You knew that this should not be a religious book but rather an educational book, teaching self-knowledge. THE LITTLE ME AND THE GREAT ME met with remarkable response, leading to two other books to form a set of three. Second in the set was MY SE-CRET POWER, a revised version of the Cinderella Story. Then came WHY AND HOW I WAS BORN, which emphasized My part in the whole sex experience.

You know it was My influence—not yours—that brought forth from READER'S DIGEST this comment about the BORN book:

> "Most impressive, combining as it does straightforward, unevasive information and a larger frame of reference which makes sense to children."

From this series, children learn something of the part I, the Creative Spirit of Love, play in their everyday lives. They learn not only *how* they were born, but more importantly *why* they were born. And this without embarrassment to parents or teachers.

People who mistakenly give credit to the creature instead of the Creator, can learn from your experience that it was not you who influenced people to buy more than a half million copies of your books all without advertising or sales effort. This was My doing. It was My guidance that brought about your decision not to accept a penny in royalties or in any other financial way to profit from the publication of these books.

You know this was no sacrifice on your part, because I brought you payment which money could never equal. I caused thousands of people to write you of how their Partnership with Me has transformed their lives. How could money ever equal this kind of inner blessing? My purpose in reminding you of My help in the past is to fortify you with courage for what I expect of you in the future: getting education to include the teaching of self-knowledge. The fact that you have been frustrated in this for two decades should not cause you to falter now. There is much proof now that the teaching of self-knowledge is absolutely essential if Americans are to be freed from slavery to self.

Now, how about the future? Where does our Partnership go from here? I know you don't want to rest on what has been accomplished thus far. You know there is much to be done before you quit this present existence. Ask yourself why I arranged for you to come into possession of several thousand acres of land. From our conversations together, I know you have been aware I had some purpose in seeing that you got land instead of cash.

My first purpose was to relieve you of the risk money would represent to you and your family. Money does things to people. Not having money you had to borrow from friendly banks enough funds to carry you thru each season. This served to put your family on guard against desiring money for their own personal use. Each member of the family knew this and was guided accordingly.

But there was another reason why I planned for you and your family to have land. Some day—and not too distant—you will be guided to start a new kind of education. You may start with a school for teachers to learn how to teach children self-knowledge which is ignored in present day education. You may follow with a model school for children of all ages to begin learning in GET SET, HEADSTART, KINDERGARTEN.

This school may be followed by other schools for primary grades, grammar, high school, college and even post-graduate. What will make this a new education will be that its main emphasis will be centered on teaching children self-knowledge, the most important of all knowledge.

To help children learn the truth about their nature, why they feel about things the way they do, why they do the things they do, they will be taken outdoors for several hours study every day that weather permits. By actual contact with things that grow, things they have probably taken for granted before,—grass, plants, flowers, trees, insects, birds, small animals etc.—children will come to respect the Creative Spirit of Love which makes all these things possible. Then when each child realizes this invisible Creative Spirit of Love is actually within him, serving as his Creator-Partner, this will accomplish two important things: 1) give each child a sense of awe and worship and gratitude, and 2) cause him to appreciate that each of his playmates has the same Creator-Partner as he. Each will readily accept the brotherhood of man and the Fatherhood of God. With this, will come a deep sense of self-respect, the kind of self-reliance described by Emerson: "True self-reliance, the height and perfection of man—is reliance on God."

Children will learn that the Creative Spirit is the Spirit of Love, because nothing will grow and prosper except when all the necessary things: the seed, the soil, the sun, the rain and the air all work together in love and harmony. Children will learn this as quickly as they learn reading, writing and arithmetic. As each child goes further with advanced studies of the regular educational curriculum, his belief in the Creative Spirit of Love as his ever-present partner in all his everyday affairs will become unshakable.

There will be little need to admonish the child to be good. Behaving properly will come naturally to a child who has been given understanding of his nature. The child, knowing he has a God-part to his nature, will be guided by the Spirit of Love. Knowing also that his playmates also have the same God-part to their nature will make for greater harmony all around. Children will grow up not conscious of a color line or any ethnic or religious difference.

Indeed, many parents will learn from their children. Soon, educators from other parts of the country will come to study the new education, and return to their own localities to introduce the teaching of self-knowledge. It will not be many years before word of the new education and what it is doing for Americans—not only children but adults—will have its effect on foreign countries. Consider what a new attitude toward America this will inspire in people all over the world. The charge that the U.S.A. is a materialistic nation will give way to the realization that your country is leading the world in spreading the self-understanding so vital to peace and harmonious international relations.

A new way of life will result from the free open society where people live in love and harmony. How much better is this way of life than communism or fascism, where people have no freedom and are compelled to follow a dictatorship which understands little about the true nature of man. How much more effective will be the efforts of well-meaning people, even radicals, when they undergird their own idealistic efforts with this new understanding of man's nature.

Now, My partner, is what I am suggesting here too much for you? Will it be too much for your children and grandchildren to take on? If you are uncertain about this, ask yourself if I have ever asked you to do more than the possible?

When you were fighting two of the most powerful organizations in the world—the Food & Drug Administration and the American Medical Association—for a period of more than twenty years, you knew you were not alone. You knew that I was with you every step of the way. Did I not bring you victory in the U. S. District Court? And after the F.D.A. took the case to the U. S. Court of Appeals, you knew I was with you and I gave you another victory there.

Again, when your powerful adversaries started new actions, and brought you to court again, you believed with an unshakable faith that I was with you, and you were brought victory again. And even though the F.D.A. continued its attack, using ample Government funds (where you had virtually none) did I not bring to your aid highly competent physicians who worked and testified in your behalf without remuneration, simply because I caused them to believe in you and your cause?

And when in desperation, your powerful opponents tried to frame you, using their great prestige and power in inexcusably scandalous ways, you had every reason to believe your Partner was with you, guiding you and saving you from another disastrous experience. And when your enemies threatened to take the case to the U. S. Supreme Court, after losing in the U. S. Circuit Court of Appeals, confident you could not afford the financial expense of defending yourself further, did I not inspire a U. S. Appeals Judge to administer a scathing public rebuke to the F.D.A. for bringing the action in the first place and wasting large sums of Government money? Was the Judge not moved to say: "Why don't you go after the big companies making false claims? I believe this defendant. I believe the medical witnesses who have testified in his behalf"? And may this not have contributed to the refusal of the U. S. Supreme Court to hear the case?

Yet, I brought you out of this long altercation with a feeling of gratitude to both the F.D.A. and the A.M.A. You realized it required their opposition as well as the Great Depression of 1932 to make it possible for you to acquire ownership of the Springs and the resort. It is not without good reason that you believe when you work with Me, all things are possible.

You would do well to remind yourself of these events of the past. Is what I am asking of you now as difficult as those twenty years of constant harassment? You were then, as you still are, an ordinary man. You knew that without My Partnership, you had no chance to survive the determined efforts to put you out of business.

What I am setting out for you now is really not too much of a challenge. The question is: Is your faith in our Partnership as unshakable as it was when you were younger? You know the answer to that. And so do I. This time you will have your children and grandchildren and many friends to join with you in the battle to teach children from the start that the Creative Spirit of Love which formed their frame never leaves them but remains with each as Creator-Partner.

Even if you feel that your present age does not permit you much time to get started on this new education, you know your children and grandchildren and friends will take the torch from your hands and carry it on to a new way of life for the U.S.A., and eventually the world.

I would remind you that Christ gently admonished his people: "You know not what spirit you are of." So vital did he consider it for them to learn that the spirit of God—My Spirit—was within them that he sternly warned anyone speaking against the presence of My Spirit in man "it shall not be forgiven him, neither in this world, neither in the world to come." Christ is saying to you and to those who take up the torch after you: "Follow thou me."

If God Spoke to the Board of Directors Member and His Wife Might it be Something Like This:

> What you are about to read is simply the imagining of one who has learned when he sincerely strives to become "an agent and instrument of Divine Providence" (Lincoln's words) his Partner will guide him, speak thru him and work thru him. The author believes this holds true for you, too.

I am asking that you, husband and wife, two human beings, imagine that you are serving as two members of a Board of Directors appointed by Me at the time I was deliberating whether to create human beings.

This may seem like stretching imagination beyond its limit, and in a sense it is, but when you consider the little you know about how the first humans came to be, you may even conclude that there is much to learn and you will come to understand how some of the fallacies got started that men have believed for the past few thousand years of man's existence.

This is by far the most important matter any member of any Board of Directors has ever had to consider. I trust you will realize how much you can gain from it.

I am asking that you try to forget all you have come to believe about people, including yourself; that, for this

Board of Directors meeting, you hold in abeyance the presumed wisdom of PTCH (pitch)—Precedent, Tradition, Custom, Habit, so you may listen with an unfettered mind. After all, is there not ample reason to question a way of life that has produced millions of little wars in every day living, two world wars in the space of 25 years (in the latter of which 50 million people were killed), and the imminence of a third and final world war which would probably destroy the earth?

Here, then, is the situation I want you to imagine, as it existed at the time you are being asked to serve on the Board of Directors, to help Me decide whether or not to create humans, with all the enormous risks this new venture entailed.

For the meetings of this particular Board, you two are the one human male and the one human female on the Board of Directors. You are Everyman and Everywoman. The other ten members may look like humans but they have come from other planets where they have been subject to My complete control, not having the freedom I am planning to give humans. (By freedom I mean being free to do wrong things as well as right things.)

In a real sense, all the other Board members are more like angels. They can do no wrong and the life they have led has been perfect, except in the sense they derived none of the satisfaction of voluntarily giving up their will to do My will. They were partners of Mine, yet there was no perfect Partnership. There could be a perfect partnership only when the partners' respect for one another is grounded in mutual trust and understanding plus the voluntary surrender on the part of the creature to his Creator-Partner. This surrender would in turn give the creature an inner joy and self-respect resulting from self-denial that could not be achieved in any other way.

I have asked them to serve on this Board of Directors of Human Creation with you because I want you as Everyman and Everywoman to give them the benefit of your knowledge and experience as humans to make up what they lack. Their viewpoint will be influenced by what they conceive man can become, while your viewpoint will be influenced by what you perceive man actually to be.

Your views and experiences will complement one another. You will be forthright with one another, and I will base My decision in a great measure on the unanimous findings of the Board of Directors. Regardless of how long your deliberations, I will not risk creating humans until all of you have considered thoroughly whether it is worth the risk and whether the time is right.

Let me set the stage for the first meeting of the Board of Directors of Human Creation. I suspect there will be many meetings before you reach a decision. The time is several billions of years ago. I had already created the Universe. The earth was but one of the planets and stars in the Universe. So that you may have some understanding of My power and wisdom, I should remind you that the Universe contains billions of galaxies, each with billions of stars and planets, some as far apart as trillions of light years.

This Board of Directors, however, is concerned only with the earth at this time. The earth consists of the mineral kingdom, rich with minerals and chemicals for the future use of man (yet to be created), also the vegetable kingdom with plants and food, and finally the animal kingdom, consisting of marine life, insects, birds, and dumb animals from small size to huge and powerful animals weighing tons.

It is at about this time in the sequence of creation that I am calling on the Board of Directors to help Me decide whether or not to create humans. As your meetings will reveal, there is much to deliberate upon, and you are apt to hold many meetings over a period of millions—even billions—of years before reaching a final decision.

The cause of the long delay centers about the fundamental question the Board must answer. Is it safe and wise to create human beings having these two irrevocable gifts and powers: 1) a brain capable of unlimited potential growth, and 2) freedom to ignore and disregard their Creator?

Bear in mind, while you debate this, that everything was serene and peaceful on earth before the advent of man. No animal hated or persecuted another animal, though in a few cases I made some animals carnivorous, as much for experimental purposes as anything else. No animal tried to gather all the food and store it, oblivious to the needs of others. When their hunger was appeased, they were content to let others alone. "Live and let live" applied to all animals with the exception of the comparative few I was experimenting with who fed on other animal life. The largest and most powerful animals (the dinosaurs, the elephants, the rhinos, the hippos, etc.) lived on the vegetation of the earth, never harming other animals.

Before you and the other members of the Board begin your first discussion, you should know something about My nature.

I am not a physical being, yet I create the physical. Moreover, I sustain and control the physical. What do I look like? How can I look like anything if I am not physical? How can anyone refer to Me as "The Man Upstairs"? In the first place, I am not a man and secondly, I am not just upstairs. I am also right here on earth with you. Indeed, I am within you.

I will tell you what I look like, in order to help you get a better understanding of My nature. I look like one of My creations: AIR. Does that help? You can't see air. You can't see Me, yet common sense should tell you I exist. How else can you explain the power and intelligence that created and controls the Universe? I am not asking that you think of Me as God in any religious sense. While you are on the Board of Directors of Human Creation, I want your minds to be free entirely of any structured religious conceptions.

Having told you what I am not, I will tell you now what I am. This is the most vital truth you can ever learn. I am Spirit. The Spirit of Love. The Creative Spirit of Love. Utterly invisible, I am yet all-seeing, all-loving, all-wise, all-powerful. You may find it hard to believe in Me because you cannot see Me. But with the brain I have given you, you must surely come to the same conclusion as George Washington, the Father of your country: "One cannot reason without arriving at a Supreme Intelligence."

Now, along with other members of the Board of Directors of Human Creation, you are to decide whether or not I should create man. If you decide in the affirmative, you must also decide what man should look like physically, also his mate. Should they look like any of the dumb animals which I created long before them? And if so, which ones? Should male and female humans propagate in the same way as dumb animals, responding just to physical urges? Or should the Spirit of Love enter into their mating? Should humans be given a higher mentality, should some limit be put on their brain development potential? And if there is no limit placed on their mental development, dare we give them complete freedom to do as they choose, which may very well mean freedom to disregard their Creator?

This is an enormous responsibility devolving on you and the other members. You are to feel free to call upon Me when you reach an impasse. You represent the Creative Spirit of Love in action. The Spirit of Love is all-powerful and all-wise, but you and the other members of the Board may have great difficulty in reaching a unanimous conclusion that it is wise and practicable to create humans with both unlimited brain potential and complete freedom. That is why I have selected the earth for this great test. The earth is one of the smaller planets, of which there are billions in the Universe. Hopefully, it will be a manageable and successful pilot project.

You, as Everyman and Everywoman, represent all of mankind and you have been invited because of your experience to give some practical suggestions to the other members of the Board. You will also have to consider, in the event you recommend the creation of humans, whether they should be a new creation or whether they should be produced through the process of evolution. If you decide on the latter, this may take many millions of years. If you decide on an immediate creation, they can be produced in the way I produce new planets and stars. Scientists and astronomers tell you that where there was no planet yesterday, there is one today.

Now, let the Board of Directors convene and discuss these matters.

The Board of Directors Meeting

The Board gathered for its first meeting. The first question considered by the members was: If humans are to be created, what should they look like?

It required little discussion for them to agree that, because of the Creator's love of infinite variety, the Love Spirit would want different colors, different ethnic groups, different individuals, yet each with the same Creative Spirit of Love incarnated in its nature. Everyman and Everywoman suggested, and the other members agreed, that the general appearance of humans should be readily distinguishable from other animals, though perhaps with some similarities according to functional requirements, and that the determination of their various colors and ethnic groupings was a matter to be determined by the Creator.

The Board readily agreed that male and female humans should be attractive, attracted to one another. The Board took notice of the fact that in the case of dumb animals the male was in most instances more attractive physically than the female, but they decided that the human female should have the greater beauty of face and form, while the human male's greater strength and more powerful physique would have an appeal for the female.

This led to the question of mating and reproduction. The Board members agreed that this relationship in the case of humans should be of a higher nature than the mere physical instinct which guides animals. The spiritual part of human nature should join with the physical and mental in the sex act. For this purpose, it was unanimously agreed that, different from animals, the bodies of humans should be so constructed that intercourse was possible with each partner facing and embracing the other. Thus, when embracing their mates, humans would be conscious that they would also be embracing the Spirit of their Maker.

The question arose: should humans, as in the manner of animals, be restricted in the use of the sex act for reproductive purposes only? It was decided that, with humans, the sex act should also provide a natural and exalted climax to the loving union of a certain man with a certain woman.

At this point, Everyman and Everywoman felt called upon to state firmly their opinion that this may be all right in theory and plan, but in practice the sexual habits of humans could not be easily controlled. Both men and women, they contended, would be guided more by their physical appetites than the spiritual part of their nature. The other members of the Board, while recognizing this possibility, explained:

"You speak from a premise that leaves God out of man's nature. It is the Creator's plan to incarnate the Creative Spirit of Love in each human's nature, so that it will be God guiding and man doing. Humans will have the intelligence and understanding to realize that there is a Supreme Intelligence and Spirit at work in the creation of humans."

Everyman responded: "That may be the Creator's plan, but most humans will be excited only by the self-part of their nature, the physical part, and God will be left out of it altogether. Humans will be greatly influenced by their physical urges and hungers."

Angel: "You underestimate the power of God to make the Spirit of Love effective in men and women. God's plan is not to limit humans to their self-part, but to make them aware of the God-part of their nature."

Everyman and Everywoman tried to explain that men and women would regard the showing of the human body as pornographic. One of the angels suggested they swing away from a discussion of sex to one of many other problems confronting them. But one angel persisted with a long, passionate argument.

"When does sex become pornographic? To show a nude infant—is that pornography? Or is it when the child reaches 5? Or age 10? Or age 15? Or is it at 20 or maturity? Or when there is a growth of hair? What makes it pornographic except one's own thinking? Why should *this* be perfectly all right (we see a female arm) and not *this,* a few inches away (we see a female breast)? Both have been shaped by the same Creator. Surely you would not say the Creator had an evil mind. If sex is evil, does this not make the Creator of sex evil? Suppose the Creator did not make sex so mutually attractive as to be irresistible. Suppose there were no such thing as sex hunger. Suppose there was no pleasure, no ecstasy, no such thing as sex appeal. Suppose the Creator made it no more than sheer duty for a man and woman to mate if they desired children. No pleasure, only duty. What would be the outcome? Sex evils would disappear. But so would children. Human nature is such that doing one's duty is not enough.

"Is not the Creator well aware of this? Is that not why God made sex irresistible? Is that not why love between humans would be infinitely more appealing and enjoyable than sexual intercourse is to animals? With animals the one purpose of sexual intercourse is reproduction, utterly impersonal. The male in heat seeks out the first female available. He seeks to fulfil an instinct. He does what comes naturally. He mounts the female. There is no embrace. Animals cannot throw their arms around one another. Love is not a factor. Only the heat of passion instilled by their Creator as a means of reproducing others of the species.

"With humans, reproduction would be the vital factor, but there is more. Passion there would be. But humans would have a greater privilege. By understanding their true nature, the passion would grow to ecstasy, for it is the climax to a personal love transcending the physical. Without the spiritual factor the sex act is animalistic. Without the personal factor of love for each other, the thrill is fleeting. To lie in each other's arms, when all is spent, without a deep feeling of love and respect breeds self-loathing and despair.

"Great unhappiness would come from not knowing the nature of man; from not having been taught that there is within each human a self nobler than the little self that wants its own selfish, self-centered way. It is because man would not be taught his true nature that he would regard sex as evil. To see a nude human body is not pornography. It is what is in one's mind that makes it pornographic.

"With the right view, one's mind is filled with admiration and worship at the majesty and creative capability of the Creator. The sight of a beautiful female figure should fill one with reverence and admiration—not so much of the creature as of its Creator."

Everyman: "You're romancing if you believe most men would think of the Creator when gazing at a lovely female figure."

Angel: "You mean they would leave the Creator out of consideration?"

Everywoman: "Just as they will do with whatever else goes on in their lives."

Angel: "This would not be true if they had been taught as children the truth of their nature."

It was clear that the Board would not quickly arrive at a decision. Ten angels who could do no evil, think no evil, say no evil, endeavoring a meeting of minds with two humans whose life experiences and knowledge of human history left them sophisticated about man's self-centered way of life. There would be no easy solution.

They differed on the principal aspects of human life. Everyman and Everywoman stood together on what they had experienced and observed about human nature. The angels, who knew only the perfection of the partnership life of man and Maker as it could and eventually would be on earth, patiently and lovingly labored to convince the two earthly people that when man learned his true nature everything would be different. The two humans, having only their own earthly experiences to guide them, lacked the vision to understand or believe what the angels were so confident could and would come about on earth.

Everyman and Everywoman brought up various problems with which they were familiar that kept humans apart, causing hatred and suffering. They leaped from one problem to another: the struggle for money, power, position, fame, free use of sex, the abuse of alcohol and drugs, prison incarceration, poverty, the millions of wars in everyday living, the wars between nations, race wars, religious wars. To Everyman and Everywoman, this was human nature. What chance was there to attain the state of peace and serenity that the angels were talking about?

To this practical couple, who felt sure their own experiences qualified them to know what they were talking about, the angels were "do-gooders" who did not know what Everyman and Everywoman knew about human nature. What this couple could not appreciate was that the angels had a vision of what humans would

be like, once they really knew what the angels knew—
that God, the Creative Spirit of Love, was within each
human. This simple truth, unbelieved by the two practical members of the Board, would make all the difference. It would take some time to get this truth across,
but it was inevitable.

Thus, the discussions continued and halted, time and
again, over eons of time. Some of the more meaningful
discussions dealt with education, religion, health and
freedom.

On education:

Everyman: "I am troubled by the impracticality of
giving humans a dual nature—a human-part and a
God-part. How will humans come to realize their dual
nature?"

Angel: "They will learn in the same way they learn
other knowledge—through education. Children will
learn from the beginning that there is another and
greater Power within them than their own. This will
come under the teaching of self-knowledge and it will
be a branch of study all the way through primary, grammar, high school, college and post-graduate. Educators
will see the wisdom of this branch of study. Otherwise,
how will people understand themselves, let alone understand their companions? Historians will write history
with an eye to the part played by the Creator in man's
affairs, instead of presenting them as if the Creator were
absent while man made his plans and fought to carry
them out. A wise teacher will say: 'Train a child in the
way he should go, and when he is old, he will not depart
from it.' "

Everywoman: "Yes, but will children actually be trained in the way they should go? This matter of giving young people an understanding of their nature is attractive and should be helpful, but what will happen when they encounter sophisticated young people who enjoy escapisms from reality in things like LSD, marijuana, and heroin? How will they resist this appeal?"

Angel: "Their own inner strength will prove their greatest immunity. They will know from training that this is the appeal of self that bids them try these escapisms and they will know where their true strength lies."

Another angel: "The educational leaders will have to understand the nature of man. This is the only way they can have love for their students. It will be necessary to re-educate those teachers whose hearts are filled with empty phrases and whose minds are stuffed with book-knowledge. The right kind of education and the right kind of teachers are both essential if God's plan is to succeed."

Another angel: "Moreover, children should be taught to question accepted practices. If not, they will learn to imitate and to worship human authority."

Everywoman: "But parents will be uncomfortable living with children who constantly question their accepted values."

Angel: "Yet parents must recognize that to condition their child's mind to fit a particular ideology—political or religious—is almost certain to arouse man against man. By teaching children to ask questions—the Socratic method of teaching—there will be understanding, brotherhood and peace. If children are not taught from the start that all people have the same Creator-Partner, how will they ever get together in brotherhood? To learn that all people have the bodies built alike inside, though outside skin colors may vary, will be acceptable to the child, particularly if it is added that the same Creative Spirit of Love is instilled in each by their Creator-Partner."

On religion:

Everyman: "Yes, that kind of learning would be nice if you could get it into education, but that sounds too much like religion. And religion will beget more divisiveness."

Everywoman: "Humans will form hundreds of different religious sects and denominations. While clergymen will preach the universality of God's part in the lives of people, most humans will confine God to religion."

Everyman: "If public schools undertake to teach children there is a higher power at work in them, some people will protest that this is teaching religion in the public schools, which will be unconstitutional."

Angel: "Won't it be enough for man to know that God is his Partner? Is it necessary to organize hundreds of different man-made religions, with all kinds of conflicting regulations?"

Everyman: "Man will learn to grow content to go to church each Sunday, or at least on Sundays when he has nothing more desirable to do, and pay his respects to his Creator for an hour or so. Until man understands his nature he is bound to create institutions and ideologies that will guarantee him security. The very desire of the little self for security will foster division and increase antagonism."

Angel: "But surely there will be progress—slow but sure."

Everywoman: "Material progress, yes. Progress with things, but not with people. A few will accumulate power and riches and live in luxury and ease. Others will live in poverty. Until man learns his true nature, there will be poverty and misery. Some men will make slaves of other men just to make money. Except as a nebulous religious concept, they will not perceive God as having anything to do with daily affairs."

Angel: "But wouldn't it be absurd to try to confine God to religion? God created the earth several billion years before creating man. Man created religions only in the last few thousand years. How can everything God does be confined to man-made religions? God figures in every phase of a man's everyday life."

Everyman: "I agree it is stupid to try to restrict God to religious matters, but that's precisely what they will do."

Everywoman: "They will also put out an inspiring book called The Bible, and call it a closed book."

Angel: "Do you mean nothing can be added? Won't this be like saying that God no longer speaks? That's almost like saying God is dead."

Everyman: "There will be some who will say that God is dead."

Angel: "Nonsense. God is creating all the time. God is sustaining each of his creatures all the time. God speaks, not spoke. God is, not was. It is not as if God had at one time spoken and then stopped. God's Spirit is within each human and will operate whenever man gets his bloated little self out of the way. Long after the Bible is published, God will continue to speak through modern prophets. Should these be excluded on the ground that the Bible is done and finished? The proper education would cause man to inquire into the meaning of existence and the significance of life, wholly independent of religion."

On health:

Everywoman: "How about health? How will humans keep well?"

Angel: "That is another reason for knowing your nature. You should know how to keep well and vigorous, so as not to fall sick, dying long before your time. You will learn that it is the Creator's plan to renew your bodies. Your Atomic Energy Commission will issue a report, after tracing isotopes in the human body that 'in a year approximately 98% of the atoms in us now will be replaced by other atoms that we take in our air, food and drink.' "

Everyman: "This means our Creator builds us a new body each year."

Angel: "Your Creator-Partner placed in natural foods, air, and water the elements needed to replenish the body, to insure its health and vigor. The Creator made certain that you would do what is needed to carry out His plan. He planted in you a hunger for food and water and air more irresistible than the hunger for sex. Suppose the Creator had not done this. Without hunger, you probably would not bother to eat. There would be no fun in it. It would be sheer duty and you wouldn't fancy doing a chore. Indeed, in the case of air, the Creator took no chances. He did not leave breathing to you. The Creator-Partner undertakes the job of breathing for you, not only during the night when you sleep but also during the day, knowing that you would be too busy following the desires of your little selves to do the job for yourselves."

Another angel: "And don't forget that, in this matter of breathing, the Creator gave you an opportunity to work in partnership with Him. He made breathing a two-way affair, out and in. Why? Was it not to give you a chance to remind yourselves of His presence within you? So that you may practice His Presence? The air contains the very essence of God. When you breathe out, you can think 'Out, ego'. When you breathe in, you can think 'In, God'. What a simple and inspiring way to remember the truth of your nature!"

Everyman: "But it will be too much trouble for people to bother to keep well. They will take short cuts like drugs and medicines."

Everywoman: "Despite the discovery of the Atomic Energy Commission that we need to replenish our bodies with food, air, and water, we will go on looking for drug panaceas to restore us to health."

Everyman: "The whole structure of the healing art seems to be based on finding cures rather than on maintaining health and preventing illness in a natural way. The customary medical curriculum will not even include the study of nutrition. It will be obsessed with mixing and compounding drugs—antibiotics and others, some of which may seem to help, but often there are side effects more harmful than the ailment they aim to cure."

Angel: "Your failure to recognize the part played by your Creator-Partner in every phase of your lives is revealed more in your misuse of natural foods than in any other way. This all stems from the failure of the healing art to recognize the Creator's part in sustaining the life He created."

Everyman: "Yes, and this will show up in the treatment of mental ailments. Psychiatrists who will study the human side of man will dismiss his spiritual side, explaining they recognize this as 'The religious sentiment.' "

On freedom:

Angel: "Is it that we will be making a grave error in giving man freedom? Yet the Creator wants to instill in each human a portion of His own Creative Spirit of Love so that man would understand his dual nature. How else would man learn that he has both a self-part and a God-part to his nature? With the freedom granted him, he would choose to be guided by his God-part."

Everyman: "This idea of giving man freedom sounds great. But they won't understand what freedom means. They will be free to do the wrong things as well as the right. Otherwise, it would not be freedom at all. Man would be a puppet if he were compelled to do what's right. Combine this kind of freedom with a cunning, ruthless mind and you have something explosive."

Angel: "Granted that it's an extreme risk to give man freedom along with a powerful brain, but we should not overlook the kind of education each child would obtain from the time he begins, all the way through college. He will learn the truth of his nature—that, along with his little self—his man-part—is the God-part of his nature. With his intellect and reasoning, the child can conclude that his own greatest happiness lies in seeking the guidance of his God-part. In the hands of wise and understanding teachers, the truth about man's nature will permeate every phase of life. The horrible things you fear as a result of man's freedom and intelligence will not come to pass."

Everyman: "I wish I could be that optimistic, but you're counting on the unseen being as powerful with men as the seen, and this is expecting too much. You assume that man will always be aware of God's presence in him. On the contrary, all too often it will be a case of 'out of sight, out of mind.' Man will make hundreds of laws for hundreds of different crimes. He will form countless organizations to raise funds for the cure of hundreds of different ailments."

Angel: "As if almost all crime and all illness did not have their origin in one cause: departure from the Creator's simple ways to insure health, peace and a long life."

Another Angel: "You overlook the one vital factor that will balance out all of man's selfishness, self-centeredness and greed. That is the Creator's plan to give each human a portion of His own Creative Spirit. This is selfless in nature and man will, through his God-part, be able to hold his man-part in check."

Everywoman: "But God cannot be seen physically.

He is invisible Spirit, and man will soon forget that God is part of his own nature despite all the assurances of His presence. He will allow his man-part to prevail. Unless man can see God in action, in the way he sees a sculptor's hand at work, man will remain an unbeliever."

Angel: "But the hand of God at work should be visible throughout nature to those who have eyes to see, ears to hear, and minds to reason. Surely if a human is taught the truth of his nature early in life, he will realize his dependence on a Power greater than his own, and with this realization he will know that he will be happier and more successful when he allows his God-part to guide him."

Everyman: "That may be true, but there is no assurance that humans will be taught these things from the time they are children. I agree with Everywoman that unless man can see God in action, he won't believe that God's spirit is present within him. It may sound shocking to say this, but I believe that the Creator will have to show His awesome Power from time to time—in such ways as earthquakes, tornadoes, typhoons, hurricanes —in ways that may be viewed by humans as destructive even though they may at times be reconstructive. Man must always be made conscious that his own power is utterly insignificant when compared to that of God. Man must be kept conscious that there is a Supreme force—in acts of God, if you please—if only to keep man humble and in his place."

Angel: "The 'acts of God' of the kind you mention are, of course, considered natural occurrences. It would be sad indeed if it required these things—a sort of divine blackmail—to cause human beings to turn to their God-part for guidance. But man may be inviting this."

Everyman and Everywoman adhered firmly to what they believed, based on their past experiences. It was difficult for them to understand that the human behavior they had been witness to and personally experienced was mostly due to the fact that children were not taught early in life and all thru their education that the Creative Spirit which made them remains with them all thru life. Man's part is to do, but if he chooses not to follow his Partner's guidance, disaster will result. Man would misuse the talents God gave him, but only because of not knowing his nature.

In the course of the many meetings of the Board, every phase of the various problems was discussed, time and again. Despite agreement on many things, it became evident there would be no real meeting of minds on some vital factors. God, of course, had been aware of the trend of the discussions. At this point, God intervened and spoke again to the Board, directing himself mostly to Everyman and Everywoman.

GOD Speaks Again

I commend you for speaking forthrightly, expressing your views to the best of your knowledge, but for the most part you were seeing thru the eyes of your self-part. This experience on the Board of Directors of Creation should have given you the opportunity to see things more clearly thru the God-part of your nature. However, I have now come to a decision.

I shall proceed with the creation of human beings. As both Everyman and Everywoman know now, I had already decided on this step. In their present form, they are living proof of My decision. My purpose in suggesting this Board of Directors imaginary concept was in the hope it will help all humans to arrive at a truer understanding of their real nature.

The truth is that a few thousand years ago, after billions of years' deliberation on the grave risks involved, I decided to no longer hold off the creation of humans. I thereupon proceeded with this new creation—humans—giving them an intelligence greatly superior to all other animals. Even more, I made each one free. Each could live in loving Partnership with Me, their Creator-Partner, or they could disregard Me. I knew well the risks involved. I knew the first few thousand years would see much suffering and anguish.

If I was aware of this, you want to know why did I decide to proceed with the creation of humans. A natural question. The answer lies in My nature. I am the Creative Spirit of Love. My Spirit of Love created the Universe. Such a vast creation containing billions of galaxies with billions of stars and planets, all moving in a precisely, ordered way, should give anyone with a reasoning mind some idea of the power of the Spirit of Love. My heart is so full of love for the creature I am about to put on earth—My very soul so yearns to live in perfect partnership with each child I create—that I can no longer defer My plan of Partnership with each one. I acknowledge that the reasons you advance to show the risk would not succeed are logical and true in the light of your experiences. I am aware that for quite a while My partners will not act as My partners but consider themselves as individuals on their own. But in good time, the truth will prevail. Their education can not long exclude My part in the lives of My children. In good time, a few daring souls will establish that an education that omits the teaching of self-knowledge is not an education at all. Children will then be taught from the beginning that the Creative Spirit of Love which created them never departs from them but lives in eternal partnership with them. I am aware that people at first will tend to believe that each human stands on his own, and that life will seem little more than a race to get things for oneself—things like money, power, position, fame.

I know they will not entirely ignore Me. They will contrive something called religion to show that they do not ignore Me. Religion will enable them to pay their respects to Me, as their God and Maker. They will build churches—some very beautiful and costly—where people will gather to worship Me. People will sing songs of praise to Me. They will pray to Me often with noble and worthy prayers, but often also for specific personal things they desire.

It will be my unceasing hope that humans, with their intelligence and understanding, will come to realize My contribution to their everyday life, from the beating of their hearts to the transformation of their food to blood, bone, muscle, brain; also, My contribution in keeping open the lines of communication from their brain to their body, so that what they do, makes sense.

My partners, look again into your own being. Dare to challenge the authority of PTCH and come to a sensible conclusion, free of religious creed, as to why I, the Creator of the Universe, decided after billions of years of deliberation to create humans, endowing them with the gifts of intellect and freedom—even to the point of disregarding Me, their Creator-Partner. Look into My nature and see that I, the Creative Spirit of Love, work in harmony and love.

Let your mind dwell on one basic truth, which in itself should be compelling: My Creative Spirit which formed your frame, also keeps your heart beating. No physician, no scientist, no human being has ever been able to determine what keeps your heart working. There is no physical connection that will explain how your heart continues to beat. It is My Spirit of Love that keeps you alive. Yes, even you atheist and agnostic. Your heart, a physical organ, is kept going by My Spiritual power. My Spirit is REAL. I chose this way of keeping you alive without any physical or mental effort on your part so that you would realize that I am the Creative Spirit of Love, and that Love can do things seemingly impossible for man to comprehend. Rise above the stupid reasoning that if man can't do something, God can't do it, either. Can man create a Universe? Can man create himself? Can man create Air?

Man is My creation. I created you to live in partnership with Me.

"Liberation from the self" is the first step toward achieving the purpose of life. You cannot achieve the purpose for which you were created—to become ONE with your Maker—unless you first achieve liberation from the self. Man's first few thousand years may be a history of failure. It will record an era of *yielding* to self—the pursuit of money, power, position, fame. You will need only look about you to see that self, while promising much, produces only mental and physical breakdowns, shortened life spans. What good is wealth and power and fame in the face of what accompanies these sought-after pieces of tinsel?

There will be many humans who believe that only great material wealth insures happiness. They will not realize that, while riches may assure that one will not go hungry for food, wealth does not necessarily satisfy the hunger for love and friendship and appreciation and health. These people overlook the fact that I work to balance things out. This is part of the law of compensation. Too much of anything is not good for man. You need the sun. Too much sun may beget a sunstroke or heat prostration. You need rain. Too much rain can cause a flood. You need food. Too much can cause illness. Too much money can make life dull or worrisome instead of thrilling and joyful. Wealth in material things need not cause one to be poor in spirit if one has learned that he holds his wealth in trust, and uses it in harmony with My plans. On the other hand, one may be wealthy in spirit without being wealthy in material things.

Once you learn that I am your everlasting Partner, you will find yourself at home with Me in every facet of your life. You will have a joy in life, a new sense of power and love for your brother-man. You will dedicate yourself to giving this understanding to others. You cannot satisfy yourself by reasoning that you listen to your conscience. I am more than conscience, although that is one of the many virtues with which you are endowed by My Spirit of Love.

You may ask: With a world of materialism all about him, how can man keep in mind the God-part of his nature? I realized this danger and planned for it. I am giving to humans an unfailing method for assuring continual realization of My presence with and within them—a method so constant and simple that they now take it for granted and give it little or no thought. There is a simple and natural way for anyone sincerely seeking to be guided at all times by the God-part of his nature.

It is the natural process of breathing. Air is as invisible as is My Creative Spirit of Love, yet you cannot live for a moment without air. Breathing is in two parts: out and in. This is not merely a physical exercise. It is true that you breathe out in order to get rid of poisonous carbon dioxide. You breathe in fresh air in order to get the invigoration I have placed in oxygen to give you new life and strength. But that is not all. You use the outgoing breath to breathe out your man-part and you use the incoming breath to breathe in your God-part, and in doing this you are benefited far more than just physically. The six-second exercise of breathing out ego, breathing in God, can be the most beneficial exercise any human can practice.

As mentioned during the Board of Directors discussion, I could have made breathing as independent of your conscious actions as is the beating of your heart.

It is a vital part of My plan that you can cooperate with Me consciously in the breathing process. This is one of the important features of human nature that should be taught to children from a very early age.

Then you will see a new earth, where poverty, disease, misery, and hate have been conquered because man will understand his nature and why he was created. Man will know that the purpose of life is to reach Oneness with My Creative Spirit of Love—an eternal life of inner peace and joy.

Man will occasionally refer to Me as The Grand Architect. This will be gratifying as long as it complements the reference to Me as the Creator-Partner of each human.

My plan for the universe is a developing plan, not static but dynamic. It is for a growing universe, one to which humans will make a distinct contribution. Each human has the opportunity to contribute to the growing Universe. His contribution helps in making his own partnership with Me perfect.

An intelligent being, such as man, is a very important and essential part of My plan. Some work will not be done unless man does it. This means I need you as you need Me. This is why ours can be a Perfect Partnership. You can learn by knowledge and experience. Your learning will be incomplete and without depth—untried and undependable—without experience.

Therefore, you must be free to make decisions, to make mistakes, however bitter, in the physical world in order to grow in knowledge of God and God's laws— both physical laws and spiritual laws.

Our Partnership can not become perfect without your contribution to the brotherhood of man. As a human, you will become aware that all humans have the same Creator-Partner. This in itself establishes the Fatherhood of God and the Brotherhood of man. It is up to you to encourage the "God-part," the "Spirit Spark" which I have placed in you. This is one reason why I have placed so many different groups of individuals on this planet. You are to help one another to promote good in each other or perish in conflict.

If God Spoke to Educators Might it be Something Like This:

What you are about to read is simply the imagining of one who has learned when he sincerely strives to become "an agent and instrument of Divine Providence" (Lincoln's words) his Partner will guide him, speak thru him and work thru him. The author believes this holds true for you, too.

I am speaking to you about the new education and the educator of the future. What is it that I am expecting of the educator of the future? That each teacher be taught to teach children self-understanding—the most important of all knowledge. Children are entitled to know the part I, their Creator, play in their everyday lives. The new education will teach this in simple, everyday truths, free of structured religious interpretations.

Educators of the future will be free from the fear that to mention the name of God as the Power which created the child is to introduce "Religion." Quite the contrary, the child will learn it is being sustained and its growth is being brought about by the same Creative Power which spent nine months within the child, building its body and brain. The child will also learn that the lines of communication between its brain and the rest of its body are being kept open by this same Power, to insure that the child can think straight, talk straight and work straight.

How unfair to keep these truths from the child! How can I, the Creator of the universe, the earth and all who dwell thereon be confined to a man-made area called "religion"? I did not and I do not create religions. Men create religions. I create people. I sustain people. I play a part—and a most important part—in their everyday lives. The evidence is clear that I work in Partnership with each human I create. Emerson was telling you a simple truth when he observed: "The highest revelation is that God is in every man."

To keep from the child these simple truths about its nature and its Creator is more than a stupid practice. It is almost criminal, in that leaving Me out of a child's life is the cause of crimes and continual wrong-thinking and wrong-doing. This tragic omission is a byproduct of PTCH (Precedent, Tradition, Custom, Habit) and requires immediate re-examination. Much of the new education will teach children things about their lives that humans cannot change or affect. Children will recognize these truths as proof that each is a creature and beneficiary of the Creative Power and that this Power works with love.

This means the child will learn of the hidden powers within him that he is being kept quite ignorant of in today's education.

As the child matures, this new instruction will vary with each new grade from GET SET, HEADSTART,

KINDERGARDEN, PRIMARY, GRAMMAR, JUNIOR HIGH, HIGH SCHOOL, AND COLLEGE, to UNIVERSITY AND POST GRADUATE COURSES.

In the early stages, much of this instruction can take place outdoors, where the child can learn in a factual, believable way that the Creative Power causes things to grow in a loving and harmonious spirit. Grass, plants, trees, flowers, vegetables, fruits, all need the loving and harmonious contribution of seed, soil, sun, rain and air in order to grow and flourish.

This is also true of children. Even if given food, shelter, clothing and every needed material, yet without love the child would not enjoy health or proper understanding. The child needs love in order to flourish. From this kind of instruction, the child will learn that the Creative Power which made the earth and made all humans is the Spirit of Love.

For a child to learn early in life that this Creative Spirit is part of his nature and will guide him to true happiness will be the most meaningful thing the child can learn. This is true self-understanding.

Using the Socratic method of instruction by asking questions, the new education will teach children My part in their everyday lives. Here are some of the questions each child will be taught to ask itself in the new education:

1. Did I create myself?
2. Do I make myself grow?

3. Do I keep my heart beating?
4. Do I change the food I eat into blood, bone, muscle, brain?
5. Do I do the other things going on in my body all the time?
6. Is any other human doing these things for me?
7. Is there not another Power at work in me besides my own?
8. Is this other Power physical or is it spiritual?
9. Is this other Power not the same as the Power which created me?
10. Does this not prove that my Creator is also my Partner?
11. Should I not always be thankful to have such a Partner?
12. Should I not seek my Partner's guidance in all things?

These questions will elicit the truth and children will be helped enormously by learning the truth of the greatness, the wisdom and the power of their Creator-Partner. Moreover, the truth will come to them in such a way as to be irresistible and not to be forgotten.

Every experienced teacher, particularly at primary level, knows what it means to have in the class a student who is troublesome to the point of exasperation. Suppose within the space of one week, this sort of "itch" or troublemaker was changed into a helper, would you not be grateful for such a transformation in which you had a part?

This kind of experience has taken place in quite a few

public schools all over the country, to the benefit of the child, the class, the teacher, the principal, the school, the neighborhood, and also the child's parents. This remarkable change took place because the child learned some very simple truths about his own nature. He learned from the book THE LITTLE ME AND THE GREAT ME:

1. He was not all bad. He was not just a self-centered Little ME
2. There was a good part to his nature—MY part, THE GREAT ME.
3. Every person has both a Little ME and a GREAT ME. Even his teacher, even the principal, even his parents.
4. He learned he was free to choose between being a Little ME or being a GREAT ME. The choice was entirely up to him.
5. He learned he was happier when he chose to be a GREAT ME.
6. He learned people liked him better when he was a GREAT ME.
7. He learned he made other people happy when he was a GREAT ME.
8. He learned that things worked better when he was a GREAT ME.

Just learning these truths about himself made the great difference. Not alone for him, but for the teacher, the class and the school.

To help children understand their nature, I inspired a plain, ordinary layman to write the story of THE

LITTLE ME AND THE GREAT ME (with the understanding that neither he nor his family were to profit financially in any way from the publication of the book). Children all over the country responded to the simple approach of the book, and for many reasons:

1. Children enjoy blowing out the self-centered Little Me, the way they blow out candles on a birthday cake.
2. They acquire a sense of being loved.
3. The idea of having two MEs makes sense to them. They know when they behave like a Little ME.
4. They get a big lift from knowing they have a GREAT ME.
5. Being free to decide which ME to be is very meaningful to them.
6. Children enjoy having their parents learn of THE LITTLE ME and THE GREAT ME thru them.
7. Children prefer to discipline themselves rather than to be disciplined by teacher or parents. They are thrilled when the discovery of self-knowledge leads to self-discipline.
8. Children respond more naturally to a positive approach than to a negative one.

Reports from teachers in different parts of the country indicate most favorable results. That most children will react this way has been proved for nearly two decades by the use of this book in public schools and in private homes. Interestingly enough, many parents learn from the book what their education failed to teach them, many of them commenting: "This book may have been written for children but it has helped me understand my true nature."

With this understanding of their nature, children know how helpful it is to seek their Partner's guidance. They learn that their own Little ME is terribly inadequate to advise them compared to The GREAT ME within them. They learn that in all things the choice is between one's Little ME and his Partner, The GREAT ME. All this better understanding is brought about without a hint of structured religion.

Virtually every person who has come into the understanding there is another Power working in him besides his own, has sought to spread this understanding to his brother-man. Without this understanding of self, how could one understand others? Eleanor Roosevelt, known in her time as "First Lady of the World" wrote: "First, I think, is self-knowledge. One must be willing to have knowledge of oneself. You must understand truthfully what makes you do things or feel things."

Those who would confine the part I play in children's lives to that segment known as "religion" do a great disservice to all people. THE LITTLE ME AND THE GREAT ME is no religious concept. It is factual truth that everyone has both a Little ME and a GREAT ME. Their Little ME is their self-part. The GREAT ME is their God-part. Some would limit My part to conscience. My Spirit includes all the virtues, not just conscience. Each person is entitled to know that My wisdom, My power, My love are all available to him. I will not fail anyone who earnestly seeks to make of his self-part, in Lincoln's words "an agent and instrument of divine Providence."

In this new education, the teacher can make the difference between success and failure. If the teacher looks upon this unfamiliar instruction with a closed mind, this may be reflected in the way the children react to it. If, on the other hand, the teacher first reads THE LITTLE ME AND THE GREAT ME more than once and decides to give it a fair trial, encouraging the children to join in the action where called for, no outside persuasion will be needed to prove that the new instruction will work.

To teach a child that the Creative Spirit of Love which spent nine months in him, building his body and brain, remains with the child to serve as his Creator-Partner does not introduce a "religious" concept. It is pure scientific fact. Nor is it a "religious" concept to teach the child that his Creator-Partner builds him a new body each year, as was recently revealed by a report of the Atomic Energy Commission. The child is entitled to know these scientific facts about himself. Present day education keeps these vital truths from the child.

The great scientist, Albert Einstein, tried to tell you that liberation from the self is the real measure of a person's value. How can anyone liberate himself from the self, if he has not learned that his nature is made up of another and higher self than the self-centered and egotistical self each person has?

When you teach the children in your class the truth of their nature, they will love you for it and will be helped by you. You will feel rewarded for contributing to the creation of the new education.

An open mind is necessary to learn the truth. A closed mind is difficult to approach. Particularly is this true in the field of education because most professional educators are held fast in the clasp of PTCH (Precedent, Tradition, Custom, Habit).

The truth will stand: I created humans to live in Partnership with Me. If properly taught, each child will seek its higher part. Those seeking My guidance will eventually come upon the truth. Each will come to know himself, and by knowing himself he will come to know and love his brother-man. Therein lies the only chance for a happy and successful life.

As an educator, you are dealing with the most important people in the world: children. Each newborn babe comes fresh from Me, his Creator. It is up to you to teach him of his partnership with his Creator.

What a beautiful and rewarding experience this will prove for you. To see children, early in life, grasp the understanding of the two Mes in their nature, and to be witness to the tremendous change this brings in children's behavior is wonderful in itself. But to see how parents learn about their own nature from their children will seem like a miracle to you.

I promise the educator of the future a new kind of joy in life. Teaching will not be boring. It will be broadening for both pupil and teacher. It will instill love in the child for the teacher, for his classmates and for all mankind. It will teach children the truth of their nature. This truth will bring you the love and gratitude of the children's parents and community. The truth about My part in the everyday lives of My human partners will change the lives and attitudes of all who learn the truth. People will no longer set Me aside for an hour on a Sunday morn. They will realize the contribution I make to their lives every moment and how to make greater use of it. Their hearts will be filled with love and gratitude for the truth.

The teacher of the future will be mindful of Emerson's description of the qualified teacher: "The Spirit alone can teach . . . The man on whom the soul descends, thru whom the soul speaks, alone can teach . . . But the man who aims to speak as books enable, as synods use, as the fashion guides, and as interest commands, babbles. Let him hush."

The new educator will not keep the truth from children, but will take joy in revealing the simple things I and I alone can do for all humans. Your school will be a different place. Your community will be a different place, and you will have a part in saving your nation. This I promise the *educator* of the future who joins with Me in the glorious and heartwarming responsibility of teaching children of all ages.

If God Spoke to the Lawyer and the Judge Might it be Something Like This:

> What you are about to read is simply the imagining of one who has learned when he sincerely strives to become "an agent and instrument of Divine Providence" (Lincoln's words) his Partner will guide him, speak thru him and work thru him. The author believes this holds true for you, too.

In your concentration on the laws of men, I am sure you do not intend to disregard My part in these man-made laws. My part is sometime spoken of as mercy, but My laws transcend mercy. If people knew My laws, there would be less need of man-made laws. My laws are almost entirely preventive. Man-made laws emphasize the punitive. I am sure you will agree that if wrong-doing can be prevented, it would be more desirable than waiting for the wrong to be committed and then punishing the offender.

Why are not more people familiar with My laws? The answer is they were never educated to learn of My laws. Yet My laws are simple and easy to understand. You may persist: "If God's laws are easy to understand, why are they not known to more people?" This is a good question and one which I would like to discuss with you now.

It is ironic that this difficulty exists because of the two greatest forces for good in your civilization. One is religion, the other education. Unwittingly, these two noble institutions are preventing people from learning My simple laws. I'll explain shortly. The effect of this unwitting misunderstanding is disastrous. Just to cite some of the harm done is to include almost all crimes, misuse of drugs and alcohol, hatred and persecution of humans by humans, millions of wars in everyday living, wars between nations, and the imminent danger of a nuclear war that might destroy the earth.

As I am the Creator of the earth and all that live thereon, you can appreciate why I am so greatly disturbed about this misunderstanding. I am appealing to you who are familiar with man-made laws to familiarize yourself with My simple laws which would eliminate most crimes and unhappiness and bring about the kind of understanding that promotes love and goodwill among all My children.

To first understand My laws, you must know something about Me, the Creator of the Universe and Sustainer of all who live therein. Your keen mind has discerned that I am not a physical being—not a man with a white beard sitting on a throne. You know that I am pure Spirit, invisible and shapeless. Yet My Spirit creates the physical, and controls the physical! Is this hard to understand and believe? It should not be for you. You will arrive at this truth by the process of elimination, in the way your first President, George

Washington did: "One cannot reason without arriving at a Supreme Intelligence." If not physical, if not visible, the Creator must be spiritual.

The fact that I am not visible to human eyes makes it difficult for many people to believe I exist. Others take My existence on blind faith. It is gratifying that 98% of the American people believe in Me. Just what they believe about My part in their everyday lives is the question. How many believe that My Creative Spirit of Love is actually within them, serving as their ever-present Partner? It seems that the general opinion is that after I created them, I left them on their own, going off in outer space somewhere where I wait to sit in judgment on them after they die.

As a thoughtful person, you have probably asked yourself on more than one occasion "What is the purpose of life? Why did God create humans?" Evidently, the decision to create humans was a comparatively recent decision, as the earth was approximately five billion years old before the first human life appeared. Why did I create humans when everything was serene and peaceful on earth before man's coming? Why did I take this risk? What did I hope for and expect from the advent of man? Or do you feel that the evolution of man took place without My having anything to do with it?

To believe the latter necessitates also believing that man evolved on his own without My approval or participation. Surely, your clear mind can't go along with that fallacious and inadequate reasoning. This would not only leave Me out of man's creation and development. It would have you believe that some apes (from which man is said to have evolved on his own) did somehow improve and transform their nature, change their body structure, acquire a mind capable of almost unlimited development and become an entirely different animal, physically, mentally, emotionally, spiritually. If some apes could do this, how about the rest of the apes? Why do they remain the same as their ancestors started, millions of years ago? Your analytical mind must have difficulty accepting this.

If the evolution of man from the ape had some basis in fact, would it not be because I, the Creator of both dumb and human animals, planned it that way? This would at once raise humans from the possibility of chance creation to having been definitely planned by Me, their Creator. This brings us back to the question: "Why did I create humans? What was My purpose?"

The answer is because I am the Creative Spirit of Love, and I planned to live in loving Partnership with a higher form of intelligence than dumb animals offered. In your legal work, you have become familiar with the phrase "a calculated risk." There has never been—nor will there ever be—a calculated risk as great as that having to do with the creation of humans. If you'll look into the interval of time between the appearance of animals and the advent of humans, you will discover a lapse of several billion years.

Why such a vast time lapse? Because I was aware of the great risk of creating man and giving him that most hazardous combination of 1) a brain capable of almost unlimited development, and 2) freedom to disregard Me, his Maker.

This was a combination fraught with tremendous risk, and it demanded long meditation and deliberation before a decision could be reached. In the few thousand years of man's existence, ample proof has been provided to warrant the long meditations and deliberations that preceded man's creation. Much misery and suffering have come with man's way of life.

Now, where do religion and education figure in preventing people from learning My simple laws that would prevent man's many difficulties? First, let us consider religion. Your dictionaries describe religion as "Man's relation to his Maker." This is simple and in itself poses no difficulty. But how about structured religions? Far from being simple and easily understood, man-made religions number several hundred different sects and denominations. Does this not in itself indicate divisiveness?

Wars have erupted between structured religions. Millions of people have been persecuted and killed in the name of religion. Much of the killing has been committed in My name and in the name of Jesus Christ—My most perfect Partner, who never even once mentioned the word religion. He gave his life in the effort to teach people their true nature—that the Creative Spirit of Love which created them, never departs from them but remains with each in an everlasting Partnership of Man and Maker.

Christ based his belief in man's partnership with the Creative Spirit of Love on simple factual evidence. Moreover, he lived in perfect Partnership with Me, demonstrating that when a human lives selflessly, My

Spirit will think thru him, speak thru him, and work thru him, achieving Oneness with My Creative Spirit. People should remember that Christ was no theologian. He was a carpenter, who was divinely inspired. His way of life—which he said you and everyone could live—was followed by many great men and women.

Some 300 years after Christ was crucified for his simple, unstructured beliefs, formal religion took over his beliefs and from them built an organized church. Since then, many other religions have been established, making his simple teachings into formal religions, differing with other Christian sects and denominations in ways that would have saddened and distressed My Partner, whose main theme was: "Why do you call me good? There is only one that is good—the Father. Of myself, I can do nothing. It is the Father within me. He tells me what to say and what to do. The Spirit of God is in you. The things I do, you, too can do."

Now, as to education. When formal education began in the U.S.A. the Founding Fathers were determined that formal religion would have no place in education, so conscious were they of the dangers to free democratic government posed by structured religions. All of the Founding Fathers had a deep belief in a Supreme Being, entirely independent of formal religion. They each maintained this personal belief in God, while they insisted the Constitution keep church and state separate.

Nevertheless, the Founding Fathers wanted to demonstrate their personal belief in God, as witness every coin and money bill bore the words "In God we trust." The Declaration of Independence explicitly refers to

God, and while the Constitution does not, implicit in this document is a belief in a Supreme Intelligence. The national anthem contained the words "In God is our trust." The oath taken by every public officer closes with the words "So help me God."

Public schools, under the supervision of thoughtful professional educators freely admitted mention of My name in an informal way, free from religious connotation. However, with the passing of time, there was growing friction between the different established religions, and some professional educators became timid about allowing My name—God—to be mentioned in public schools.

The result was when some forward-looking educators introduced the teaching of self-knowledge in some public schools, they were halted by the Board of Education. The principals and teachers wrote letters relating the remarkable experiences when young children learned their dual nature, but the Board of Education was adamant claiming the book used was a religious book because it mentioned God.

The point that weighed with the Board of Education was not whether children were helped by learning something about their nature. The evidence was clear that some of the children had been transformed by learning that My Spirit of Love was within them serving as their Partner. What the Board was influenced by was that the mention of My name or just mentioning there was a higher power in each child than his own made the whole approach "religious."

The result of this mixup between religion and education is that children—even college students—are taught every kind of knowledge except the most important of all: self-knowledge. The Board of Education may not have realized that they were in effect confining Me—the Creator of the Universe and all living things therein —to a small area in man's life known as "religion."

This defeats the very purpose I had in creating humans. I planned to live in Partnership with each of My children. Education was to be the natural place for My children to learn that My Spirit of Love which formed their frame and built their brain remains with them, serving as their Creator-Partner. They would learn our Partnership works very simply: "God guiding, man doing." Children would readily accept the teaching of self-knowledge, realizing the vital part I take in keeping their heart beating and doing all the other things in their body which they cannot do for themselves.

But the Board by confining Me to religion, did more harm than they realize. Most crimes, most wrongdoings, most suffering have their origin in man's lack of self-understanding. If children learned of My presence within them, they would seek My guidance in all things the way Lincoln did, and as did also the Founding Fathers before him.

You who are trained in the laws of men may also know My simple laws which encourage man to yield his will and wisdom to that of his Maker, in this way finding his highest happiness. You may probably know of My law which says "Too much of anything is not good for man." Too much of the sun, too much rain, too much food, too much money, too much power—not any of these in excess is good for any person.

Another of My laws is that any wrongdoing carries with the pleasure it gives, its own punishment. As My partner Emerson put it, "Crime and punishment grow out of one stem." No one—and I mean no one—can reap the benefit of any wrongdoing without also reaping the punishment. The punishment may come long after the wrongdoing and it may seem dissociated from it, but it is inevitable.

In your practice of law and in the meting out of justice, I beg you to consider whether the people involved have ever been taught understanding of their nature. If they have not, be merciful and see they get instruction. You do not help people if you fail to point out to them the truth of My presence within them. This is factual, not religious teaching.

You love your country, and you cannot be blind to the alarming signs of decay showing up in almost every facet of its affairs. The way out is the teaching of self-knowledge all the way thru education beginning as early as possible in the child's life. Your intelligence tells you there is some Power other than man's which created and sustains him. Children are entitled to learn this truth, as a matter of self-knowledge free of religious connotation. Knowledge of the law should mean knowing My law as well as that of man-made laws.

You know that Abraham Lincoln was a lawyer, and while he never joined a specific religion, he had an unshakable belief in Me. He continually sought My guidance and wisdom, asking himself "What is God driving at?" He courageously admonished the Americans of his day that they had become slaves to self: "We must disenthrall ourselves and then we will save our nation." To disenthrall, as you know, is to become free of slavery to self.

As lawyers, you must be impressed with Lincoln's forthright statement as President, regarding his own wisdom and that of Mine:

> "I should be the veriest shallow and self-conceited blockhead upon the footstool, if in my discharge of the duties that are put upon me in this place, I should hope to get along without the wisdom that comes from God and not from man."

My lawyer partner: For your country's sake, for the sake of your brother-man, and for your own happiness, I plead with you to do what you can to promote the teaching of self-knowledge in your public schools. As lawyers, you know ways can be found to teach children the truth of My part in their lives free of structured religious interpretations. To teach American children their true nature, so that they have an honest understanding of what makes them do things and feel things is surely no violation of the Constitution.

Consider the wisdom of your great scientist, Albert Einstein: "The true value of a human being is determined primarily by the measure and the sense in which he has attained *liberation from the self.*" (underscoring Mine).

Seek My presence within your own heart and mind, and as with Lincoln, I will fill you with wisdom and power and love for all mankind.

If God Spoke to the 38th President Might it be Something Like This?

> What you are about to read is simply the imagining of one who has learned when he sincerely strives to become "an agent and instrument of Divine Providence" (Lincoln's words) his Partner will guide him, speak thru him and work thru him. The author believes this holds true for you, too.

If ever a man should ask himself the question which the 16th President continually asked himself: "What is God driving at?" it is you, Gerald Ford, sworn in as President, this 9th day of August, 1974.

A few short months before you took the oath of office as the 38th President, neither you nor any of the more than 200 million people in the U.S.A. had the slightest idea events would shape themselves so as to elevate you—then one of 500 Congressmen—to the most powerful office in the world.

One need not be a religious person to realize that a Power greater than his own or that of any man, has brought about this startling event—so startling as to have been considered utterly impossible less than a year ago.

Because you, Gerald Ford, have always been honest with yourself, I can speak to you, believing you will take on, if you have not already done so, the practice of the 16th President in talking with Me regularly. Abraham Lincoln was not a "religious" man in the sense people speak of religion. He had no specific religion, never having joined an established church. Yet I am revealing to you that no person since Christ lived in closer Partnership with Me than Abraham Lincoln.

Surely, at this very moment, you are asking yourself "What is God driving at?" The first answer that may come to you is the answer that came to President Lincoln, when he first took the oath of office as President. This first answer was "God wants you to preserve the Union."

What your 16th President said more than a century ago remains true today: "America is the last best hope of earth." My first desire in placing you here at this time is for you to preserve your beloved country.

How? What are the first steps to bring about the preservation of the U.S.A.? Are these to control inflation, promote business, reduce taxes, restore confidence? These things are all desirable, and your experience as a practical politician will keep you aware of the need to bring them about.

But are these the first steps to be taken? The first step is the same one your 16th President sought to take but failed. Lincoln tried to lead his people back to God. "We have forgotten God" was his outspoken comment to the American people. Lincoln did not make the mistake so common with most Americans of restricting Me to the realm of religion. He knew that God transcends religion no matter what its structure.

Because Lincoln realized that the Creator could not be confined to man's religious concepts, he consulted Me on all matters in his life. He followed Christ's way of seeking My guidance and My will in all things, believing he should not be satisfied with the wisdom of men when God's infinite wisdom was available to him. To Lincoln, consulting with God was a matter of understanding one's nature. Your 16th President believed with an unshakable faith that the Creative Spirit of his Maker was within him, part of his very nature, as was true of every person. "The kingdom of God is within you" the Master Teacher had assured you.

Lincoln believed every child should learn the truth about himself. He did not get it in formal education (of which he had only six months) but because he wanted this more than anything else, he got it in direct guidance from Me. Lincoln believed the place for a child to learn the truth of his nature was in education, so that each child will understand that his Partnership with God is simple truth, not just a religious concept.

It was clear to Lincoln that the person who does not know that My Creative Spirit of Love is part of his nature is at a distinct disadvantage. Lincoln's contemporary, the great American philosopher, Ralph Waldo Emerson, called it "a defect . . . that the Moral Nature, that Law of Laws whose revelations introduce greatness —yea, God Himself—into the open soul, *is not explored as the fountain of the established teaching in society.*"

Almost all of man's troubles stem from this defect, as without My wisdom and guidance, man leans on his own understanding. This limitation, which man puts on himself, leads him into the pursuit of material things to insure his happiness and a successful life. His God becomes money and power. History is replete with illustrations where men with talents and courage achieve success for a brief span, only to meet a tragic end. You, Gerald Ford, became the 38th President because the 37th President trusted his own wisdom, apparently feeling he had no need of Mine.

Contrast this attitude of the 37th President with that of the 16th President. Abraham Lincoln openly acknowledged:

> "I should be the veriest shallow and self-conceited blockhead upon the footstool, if in my discharge of the duties that are put upon me in this place, I should hope to get along without the wisdom that *comes from God, and not from men.*"

When you, Mr. President, dedicate your efforts to giving children early in life the truth about their nature, you will be laying the groundwork for a way of life that will arrest the decay that has been going on in your country for many years. Lincoln warned of this decay repeatedly, even to the extent of proclaiming a day of "National Humiliation, Fasting and Prayer."

Do you, Mr. 38th President, have the courage to say the same things to the American people as did the 16th President? Your people need these truths now more than ever. Members of Congress need these truths now more than ever. I suggest you read and call attention of your people to Lincoln's words (page 350).

You will gain heart from these courageous words of

the 16th President, and you will dare to remind the American people of Lincoln's belief that My Spirit was within him as it is in all humans. Moreover, you will find in Lincoln's words the way to save the nation: "We must disenthrall ourselves and then we will save our nation." To disenthrall is, as you know, to free oneself from slavery to self. The person who has not learned of My Presence and Partnership with him is in danger of becoming a slave to self.

People will be looking for My Presence within you, Mr. 38th President. When you speak, they will be hoping to hear Me speaking thru you. When they see you, they will be hoping to see evidence of My invisible Spirit of Love. Every word you read of Lincoln in the few pages (beginning p. 350) will help you in your struggle to save the nation. People will rally to your aid in everything you say and do, as long as they feel My presence within you. This is the way I created them and they will respond to that of God in you.

When you promote the teaching of self-knowledge in the public schools, so that children can understand their nature the way Lincoln understood himself, you will find that parents will learn from their children that My Creative Spirit of Love which gave them life sustains them from moment to moment. Your whole nation will respond to their President as if with one voice.

Your closing words when you took your oath of office as the 38th President were "God helping me, I will not let you down." You were talking to the American people. I am speaking to you now, assuring you that you do have My help. I will be with you always and I will not let you down.

August 27, 1974

Dear Mr. Austin:

Dean Burch has shown me the words you were
inspired to write as an additional chapter in your
forthcoming book, Your Perfect Partnership.

I am deeply grateful for your goodwill and I
assure you that my petition for Divine guidance
expressed the very core of my belief. My
greatest hope is that all my efforts for this
country and its people will be rooted in the
same source.

With warm personal regards,

Sincerely,

Gerald R. Ford

Mr. Lou Austin
Capon Springs and Farms
Capon Springs, West Virginia 26823

Author's note:

The letter from President Ford regarding this particular chapter in the book was quite unexpected. We are most grateful for it, revealing as it does the President's simple yet profound spiritual understanding and his constant search for guidance from his Creator-Partner.

The chapter and the President's letter came about in a rather unusual way: On the morning of August 9th, the day Gerald Ford was to be sworn in as President of the United States, I awoke about four A.M. and I reached for the pencil and pad I keep handy, as I realized a message was coming thru from my Creator-Partner.

What came thru was this chapter "If God Spoke to the 38th President." The manuscript for the book YOUR PERFECT PARTNERSHIP was about ready to turn over to the printer but had been strangely held up. After I typed the pencilled memorandum that had come thru so early in the morning of August 9th, I naturally assumed it was to be incorporated in the book, wondering if this was not the reason for the strange delay in getting the manuscript to the printer.

As is my custom, I submitted the proposed new chapter to about a dozen friends here to get their reaction. Each of them approved holding up the book if necessary in order to insert the chapter in the forthcoming book. Even more interestingly, however, each of them without exception volunteered the suggestion that a typewritten copy of the chapter be sent to President Ford even before the book was published.

I sent the proposed chapter to the White House. A friendly and understanding Counsellor to the President deemed it worthy to be called to the President's attention. The letter from President Ford followed in a few days.

We Americans are free to differ with our President as to his politics, his treatment of inflation, taxes, big business, big labor, amnesty and other problems, but should not all of us feel a sincere sense of gratitude for the mysterious way in which God performed before our very eyes one of His great wonders?

In the wake of the depressing years that have engulfed this nation recently, God has, as it were, plucked a man from almost out of nowhere to become our President, apparently because He felt our greatest need was for a leader of complete integrity, whose "petition for Divine guidance expressed the very core of my belief" and whose "greatest hope is that all my efforts for this country and its people will be rooted in the same source."

Should not our individual differences as to the material problems that confront our nation give way to the evidence of God's desire that this country still remain "the last best hope of earth" as Lincoln believed it was God's plan to be? Have we not clear evidence on the record of our new President's expressions and behavior since taking office—and indeed on the open record of Mr. Ford's utterances and behavior during his entire career—that his earnest desire is to follow the way and faith of Lincoln, whom he regarded as America's greatest President? Surely, one of Lincoln's most unforgettable phrases is burned indelibly in the mind and heart of President Ford: "Encompassed by vast difficulties as I am, nothing shall be wanting on my part, if sustained by God and the American people."

Let us rise above the materialism that has surrounded us for all too long, and follow Lincoln's way of seeking God's guidance on all things. This common sense practice will bring our people together in harmony and love.

I should add that on receiving the letter from President Ford, the question arose as to whether it should be included in the book (then in the course of being set in type). I wrote to the White House, asking for permission to include the President's letter along with the new chapter.

I explained that this was not a commercial proposition. No one has ever received or will receive royalties or other financial payment or material compensation for our books. The Partnership Foundation has no payroll, all services and overhead being provided without charge, so that all receipts go directly to the Foundation, whose purpose is to promote the concept of the Partnership of Man and Maker, in the way Lincoln believed—free of structured religious interpretation.

The permission we sought was granted, and this is how President Ford's letter came to be included in this book.

If God Spoke to Married Couples Might it be Something Like This:

What you are about to read is simply the imagining of one who has learned when he sincerely strives to become "an agent and instrument of Divine Providence" (Lincoln's words) his Partner will guide him, speak thru him and work thru him. The author believes this holds true for you, too.

Those who go by statistics say you have two strikes against your marriage lasting. They quote figures to show that two out of five marriages end in divorce; soon, it will be one out of two. Some cynics go further, reasoning that most of those who remain married are not really happy together, but remain married because it would be more trouble to get a divorce.

This situation has convinced many people that the institution of marriage is a failure. As the Creator of people, who planned marriage and family life as part of the Partnership of Man and Maker, I must speak to this unfortunate and mistaken conclusion.

I will speak forthrightly and, it may seem, critically, though it is not My aim to sit in judgment on anyone at this time. What is responsible for the failure of marriage is the way of life that has been handed down from one generation to another. Your present generation is really the victim of this ill-chosen way of life.

Some who know, call for a re-examination of PTCH (pronounced pitch) which stands for Precedent, Tradition, Custom, Habit. Respectable as these are, research into them is required now and then lest they become obsolete and resist progress and better understanding.

Try to keep in mind you are My children. I created both of you. You were nothing—you did not even exist until I selected that one certain sperm and that one certain ovum to form a certain cell (one out of a billion possibilities) and then spent nine months in you building you a body and a brain. I sustain you both. I am in truth your Partner. I love you both. I want your marriage to work.

To make your marriage work, the necessary ingredient now missing must be restored. That missing ingredient is Me, your Creator-Partner. You may believe you believe in Me—God. But do you really believe that I am the Creative Spirit of Love? Do you really believe that My Spirit is within you as part of your very being? This means there are two separate though integrated forces at work in you—two separate parts to your nature. One of these is your God-part, the part that was first at work in you, creating you. The second is your self-part—the part you think of as you, and which most people believe is the one and only part of their nature. It is this enormous fallacy that PTCH has handed down from one generation to another, which is responsible for almost all of man's troubles.

Is it not obvious that both Creator and creature are within you, working as a Partnership? Is there any truth more vital for any person to know about himself than this simple truth? Yet it is left out of education. All other knowledge is taught but not self-knowledge. Professional educators leave Me out of education, insisting at the behest of PTCH that I must be confined to "religion."

Why not pause right here and consider just some of the things which I, your Creator-Partner, am doing this very instant in your body to keep you going? Things you cannot possibly do for yourself or which anyone else can do for you. There is no end to them. Let Me remind you of a few:

1) It is My Spirit of Love in you that keeps your heart beating. 2) I transform the food you enjoy into blood, bone, muscle, brain, etc. 3) I work your sewage system, despite your unwitting interferences. 4) I revitalize your body so that you can reproduce and enjoy your mate completely. 5) I keep open the lines of communication between your brain and the rest of your body so that you can think straight, talk straight, work straight. 6) I breathe for you every moment the breath of life. This should be meaningful to you at least in your hours of sleep when you are unconscious. But why go on? You just can't do without Me working within you—not for a moment.

Nor is there any way you can evade acknowledging My presence in you and My part in your everyday affairs, if you are honest with yourself. Oh, there are some smart folks who try to avoid admitting the simple truth by attributing everything I do in your body to biology—the forces of Nature.

Who created biology if not My Creative Spirit of Love? Biology is simply My plan to keep things moving and developing in life, just as I planned reproduction. My chief reason for creating sex was to keep My world peopled, so that I wouldn't constantly have to go thru the process of forming the physical structure of man (and woman) as I did at the beginning. Biology is My tool. Everything you see in nature, everything that is going on in your body right now is the result of My plan. Can you really doubt that this is the work of a Power infinitely greater than man's? Or do you find it easier to believe it is all the work of happenstance and that in fact there is no plan?

I find it amusing when a grown person who should know better turns on Me. Picture, if you will, a newborn infant shaking his fist at the heavens, and crying out "I don't believe in you. I don't need any God to lean on. I can stand on my own." Some who wouldn't speak this way nevertheless live this way. It's really not their fault. They were not taught self-knowledge in school or college. The reason given by professional educators for this failure is truly ironic. They say to teach self-knowledge would involve admitting there is a higher power at work in each person and this would introduce religion into education.

How absurd! By what reasoning could the Creator be confined to a pigeonhole earmarked "religion"? I created the earth several billion years ago, whereas I delayed creating humans until a comparatively short time ago and they in turn contrived many different structured religions out of the simple natural religion made up of man's relation to Me, his Maker.

Why have I gone into this matter with you now? Because all the troubles you have experienced in your married life are mostly due to your not having learned of My presence and Partnership with you. I am not talking religion. I am talking simple, everyday truth. Is it not ironic that religious divisiveness is responsible in great measure for the failure of education to include the teaching of self-knowledge in your public schools?

If you can listen to me in a "Father to child" relationship, you will surely understand better what I am saying to you. It is important that you do this if we are to save your marriage and turn it into an understanding, loving experience. I suggest you go back in your mind to the first time you two came to believe you loved one another. You may sincerely believe that your coming together was of your own doing, and that it was your own initiative that brought about your marriage. This is only partially true, as it overlooks My part in your lives. It was My Creative Spirit of Love that arranged for your paths to cross. You decided to follow the same path together and this resulted in your marriage.

This was My Creative Spirit of Love at work. To regard your coming together as happenstance is to discount our Partnership. You may ask why I do not use My wisdom and power to compel your better understanding of My part in your lives. The answer to that lies in the freedom I give to each human being to choose his way of life. If freedom means anything, it means being free to do the wrong thing as well as the right.

Your professional educators have exercised their freedom to ignore the part I play in the everyday lives of My children. These well-meaning men and women need a different education. They must learn to distinguish, as did the Founding Fathers, between what is structured religion and what is self-knowledge. The Founding Fathers had an unshakable belief in a Supreme Being but were adamant against the teaching of religion in public schools. They regarded their belief in a Supreme Intelligence not so much a matter of religion as of reasoning and common sense.

When you first decided you loved one another, do you remember what was the principal factor in your love for one another? Was it sex—the desire to make your flesh one? This would be a natural reaction. Is there a more powerful urge I have implanted in all living creatures than the sex urge? This is particularly so with two humans in love. This is the way I planned it. Yet most marriages founder on the rocks of sex, due to sex incompatabilities and misunderstandings. These occur because My Creative Spirit of Love is left out of sex relationships. My Spirit is left out because most people were not taught that I am a part of their nature. Without this vital self-knowledge, the sex relationship is without spiritual understanding. Sex becomes almost completely physical.

This spells sure disaster. How can a marriage last without the participation of the Creative Spirit of Love? Indeed, even the physical enjoyment of the sex act soon loses its appeal without the spirit of love.

Some marriages have difficulty surviving because of money—either the absence of it or a surplus of it. You may find it hard to believe that too much money often causes more trouble than too little. Married couples who practice their Partnership with Me have no difficulty getting along with less money than others would feel was actually needed.

Where true love takes second place to love of money, where My Spirit is given lip service on a Sunday morning, the desire for more money can play havoc. This love of money can spring from the man's notion of a "successful" life, or it can come from his wife's desire for comfort, luxury and social standing. Where it's the man's idea, the wife may thru faith and love, temper the husband's money-gathering ambitions. If, however, it's the wife who loves money more than she loves Me, her Creator-Partner, she may get what she's after and it may satisfy her for a while, but what about the ultimate success of her marriage?

Being able to transcend "the Joneses" cannot insure a happy marriage, or a "successful life." My children should all learn of My unbreakable law which says: "Too much of anything is not good for man—or woman." Only a few people hold to this law but they are among the happiest. Most of the people who claim to believe in ME don't hold to that law. They hold to Me with one hand and to Mammon with the other. This is not a tenable position and in an emergency, they come to Me on their knees.

It is too tragic to be amusing that some think they can outsmart this law. They delude themselves they'll know how to handle the extra money, not realizing it's the very gathering of more and more money that can't work for their happiness. If, as he gathers, he shares with others,—with those who have helped him and with those in need, so that he is in truth not gathering for himself, but for his brother-man, then the joy that comes from sharing will be his.

What I am saying to you is simple: Money, above your own actual needs, is deluding. It can give you happiness only when you start giving it away. This is not to say one should not work for a living. Every able-bodied person should do that. This gives him the feeling of making his own way, of sustaining himself and his family. This is a natural and worthy desire. It's when he is led to believe that the more he makes the more "successful" he is regarded and the more respected he becomes, that he conflicts with My Law that too much of anything is not good for anyone. People think more is better, but the truth is enough is best.

Because of PTCH, you have been persuaded to honor wealthy people. They are pointed out with a sort of reverence: "He's worth several millions. He owns several big estates." Instead of honoring him, you should feel compassion for him. PTCH has sold him a bill of goods. All too often, he traded in his happiness for money. He has to put on the front of being happy. Inside, there is neither happiness nor peace of mind. Oh, he has material security. So, too, does the miser who, sitting under a low lamp, counts his money. What kind of security is that? If he didn't believe that most people envy him his wealth, he would have nothing to give him satisfaction. If the American people learn to lose respect for the gatherer of money, some wealthy people would be driven to suicide, unless they first learn the true nature of man and why I created him.

I am not directing My anger at any of My children. It is the stupid nonsensical notion, fostered by PTCH, that I created man to engage in a race for money, or power, or fame. If you were on My Board of Directors at the time we were deliberating whether to create man, would you have ascribed to money-gathering a good reason for creating humans? Would you have thought highly of the current practice of paying honors and respect to the wealthy as symbols of success in life?

Let Me suggest to the wife who keeps prodding her husband either in subtle ways or by nagging that she ask herself whether more money would make up for the tension and loss of vigorous health threatening her husband by an unceasing pursuit of money. If he shows a real sense of responsibility in the support of his family, and at the same time shows real affection for his wife and children, it could be risky business to persuade him to devote more time and thought to the gathering of money.

It may well be that neither of you know just where to start to regain the happiness you first enjoyed in your married life. Let Me direct you to a very simple beginning. It has to do with the art of touching. Learn the magic I have placed in the human touch. It will work wonders for any couple sincerely desiring to regain the love that was once theirs. The next time the opportunity offers itself, reach out and touch your mate. A touch of the hand or arm or shoulder as you pass by or sit near may be enough. You need not say a word. You may not even have to look at your mate. Just a touch, only a touch, but how meaningful it can become.

It may be that you will find this first step not easy to take. Let Me direct you to a way that never fails if sincerely tried. It's the six-second exercise: Breathe out Ego, breathe in God. With your outgoing breath, think to yourself "Out ego." With the incoming breath, think "In God." Practice this six-second exercise. This natural exercise is My plan to help you get your self-part out of the way of your God-part. It's your self-part that finds it hard to give love.

To give love comes natural and easy for your God-part, for God is the Creative Spirit of Love. Almost all your unhappiness can be traced to your self-part. When you know for a certainty that your self-part is but a small part of your nature—though it tends to believe it is the whole thing—you are likely to appreciate the advantage of having for a Partner, an all-powerful, all-wise and loving Creator. My presence and Partnership makes it easy for you to reach out and touch your mate.

It won't be long before your self-part finds happiness in becoming a channel for your God-part to work thru with love. Indeed, your self-part will become transformed, as Lincoln stated, into "an agent and instrument of divine Providence." The simple touch will soon become as meaningful to you as to your mate. A loving touch finds its own ways to follow up. You both will look for ways to be kind to one another, as you did when you first met. This does not mean you believe all the things the Madison Avenue advertising experts tell you, though they do make sense playing up the appeal of a clean breath and a clean body. If these are so essential in your association with others, how much more so do they apply in your relations with one another?

In creating humans, I planned that the appeal of a woman for a man should be quite different from the appeal of a man for a woman. I made it natural for a woman to be drawn to a man for his strength, for his courage and ability to perform physical work. On the other hand, I made it natural for a man to be drawn to feminine charms and the beauty of face and female form. You need no one to tell you that I planned for husband and wife to be drawn to each other physically.

I implanted in both man and wife the urge to make their flesh one. Both should know, however, that this urge in humans transcends the physical. There must be a spiritual foundation to married and family life. I would not have made the sexual urge so irresistible for humans, otherwise. Of all the senses, is not the sense of touch (feeling) the most compelling?

With dumb animals, I limited the sex urge to physical instinct, as the one purpose there was to reproduce. However, I did experiment with a few animals to whom I gave some spiritual understanding. These animals would not mate except with the one chosen companion. All others were rejected. With the arrival of offspring, the family life of these animals was loving and devoted. Take geese for example. Geese mate for life. Mother goose chooses the site for a nest, builds it, lays and hatches the eggs. Father goose fearlessly stands on guard and drives away any invader, man or beast—or at least tries to. When the young are hatched, Father Goose is as fussy with the goslings as a mother hen. With some other animals, I had the expectant father help build the nest and join in bringing food to the young ones.

With the success of these experiments, I proceeded with My plan to instill in man and wife My Spirit of love, which, with their higher intelligence would insure the success of marriage and family life. Therefore, I gave to humans a deeper loving dimension in their sexual relationship than that which I gave to dumb animals. Sex was to be more than an irresistible method to keep My earth peopled. For humans, it would also provide a natural and exalted climax to the loving union of one certain man and one certain woman. The spiritual contribution to the loving union of man and wife added an ecstasy that mere physical participation was bereft of. Without true love, physical intercourse is distinctly limited in gratification.

It is in this area that many marriages founder. And it is in the art of touching that much can be done to heal the breach. With husband and wife who feel themselves drifting apart, a loving touch may serve to recall earlier days when a touch would lead to an embrace, and the embrace to a gentle caress, with the husband stroking his wife's head and face, her curving neck and bosom, all naturally leading to the most sensitive and expressively enchanting touch of all—the blissful spot I planned for· true lovers to meet.

But there must first be a desire for understanding.

For this, your mind should be allowed to dwell on your mate's good qualities, not the deficiencies and shortcomings. Let your mind center on the things for which you should be grateful and which you have probably come to take for granted. Because it is your self-part that is critical, it is well for you to let your God-part take over and look kindly on your mate, reaching out to touch a hand with loving kindness.

With time, the art of touching opens other doors, which often stay closed if touching is not practiced. Take a situation where either husband or wife is stimulated by a certain book, play, story or person, picture or whatever, yet no outlet for the aroused emotion is made available, thus inviting an extra-marital experience. By its very nature this tempting situation must end in regret even if it ever produced the pleasure it promises. If the art of touching had been practiced, the stimulation aroused would have been directed to the other partner and the emotions of both would be satisfied in a natural and loving way. Nor would their happiness be limited to the specific incident, but would promote better understanding and affection in the days to come.

For couples who have allowed themselves to lose close ties to one another, the art of touching may seem too difficult and improbable of success. It may be that they have become separated by a chasm of misunderstanding, with no bridge of communication. However difficult it may seem, such a bridge can be built when either of them—preferably both, but at least one—is prepared to use the simple, effective tool: touching in a spirit of genuine love. How is this to be done? Get the self-part out of the way and the Creator-Partner will show the way. Remember, what may seem impossible for your self-part is readily achieved by your God-part. You need but strive for liberation from the self and I will rise to help you.

When you have disenthralled yourself—freed yourself from slavery to self—you will come to believe in your true self and practice the art of touching. And when the results seem miraculous, you will know it is not you who is doing the touching and loving but your Creator-Partner working thru you. My Creative Spirit of Love will inspire communication between you both, so that the love you had for one another in your earlier days will make itself more noble in every phase of your lives. Just to reach out and touch will cause you to grow and explore and love. But there is also reaching within to touch the heart.

In every other respect than sex, people come to know their prospective mate very well before marriage. They know each other's looks, smiles, voices, general appearance, viewpoints, and the impressions others have of them. These all contribute to the feeling of love each has for the other. In short, they know each other in all respects except the most intimate and important: Will their sex relationship prove compatible?

The importance of this question can be better appreciated when it is learned that sex incompatibility is the greatest cause of marriage failure. Should two people sign up for life without first knowing surely that their sex life will be compatible and loving and gratifying?

The one answer to this very important question is for

both the man and the woman contemplating marriage to first make sure each understands his or her own nature. Self-knowledge would give each the assurance that within them is a Power infinitely greater than their own. This is My own Creative Spirit of Love, which gave them life. This understanding of self would extend to understanding one another. Their sex relations would fall into this pattern of understanding and helping one another.

But how about those married couples who have only recently come into this self-understanding? How can they arrive at a truer understanding of what their sex relations should be? The art of touching will lead them to this. Gentle and loving helpfulness one for the other will come naturally. Each will be wanting to help the other. Getting the self out of God's way is the answer to all problems. The Creative Spirit of Love which planned the right sex relationship for married couples will bring this about if the self is submerged to the God-part of your nature. God works gently and with love.

My presence and Partnership may give the necessary help in cases of impotence and lack of feeling in sexual relationship. After all, I created sex. I planted the urge in you both to make your flesh one. I planned the steps leading up to this: the touching, the fondling and caressing. I planned for My spirit—the Creative Spirit of Love—to join in every step of the way.

When you leave My Spirit out, you may for a while be satisfied with mere physical friction but it won't be for long. The reason is simple: I made you more than animal. I made My Spirit part of your nature. When I am left out of your thoughts and plans, some deficiency in your life begins to show up. This is true in all aspects of your lives and your sex life is no exception. There can be no true thrill in sex, let alone ecstasy, without the love that only the Creative Spirit can provide.

Love that does not encompass the spiritual is really only physical love. Touching someone without the spiritual part of love may seem better than not touching, but it has distinct limitations. Whereas the love that combines spiritual with physical feeling gives unspeakable joy to both giver and receiver.

While the most compelling of all the senses is the sense of touch, Love, the invisible selfless feeling of the heart, is far more potent than all the other senses put together. Surely, you must realize it is My Creative Spirit of Love that gives you the power to love and reproduce.

Touching brings about a revelation of the divine within human experience. Husband and wife really want to love one another. My presence inspires that belief. When you touch one another, you are also touching God. When you believe in My presence you come to believe more in yourselves and in one another. Without the Spirit of Love, your feeling for one another declines. Let Me remind you of Acts 17: 27-28): " . . . to seek God, and it might be, *touch* and find Him, though indeed He is not far from each one of us, for in Him we live and move, in Him we exist."

Nor is touching to be restricted to one another.

Touching the arm or shoulder of a member of the family or a friend is a gesture of friendship and goodwill. The ease and naturalness with which you are able to do this promotes the ease with which you two touch one another. Practice the art of touching and the two of you will never be the same. With this practice, you come to seek My guidance in all things, and this makes all things different. My Spirit touches you and you now see Me—the Creative Spirit of Love—in each person. You become more open, more human.

Your self-part's way of isolation, loneliness, greed, suspicion and hate depart from you for good, and you feel yourselves touched by the needs of others. You want to be the means of their finding light in the dark. You communicate to them your belief in My presence and they discover for themselves the light that shines in the dark.

My Spirit within you offers liberation and inner peace. This is more than a coincidence. It is an unshakable conviction that things are right with you. You are most human—and most divine—when you are working your Partnership with Me. When you touch someone, you celebrate My presence within you and the one you touch. This is creative loving. When you feel close to Me, you are close to one another and to other people.

You touch God most deeply when you touch others in selfless love. My presence within you can be as personal as your experience of loving and being loved. Love is the extension of others into your world and you into theirs. My Spirit is within you not as an invisible person or as "The Man Upstairs" but as the Creative Spirit of Love, serving as your Creator-Partner.

You will know that when you become deeply involved with Me, you touch the world around you and people will respond. To believe in God is to believe in the divine presence within you. Your faith becomes bright and beautiful. You joyously help others to understand that God is within them. You have learned to touch flesh and with it life, work, love from the inside. You recognize all of them for what they are: My plan for your way of life.

Another joy that will be restored to you, greatly enhanced, by the practice of touching, will be the quiet inner tranquility that will come upon you from little acts of consideration and self-sacrifice for your mate. Giving this kind of joy to your married partner begets even greater joy for you from your eternal Partner.

Everything is changed though things may still look the same. Thru the art of touching, you come to understand what the Master Teacher meant when he said "The spirit of God is within you."

* * *

If God Spoke to the Money Gatherer Might it be Something Like This:

> What you are about to read is simply the imagining of one who has learned when he sincerely strives to become "an agent and instrument of Divine Providence" (Lincoln's words) his Partner will guide him, speak thru him and work thru him. The author believes this holds true for you, too.

AN AESOP'S FABLE FOR BUSINESS MEN

Once upon a time there was a very successful businessman. He was a self-made man. Not in the sense that he actually created himself, although some people thought he gave that impression. He had worked his way to the top from a rather humble start and enjoyed the admiration which this accomplishment evoked.

"Success" in the judgment of our self-made hero was appraised pretty much by two things: money and position. He did not believe people inquired: "Does anyone love this man?" or "Does this man love anyone other than himself?" These things had nothing to do with success, in his opinion. "Success" was a simple matter—nothing complex about it. If you had money and a position of authority and power, you were a "success".

Our "successful" man hobnobbed with other "successful" men, and it was assumed that these men with money and position were happy. But alas, this was not always the case. In fact, it was rarely so. Most of our "successful" man's "successful" friends seemed to have some secret sorrow which neither money nor position could relieve.

In the case of our hero, it was a growing uncomfortable feeling that something was missing; that he had not made his life worthwhile; that he had somehow not used his talents to their greatest extent, or at least had not used them for the benefit of anyone but himself.

He gave to charity regularly, often accepting posts to raise money which demanded both time and effort without compensation. He attended church and was a generous giver, but somehow he could not get away from the persistent thought that this activity and generosity were a sort of window-dressing. Publicity in newspapers and on radio and TV helped dim this guilty feeling, but could not quite erase it.

One day, the same blow that strikes so many nationally successful men—heart attack—struck down our self-made man. For weeks he lay on the flat of his back. At that he was lucky. Once during his illness, it appeared that his heart stopped beating but energetic work by skillful medical men got the heart going again.

During that brief interval, when it seemed to others as if he were gone, our hero had what some would call a dream. However, *he* knew it was not merely a dream. He was sure· that something actually happened, although he could not understand how it could occur in the few seconds when he hovered between life and death.

He heard a voice saying, "This is your partner."

He responded, "Then you must be Uncle Sam, to whom I must pay out taxes each year." This was one of his favorite complaints. He didn't enjoy paying taxes.

The voice came back gently: "No, it's not Uncle Sam. But you're close. Not uncle, but father. *The* Father, the Creative Spirit which gave you life."

"What do you mean when you say you're my partner?" asked the "successful" man.

"I do all the things necessary to keep you going."

"I've made my own way. I don't need anyone to keep me going."

"Your heart just stopped. Who started it again?"

"The doctors."

"Ask the doctors who keeps the heart beating."

"What do you mean?"

"The doctors will tell you they don't know. They can't explain what causes the heart to beat. There is no physical explanation."

"What makes the heart beat then?"

"I do."

"Who are you?"

"The Creative Spirit. I am Spirit but I control the physical. In fact, I make the physical. I created you."

"You say you're my partner. I don't understand what you mean."

"Keeping your heart beating is not the only thing I do for you. I keep the lines of communication open between your brain—which I built—and the rest of your body, so that you can think straight and talk straight. You could be a babbling half-wit if I didn't do my part."

Our "successful" man was jolted. Then his reaction seemed to shape itself in his mind. "You know, I never gave that a thought."

"That's true of most people," replied the voice, "and that's what's causing you trouble. You just don't understand your own nature."

"I always understood these were biological doings," persisted our hero, but the voice again challenged:

"Who created things biological? Suppose people denied you credit for your factory products, claiming they're being made by automation, ignoring the fact that it was you who put in the automation and took all the other steps necessary to manufacture."

"I get the point."

"Would you be interested in learning what else I do for our partnership?"

"You'll probably make me ashamed I hadn't thought of them before."

"It might be even worse than that. You may end up realizing that the body you call yours is not yours at all. It's mine."

"You wouldn't go so far as to say that!"

"*I* wouldn't, but *you* may. And you would be right."

"But I'm the one who makes the decisions. I do the things I choose to do."

"Yes, that's true. That's part of My plan. But that's because I have made you trustee of your body—or the body you call yours."

"This is getting a little too much for me. You really mean that this body which I have always believed mine is really not mine but yours?"

"That's correct, and now I must explain the situation. First, you'll agree *you* did not create your body. *I* did. I formed your frame, starting with a cell which I made by uniting one certain male sperm with one certain female ovum. I'll give you the great satisfaction of knowing that you were chosen out of billions."

"What do you mean?"

"I had to select one out of some 250 million sperms from your father's life blood, and one out of some 10,000 ova on your mother's side. This combination that would produce you was one out of 2500 billion. So you now know that you are a truly chosen person. You are here for a purpose."

"That's tremendous. What a help to the morale!"

"Once the cells of your creation were joined, I started building you a body. You are familiar with some of the steps in this creative job, so I won't go into them now."

"I wish I hadn't regarded this as just biological."

"This was not *your* fault, but that of education."

"Why would education cover this up instead of frankly teaching this is the work of the Creative Spirit?"

"Education is fearful of anything sounding religious."

"But if what you say is true, it is not religious. It's simple truth."

"Education is guilty of far worse errors than that."

"In which way?"

"When teaching physiology, including sex education,

children are made familiar with the creation of a baby. Thus they learn the Creative Power is at work building a human body."

"Yes, this is evidence that you are present in the child doing your work."

"And that is just where a tragic omission occurs. When the child emerges from the womb as a live infant, educators seem content to leave the child under the impression—utterly false—that the Creative Power which was present forming the baby's body thereupon departs, leaving the child entirely on his own."

"I see what you mean."

"But do you? How could I leave the child? Who would be there to make the child grow? Parents can't make the child grow. Nor can anyone else. The matter of growth is entirely in *My* hands. Humans can care for the child, feed and clothe and house it, but they are helpless to bring about growth."

"I see."

"Consider all the other things that have to be done to keep the child going—the things I am doing for you and other grownups. I started to tell you of some of these. Or would it embarrass you to learn of them?"

"Not if they are facts. I'm not one to run from the truth."

"Good. You already know I created the body you call yours. Have you thought that I am the one responsible for keeping that body going? I work 24 hours a day at this. Not only do I keep your heart beating day and night, I breathe for you during the hours when you're taking it easy, sleeping. When you're hard at work making money, it is I who keep open the lines of communication so that your brain can solve problems and you can be a success."

"It's a strange thing we never think of this."

"It's even stranger that you have been able to kid yourself into taking credit for things that really belong to Me. You don't even give Me credit for doing the dirty work."

"What do you mean—dirty work?"

"You enjoy eating—several times a day. It's fun for you, eating tasty foods which incidentally I have caused to grow. You never once think that it is I who has to do the work of breaking down the food you enjoy eating, through an intricate process no man-made factory could ever duplicate, in which fruits, vegetables, meat, milk, grains, nuts and other foods are transformed into blood, bone, muscle, brain."

"That's right. We never give it a thought—almost never."

"And as long as you asked about dirty work, it is I who makes your sewage system function (which incidentally I was the one to build), so that poisonous waste is not left in your system to do you harm. If you don't think that's dirty work, you haven't really let your mind dwell on it."

"You were right. I am embarrassed. In fact, I'm humiliated. Why have we been taking these things for granted?"

"The fault lies with your education. And I'm telling you right now that until you change your system of education, things will not get any better. In fact, they're getting worse, as you must know from the increase in juvenile delinquency, crime and mental breakdowns."

"You lay this at the door of education?"

"Think about it. Your system of education leaves out the most important thing for a person to learn."

"You mean while teaching a lot of other knowledge, it teaches no self-knowledge?"

"Precisely. There is nothing more vital for children to learn early in life than the truth about their nature. Today's education ignores My part in the outer world as well as in the child's physical and mental make-up."

"A half-truth can be more damaging than an outright lie."

"I created man and gave him a brain so that he could reason, but education slants his thinking so that he considers only his own handiwork. Even worse, the child is left to believe that the intelligence and power of the Creative Spirit which built him and gave him life is no longer available to him, and that he must forever be on his own."

"Is that why the world is in such a mess?"

"There's the reason—as simple as ABC."

"Could it have been a mistake to have given us the freedom to choose wrong things?"

"That was one of the things I deliberated over for some billions of years before I decided to go ahead and create man. I finally took a calculated risk, counting on man's brain and my Spirit combining to properly direct his choices."

"This doesn't seem to have worked thus far."

"But had I not given man freedom to choose the

wrong things, he would not be truly free. If freedom means anything, it means being free to do the wrong as well as the right thing."

"I agree. Otherwise, we would be like puppets on a string."

"Perhaps you may have observed that I retain My powers of balance. As soon as man does the wrong thing, I set out to balance the error and re-establish the correct balance. Some of you term this the law of compensation."

"This takes time, though."

"Yes, as you look at time. As I measure time, you are here on earth but a fleeting second. However, in cases where man harms his own body—or is harmed accidentally—I set out at once to correct the damage. If, for instance, your skin is torn or a bone broken, I rush new material (which I make in your own body) to the wounded spot, and effect a prompt recovery."

"Further proof of your presence within man. I am beginning to realize what you mean when you say a faulty education is to blame for much of the world's troubles."

"The question is, are you realizing by now whose body it really is—yours or Mine?"

"Just from the few examples you've given, I'm catching on."

"If a partnership is composed of two partners,—one who built the physical plant and the machinery which operates it; who works 24 hours a day to keep it going, even if he·remains a silent partner and lets the other fellow run the business without consulting him, whose was the greater contribution to the business? Whose plant is it?"

"You've made your case, but you know I can't see you."

"Must you see Me?"

"Well, it would be easier to believe you are real if I could see you."

"You demand to see Me with your eyes. Can you not see Me with your understanding?"

"I should be able to, but if I could see you as I see the hand of a sculptor at work, it would eliminate all doubt."

"You have eyes and see not, ears and hear not, yes, even a soul and understand not."

"That is not as true as it was a few minutes ago."

"You are in a hospital. Babies are born here every day. When you look at a new-born infant, don't you see Me? When you see dedicated doctors and nurses at work, don't you see Me? Or are you so fiscal-minded that you think only in terms of money?"

"I mean no irreverence, Mr. Creator, but if you were a human being, I would say you certainly know how to hurt a fellow."

"Why?"

"After all, no one ever told me I was a partner in a partnership. I thought I was my own boss. That's the way I looked at things and I acted that way. The partner you speak of was not only silent, He was invisible. He never showed up, He never said a word or communicated with me. Not once was I apprised of the partnership. This partner never let me in on the truth.

He could have said 'Look here, we're in this thing together. I have even more interest in the success of this business than you.' How was I to know? To have someone suddenly appear and claim to be my partner when as far as I've been concerned he might be both deaf and dumb and on another planet—I'm not sure it's fair to give me such a panning."

"That's what I like to hear. You've got your spunk up. Now, how about doing something to correct the situation? Wouldn't you be interested to know what I'm expecting of you—why I started your heart beating again?"

"I'm excited. More so than I have ever been about any business project. I want to do something worthwhile before I go," said the self-made man.

"We'll work together—a real partnership team. I need you as you need Me. But I must warn you. Your friends may turn against you. They may crucify you. It's been done before. The greatest partner I ever had, whose mission it was to tell people of their own partnership with Me, he suffered the penalty. Then, there was Lincoln, who told his countrymen repeatedly that without My guidance he could not succeed; with it he could not fail."

"But surely they wouldn't pick on a nobody like me."

"I like your humility. But let Me assure you that even if this means your passing from this scene, you will return. This one existence is not the end of things. The whole purpose of life is to reach oneness between the self-part of you and your God-part, for the two partners to become ONE. One existence is not enough to do this. Many will be needed before you reach the pinnacle. You have lived before. You shall live again. Your spirit will return and inhabit another body, so that the struggle to achieve oneness with your Partner may go on."

"I'm not sure I can go for that. That sounds like reincarnation and that's beyond me."

"Wouldn't it be an unfair Creator to allow crippled and half-wits to be born, suffer and die—dismissing them with a wave of the hand as if to say 'Sorry, this is all for you.' This is just part of their battle for Oneness. They too shall return and try again—the next time probably in sound wholesome bodies."

"I have no fear now. Tell me what you want me to do."

"It's really simple, though you will find it difficult to get it done. I want you to join with other successful men to wage a battle to give each child early in life understanding of the truth of his nature; to let each know he is in partnership with Me."

"This sounds simple and I'm sure it would be simple if children were started off right, but to try to get men of my acquaintance to believe it, that's a formidable task," said the business man.

"But now that you believe, is the task any more formidable than some you and your friends have overcome in their drive for money?"

"I'm afraid it is. I shouldn't say afraid, because with you as our Partner, we will know no fear. But I know these men. They believe in themselves and what I will be trying to do will, in their opinion, be robbing them of credit and giving it to God. This won't sit well with them."

"The more difficult the task the greater the inner joy

in achieving it. While most of your friends will turn you down, one or two will join with you, and yours will be the strength of a hundred ordinary men."

"As I understand it, our job will be to get education to include self-knowledge in its curriculum."

"Precisely. They teach all other forms of knowledge but leave out the teaching of self-knowledge. Does that make sense?" asked The Voice.

"It does not. If a person cannot understand himself, how can he understand others? A child should learn at once that he is made up of two separate entities—separate but integrated. One is a little self all his own, entirely different from any self that ever lived. This little self by nature is self-centered and selfish, always wanting to be first, craving attention, security and all that goes with it."

"True, and when he learns this, he should be taught also that this is not *all* of his nature. Compensating for this selfish and self-centered part, there is his share of the Universal Spirit—selfless, loving, seeking the happiness of others—the only means of obtaining true happiness for the self. To help him understand the presence within him of the Universal Creative Spirit, he should be taught to examine into the things being done for him constantly by this other Power—things that keep him going, yet which he cannot do for himself."

"As it comes to me now, life is a constant and unceasing battle between one's self and his God-part. Unless a person knows this and understands its implications, he will not know true happiness. He will always let the desires of his little self rule him. This is bound to bring him into conflict with the little self of others who are also leading misguided lives."

"He will not know the purpose of life. He will not know why I created him. Had he been taught the truth about his nature, he would understand what Lincoln meant when he said: 'We are all agents and instruments of divine Providence.'"

"Not one person in thousands knows this. This is the root cause of almost all our troubles. I wonder why this has not been taught before. We have many brainy men but they seem to have been occupied in finding ways to sustain man's exaltation of his ego, not in seeking the truth of man's nature," said the man.

"Perhaps you understand better why there was an interval of several billion years after I created dumb animals before I decided to create man. The danger of giving man such a powerful brain capable of almost unlimited development—combined with the freedom I gave him to do what he chooses—this required the utmost deliberation."

"And the mess we have made of things justifies your long deliberation. Do you feel that the future of man will justify your ultimate decision?"

"This is one of the reasons I started your heart beating again. I am counting on your help to justify My decision. You are a successful man. You are well regarded. You can help direct men to the truth about their nature. People today are trying to solve their problems by use of *their* intelligence alone, leaving out of the picture the infinitely greater intelligence I place at their disposal all the time."

"How can they be expected to understand this if it was not taught them in their education?"

"That's the point. Over the years, many men with understanding have tried to point to the truth of man's nature. In your country, Washington, Jefferson, Franklin, Lincoln and Emerson did what they could. Lincoln and Emerson never ceased to call attention to and *live* the life of partnership with the Creative Spirit. Had it not been for Franklin, the United States might not have been formed. At the time the 13 colonies were trying to form a union and not getting anywhere because the representatives of each state were looking at the situation from the standpoint of their individual states, Franklin was inspired to arise and say: 'In this situation of this assembly, groping as it were, in the dark to find political truth, and scarce able to distinguish it when presented to us, how has it happened, Sir, that we have not hitherto once thought of applying to the Father of Lights to illuminate our understandings?' "

"That's interesting. What happened?"

"From that moment, harmony prevailed and in the space of seventy working days thereafter, the Constitution was prepared. The delegates had completed the framework of a system accurately described by a historian: 'new in human experience, well-suited to the American situation, equitable as between states, and so wisely conceived that it has survived over 180 years, during which all important nations of the world have revised their forms of government.' "

"I can understand now why Gladstone, the great British statesman wrote 'the American Constitution is, so far as I can see, the most wonderful work ever struck off at a given time by the brains and purpose of man.' This was surely done under the guidance of the Creative Spirit," said the self-made man.

"Let your wealthy friends ask themselves what inspired Franklin to retire from making money at an early age so that he might devote himself to the welfare of others, trying to repay, as he put it, for the many blessings he received. They will find Franklin's belief in the Partnership of man and Maker expressed in this statement to the Assembly, striving to form the union of the thirteen colonies: 'I have lived, Sir, a long time and the longer I live, the more convincing proofs I see of this truth, that God governs in the affairs of men.' "

"My efforts will be mighty feeble alongside of men like Franklin, Emerson and Lincoln."

"Yours will not be so feeble as they will be different. I look to you to reduce to the lowest possible denominator the simple truth each of these men was trying to express in what seems to you a more profound manner. You are to present this truth in a way even children can understand it," said The Voice.

"Surely Lincoln spoke in simple language."

"Yes, he did. He frequently stated that he always sought guidance, explaining that his own wisdom and that of the best minds about him were insufficient for the day. But you must find the means of putting this truth in ABC simplicity. It will come to you, perhaps through someone else, but it will come."

"I believe. Help thou mine unbelief. They that wait upon the Lord will be given the necessary strength and wisdom, I am now certain," came from the man.

"As Franklin stated, 'If a creature is made by God,

it must depend upon God and receive all its power from Him.' "

"Are you giving me the chance to help build a new America?" asked the business man hopefully.

"That is correct. With a new America will follow a new world. But tell me, are you prepared to use your wealth and to spend yourself completely in this task?"

"I welcome it. I am filled with desire to try it."

"Your best friends may turn against you."

"I suspect this may be so."

"But not all. Here and there a few will join with you. After all, what you plan to do makes sense. It is truth."

"And all I have against me is precedent, tradition, custom, habit. Every new idea has to fight those enemies. But truth cannot be denied."

"When things look bleak, and brilliant men prefer their own intellect to Mine (forgetting that they owe their own intellect to Me) remember that I am always with you."

"This I hope never to forget. Give me a sign I can remember."

"I will. But it will be more than a sign. It is a way that will strengthen your resolve and inspire you and give you added physical and mental strength. It will be a way to defer old age. You will grow younger."

"I do not deserve such a blessing."

"With every breath you take, you will think of Me being with you. I created breathing for that purpose. I made it in two parts—out and in."

"I breathe out to get rid of toxic substance. I breathe in to get the pure air I need to live."

"But here is the secret. I also intended breathing to be man's way to remember his true nature. With every breath out, think 'Out, ego.' With every breath in, you think 'In God.' "

"What a good advertising man could do with that idea!" the business man enthused.

"It *would* make a good theme: 'Breathe out ego, breathe in God.' "

"With that for a reminder, I should not forget you are always with me, as my Partner."

"If that sounds beautifully simple, let me tell you how simple life can be. At the root of all of man's troubles is the tragic omission of My part in man's nature."

"You mean if we correct this one defect, we correct everything?"

"Does that sound too simple to believe? Think about it. The same Creative Spirit that made the universe is present in man as his Partner. If man sought to do the will of this Spirit, how could he go wrong?"

"It's because he does not know that this Spirit with all its power and wisdom is his ever-present Partner that he relies on his own intelligence and his own will."

"Consider what this change from one partner to another will mean. As a business man, think of the billions of dollars spent in trying to correct the wrongs of your present way of life—just in crime alone, not to speak of illness and mental breakdowns."

"This should appeal to my business associates. Prevention makes sense as well as saving dollars. My guess is that with an expenditure of $1000 in right education, we will be able to save a million dollars. Multiply this a thousand times and we save at least a billion dollars."

"Even more, the difference in the lives of people—their new-found joy and healthful vigor. Knowing the truth will make them free, whereas they are now slaves to self," said The Voice.

"I realize now what Lincoln meant when he said 'We must disenthrall ourselves.' He meant we must free ourselves from slavery to self. He was not referring to money, but rather to the spirit. Yet the truth is, the teaching of self-knowledge to children early in life would mean tremendous savings in dollars now wasted." said the business man.

"Prevention would also extend to illness. Your great schools of medicine teach how to treat and cure illnesses. The change of emphasis from self to your God-part would affect the practice of medicine. The emphasis would be on prevention. Think of the savings there, both in health and in money."

"In just the few minutes we have been conversing, I have been quietly practicing breathing out ego, breathing in God. You know, I have never really breathed before. I've been letting You do this for me."

"I could have made breathing as independent of you as I did the beating of your heart."

"Why didn't You?"

"I chose this way because I counted on man's being able to reason out why. He must eventually discover the reason why breathing is a two-way affair in which both partners join."

"In just these few minutes I have felt the power that lies in breathing out ego, breathing in God. I feel both my mind and body taking on new life, as if cleansed and uplifted. Am I romancing about this?"

"No. This is what I planned. Air can be likened to Spirit. Neither air nor spirit can be seen, yet both exist. Air is the perfect combination of the physical and the spiritual."

"We all know air is real. It has both weight and volume. Air supports airplanes weighing many tons. Air plays a part in the construction of every product made."

"This is the material side of air, but greater by far are the spiritual qualities of air. In the air you breathe is the soul of the universe. With every breath you take, you breathe in the Intelligence which directs the course of the planets through the vast reaches of space. Every breath of air carries with it not only life itself but the very love and power of My Creative Spirit."

"The things we humans take for granted! I suppose nothing more so than air. I have probably not given a thought to the air I breathe—for I don't know how long. Now, it will be different," said the man.

"Before breathing *in,* you must first breathe *out.* In this way you empty yourself of ego. When you get ego out of the way you can't help but breathe in God. First breathe out ego, then breathe in God. Breathe out care, breathe in peace of mind. Breathe out weakness, breathe in strength."

"If only air had a color, we could see it and perhaps not take it for granted."

"Though you can't see the air, you know it is there. Apply a two-inch wide strip of adhesive tape over your mouth and nostrils and in a few seconds you will be in a panic to pull off the strip. You must get air. Is the Creator of air less real than the air He created?"

"Air surrounds us everywhere. We cannot be where air is not. Why don't we realize we cannot be where the Creator is not?"

"It is through air that you both hear and speak. Do you think you are able to converse with people but unable to converse with the Creator of both air and people?"

"Not now, I don't. I can see now you made air to be the connecting link between man and his Maker, and you didn't want anything to interfere with this lifeline. You did not give us any choice in the matter. We cannot escape breathing, as You do it for us when we forget."

"True. You may for a while do without My other gifts: food, water, sun, sleep, but you cannot do without air for more than a few seconds."

"I feel myself growing stronger as I practice this simple breathing exercise. Obviously, no great change can come about in a few moments, but I feel certain sincere steady practice will do the work. I want to make a good Partner to you."

"You have just undergone a most traumatic experience. No one has ever been closer to death and been revived to even greater health than before. Are you sure you are not speaking now out of an overflowing grateful heart?"

"Perhaps, but even more out of the inspiration You have given me to tell the truth about man's nature so that it becomes an important part of education. I can see a whole new world. I can see our nation without juvenile delinquency or crime, with very little illness or mental breakdowns. I can see people with love toward one another, living in vigor and health to a much longer age. All because they have learned the truth of their nature."

"You are catching fire. This is the first step, as nothing can ever be achieved without enthusiasm. You believe in the duality of man and you want now to bring out the best that is in him. You want to do this for your fellow-man, but it is also the one way for you to find your own happiness. While you give children the truth, don't neglect the grownups. Teach them the simple breathing exercise. They will learn that life is a series of breaths. To breathe is to live. Without breath there is no life. This was true from the beginning. An infant emerges from the womb, sucks in life-giving air, lets out a wail, and begins life on earth. The aged person gives a faint gasp, ceases to breathe, and life is over."

"The most difficult thing about all this is to get my little self out of Your way. Coming so late in my life, this new truth will have tough going against the confidence and egotism built up over the years."

"I understand this. But if your desire for guidance is strong, if you believe that the concept of the Partnership of man and Maker is the truth, the many times you fail will only serve to add to your faith. I anticipate there will be times without number when you will forget that I am with you and you will run things yourself."

"That's what I'm most afraid of. I can take the opposition from my friends, but I know I'm going to get in Your way some of the time," admitted the man.

"There will be even more occasions when you will forget to practice breathing out ego, breathing in God.

Your Partner expects this. Though you fail again and again, I will reach down, take you by the hand and help you start again. But remember this, you cannot hold to both ego and God. Both cannot be your masters."

"This I realize. I should not ask this, but will the Partnership of Man and Maker work in every kind of problem?"

"What are the great problems of today?"

"The first I guess is in the field of money. Most crimes are committed for money. The next is probably sex. Then there is illness—physical and mental. Excessive use of liquor, drugs, cigarettes, may be next."

"Tell me, do not all of these troubles spring from the desires of the little self?"

"I would say they do."

"Can you conceive of the God-part of man's nature falling for these desires?"

"No, I cannot." the business man responded.

"Take the matter of money. Every man with a sense of responsibility knows he must do his part to support his family. He must earn money to pay their way. But it is the stupid belief of his little self that the more money he is able to get, the happier he and his family will be—this is what gets him into trouble. He need but look about him to realize that too much of anything is not good for man. That is the Law of Laws. It provides for compensation and balance in the life of man."

"Too much of anything is not good for man—we should know that. We need the sun, too much can bring heat prostration or a sunstroke. We need rain, too much can bring a flood. We need food, too much gives us trouble. These are obvious truths. Why have we persuaded ourselves this law of balance would not apply to money? I realize now that very few of my wealthy friends are really happy." admitted the man.

"When a man gathers too much money, My law of compensation starts to take out of the man what I have allowed to go into his bank balance. The law of balance permits him to swell his estate but it may take his life or bring on untold suffering."

"How about if wealthy men used their money to help others?"

"Then they are not gatherers. Their hearts are not where their treasure is but with the people who need help. This means their God-part is in control, not their little self. They get their happiness by trying to give happiness to others."

"These are the men I must look for, to work with me in getting the new education into our schools. They may get the thrill I have now in just the thought of helping to build a new America."

"Emerson has told you that an inevitable dualism bisects nature, so that each thing is a half, suggesting another thing to make it whole; such as spirit, matter; man, woman; odd, even; subjective, objective; in, out; upper, under; motion, rest; yea, nay; Creator, creature."

"Are you saying that because the world is thus dual, so is everyone of its parts?"

"The same dualism underlies the nature and condition of man. He is a duality, not the individual he has been led to believe. He is in individual partnership with Me, his Maker."

"How come our great thinkers don't bear down on this vital truth?" asked the man.

"The truly great thinkers do. Emerson dwelt on this facet of man's nature incessantly. He said, as you may recall, 'the highest revelation is that God is in every man' and he termed it a 'defect . . . that the Moral Nature, that Law of Laws whose revelations introduce greatness—yea, God himself—into the open soul, is not explored as the fountain of the established teaching in society.' "

"So that more than 125 years ago, Emerson was urging education to do the thing we're going to set out to do."

"You will find that to Emerson My presence in him as his lifelong Partner meant everything. He said 'That which shows God in me fortifies me. That which shows God out of me makes me a wart and a wen. There is no longer a necessary reason for my being.' "

"I can't help but wonder where our present day thinkers are that they neglect these evident truths. People rush to psychiatrists to get their problems solved, when the answer is right there within them."

"That's why psychiatry as presently practiced is a dismal failure. It is all based on the man-part of man's nature, with no consideration to the God-part of his nature."

"You mean they show no recognition of the Creative Power?" inquired the business man.

"Oh, they casually pay lip service to what they term 'the religious sentiment,' tossing it over their shoulder to get it out of the way."

"Frankly, I find myself confused by the hundreds of different religions."

"You are confused more by sectarianism than by religion. Emerson stated 'Religion is the relation of the soul to God, and therefore the progress of Sectarianism marks the decline of religion. For, looking at God instantly reduces our disposition to dissent from our brother.' "

* * * * *

The successful man recovered. During his recuperation, he sought guidance from his Partner, and was given a course of action which involved resigning from his post as Chairman of the Board of Directors of a large corporation. This was the termination of the Little Me's grasp on his life. He told some intimate friends who were also men of means that he wanted to make the rest of his life worthwhile. "No doubt what happened to me was a dream, but it was real enough to change my thinking. We can no longer deny that something is wrong with our way of life.

"The truth is forced upon us by the alarming increase in crime, in juvenile delinquency, in mental breakdowns, in suicides even among the young. We are a decaying nation, and I love my country too much to stand by and gather more money while the nation decays. Escaping from reality is no answer; drugs and alcohol provide no answer. Divorces are reaching the point where, out of every five marriages, two end up in divorce.

"How many people are truly happy? With all my wealth, I have not been a happy man. Now that I know the truth of my nature and the purpose of life, I have a feeling of deep contentment and inner peace. I invite men to join with me to give children early in life the truth of their nature. As Lincoln said, the way to save our nation is to free ourselves from slavery to self. As of right now, I am no longer a money-gatherer. I am devoting myself to helping the children of my beloved country to learn of their Partnership with their Maker."

* * * * *

If God Spoke to the Physician Might it be Something Like This:

> What you are about to read is simply the imagining of one who has learned when he sincerely strives to become "an agent and instrument of Divine Providence" (Lincoln's words) his Partner will guide him, speak thru him and work thru him. The author believes this holds true for you, too.

You know the human body. You have studied it. You have worked on it for many years. I know it, too. I created it. My Creative Spirit of Love deliberated for several billion years before creating the human body. I also sustain the human body. You possibly may have forgotten this. I have created and sustained human bodies by the hundreds of millions.

A physician's aim is to heal. People have especial respect for the physician because of the nobility of the service he seeks to render the afflicted. In your faithful devotion to your patients, have you not occasionally wondered why My part in creating and sustaining man is ignored or at least taken for granted in the study and practice of medicine? I do not place responsibility for this at your door. I know medicine has been taught this way in the medical schools for years.

But, I am constrained to ask, how could the medical

books teaching students about the human body disregard the part the Creator plays in building and sustaining the human body? When medical students are taught to explore human cadavers and witness for themselves the planned construction of the inner body, should it not be natural for the medical professors to call attention to the perfect architecture, planning and workmanship revealed? To point out how the billions of cells and blood vessels, the soft, tender flesh and hard bones, the different vital organs like the heart, lungs, stomach, intestines, liver, together with the glands and muscles, are all held together and bound in the body by skin which, while tight and firm against seepage or loss, is able to breathe and exhale waste material from the body. Why should a few simple questions not be asked of the students: what is the nature of the intelligence which could design and create such a miracle as the human body? Can you believe man would ever have the genius to do this? Would this not be tantamount to believing man can create himself?

How could the brilliant professors of medicine omit from their teaching the contribution of the Supreme Intelligence to the growth of man from the moment I join a male sperm with a female ovum to form a cell? How could My work of building a human body from that tiny cell be treated so casually? And after the nine months' building operation performed by My Creative Spirit (without help from man) for you as a physician to join with Me in gently easing the newly created infant from its mother's womb on to the outer earth, why is the Creator's part in this vital operation hardly ever mentioned?

I have other questions to ask of you, My physician partner. How about My part in replacing wornout tissues with new ones? You used to be taught that every seven years, each person acquires a new body. Now, thru a report of the Atomic Energy Commission, after tracing isotopes in the human body, you learn "in a year approximately 98% of the atoms in us now will be replaced by other atoms that we take in our air, food and drink." Surely, you have caught the significance of My building every human a new body each year, and that My building materials are "air, food and drink."

Is it not clear from this that the greatest contribution the physician can make is on the side of prevention? By ignoring the contribution I planned to make to the health of My human creatures, and putting most of your emphasis on curative efforts, you unwittingly permit people to get sick and then proceed to help them with powerful drugs. If business men conducted their business this way, so that their most valuable machinery was permitted to go bad, instead of keeping it in good shape, there would be far more failures than successful businesses. Should not physicians spend more time and study in preventing illness? Your patients would be better off and would be far more grateful for this kind of help. You yourself would derive greater satisfaction working with Me in the art of healing than when you ignore Me, as your training does.

I know that most physicians are noble men and women, who have chosen to become healers out of the sincere desire to help their fellow-man. Yet, there may be a few influenced by the ambition to become wealthy. I am also aware that there is very little chance of a physician becoming wealthy by keeping people well. One of the first questions a student desiring to go to medical school should answer is "Why do you want to become a physician?" If the answer does not indicate "I want to work with the Creator to keep His other children in good health," he surely should not be at the top of the list. As a physician, you know that the inner rewards coming to you from grateful patients can never be equalled by money. The art of healing must include knowing the place of food in replenishing wornout body material. Undergirding this understanding is a knowledge of nutrition. This means food grown without artificial fertilizers and insecticides, and prepared without additives, preservatives and supplements. This is food the way I cause it to grow, containing the essential elements to replenish the body parts that wear out with time.

What would be the result if physicians placed more emphasis on prevention? The first result will be the universal increased respect and affection people would have for their physicians. The relationship between physician and patient would become very close indeed. When the physician is employed by the whole family to keep them well, he becomes in a real sense a member of the family. The well-known "bedside manner" is raised to its highest genuine level. The physician becomes more than a professional advocate of medicines and general repair work. The family will naturally seek his judgment on emotional factors in health. Keeping a person well means more than keeping his physical body well. It means keeping his mind well. And this is only one step removed from keeping his spirits well. The physician practicing general medicine would be doing far more for the family than prescribing drugs and antibiotics.

By reminding his patients that the Creative Spirit of Love which built their body also provided the means of sustaining that body and keeping it well and vigorous, the physician, acting preventively will direct their minds to natural means of keeping well. This is bound to lead to the study of natural foods, pure spring drinking water, breathing exercises and particularly the part air can play in working one's Partnership with Me.

It is difficult to understand how medical college professors have persisted in their refusal to teach nutrition. This may be due to some short-sighted professors of medicine who fear that medical men would not be able to earn a decent living if their patients learned how to take preventive measures to keep well. For years, these medical professors scorned natural food as having any influence on health. They preferred to attribute illness to germs. In recent years, they have been forced to acknowledge the health value of vitamins and mineral salts which I have placed in natural foods.

Then there is the matter of the health and vigor of the physician himself. Government statistics on this show that the rate of illness and mortality among physicians is close to the highest of any profession or business. Long hours and interrupted rest at night were used to explain away this high rate, but most of this extra service no longer obtains. If physicians studied the value of My natural means in keeping the human body well and vigorous, they would themselves enjoy more vigorous health and a longer life span.

The change from doctoring with man-made medicines to use of My natural gifts for health will improve the whole nation, physically, mentally, emotionally and spiritually. The healing art will take its place among the noblest of professions, a place deserved by many physicians even today.

Of course, the need for surgeons will still remain. Not only to take care of accidents but also to mend the damage done by unpreventable ailments as well as by wrong living. All mankind owes a debt to the great advances in the technique of surgery. People are discovering the remarkable benefits resulting from acupuncture, when performed by trained, competent medical specialists.

When the teaching of nutrition and other natural aids to health is made a part of the medical college curriculum, perhaps students will also be taught the part I, the Creator-Partner of all humans, play in the maintenance of health and vigor. As students learn the intricacies and complexity of the human body, they may be instructed to give consideration to the Supreme Intelligence which created this remarkable machine.

Physicians and scientists are making great advances in mending and even constructing artificial body organs. Indeed, some talk confidently of making a new heart to replace a badly wornout one. But making a new heart is one thing. Keeping it beating is another. This is My contribution. Science has never been able to discover what causes the heart to keep beating.

When students learn there is no physical connection to explain why the heart keeps beating, perhaps they will understand that it is My Spirit alone which makes the heart beat. This one simple revelation may be enough to convince everyone that while no one can see Me with their eyes, it is My invisible Creative Spirit of Love which keeps all mankind going. Think about this, My physician partner. There is no physical explanation as to what makes the heart to beat. Could this be just chance or because I planned it that way? For all any physician can do or for that matter any mortal, each human heart can stop beating this very moment. What keeps your heart beating is My invisible Spirit—the Creative Spirit of Love.

As a healer, you should stay close to Me, as also should the healer of the mind. Both body and mind need our joint care. As you know, one affects the other.

When physicians were competed with by charlatans promising all kinds of cures, there was need for the protection of physicians, and in that respect your American Medical Association performed a needed service. But has the time not come for the A.M.A. to promote the practice of preventive medicine? To lay out a system whereby families can pay physicians to keep them well rather than wait for them to fall sick?

A transformation in teaching and practicing medicine is surely needed. As a physician, do you not want to take a hand in bringing this about as promptly as possible? You will not make as much money, but then the accumulation of money should never be a standard of a physician's success. When you become a true healer and preventer of illness, all your patients will rise and call you blessed. And so will I.

* * * * *

In all fairness to the family physician, it should be stated that the very fact he has chosen to be a family physician is testimony in itself, his first interest is not the making of money but a sincere desire to help keep the family well. Too often, people do not co-operate in preventive measures, regardless how often their family physician advises the proper steps to take. Some patients, for reasons they themselves know best, are different persons when in the hospital than when at home. They enjoy all the service they get in a hospital, whereas at home they have to wait on themselves.

Then too, physicians should be credited with the many preventive measures taken in the past, in saving infants at birth, in sponsoring successful vaccines, in exposing the dangers of drugs, tobacco and alcohol, excessive salt intake, obesity, etc.

The great job remains to be done, however. This is the change that must take place in the kind of instruction given in the medical schools. Consideration should be given to the wisdom of having, as full time professors, non-practicing physicians. Medical knowledge learned out of books must be augmented by actual practice if a physician is to qualify as instructor for medical students. There should be a course introducing the Creator's part in the construction of the human body and in its maintenance of health, as well as its contribution in curing disease. Many physicians do openly admit to their patients: "Don't thank me. My part was insignificant in getting you well. It was God who did the curing." The proper training of medical students would make them conscious of the truth: that He who made the human body is best able to both prevent and cure illness.

* * *

If God Spoke to the Psychiatrist Might it be Something Like This:

> What you are about to read is simply the imagining of one who has learned when he sincerely strives to become "an agent and instrument of Divine Providence" (Lincoln's words) his Partner will guide him, speak thru him and work thru him. The author believes this holds true for you, too.

I know you are a person of extraordinary brain power. I also credit you with a sincere desire to be of service to people who are troubled and depressed. You are to be commended. Indeed, I had hoped for something like this in creating you and endowing you with a brain of such potential development.

You have made great sacrifices and spent much time in research and study to learn the nature of man. Why have you not also made some inquiry as to the nature of the Supreme Intelligence which created the Universe and all life therein, including yourself? Surely, you have given much thought to this Creative Power which spent nine months within you, building you from a cell into a human being? You must have devoted much study as to the nature of this unknown, invisible Creative Spirit and whether, after having built your body and brain, causing you to be gently eased out of your mother's womb, this unseen Power departed from you or remains with you to guide you and do the many things in your body you can't do for yourself.

Are you satisfied with the explanation offered by some that what goes on in your body and mind is due to biology, which tends to leave Me out? If you were asked "Who created biology," how would you answer?

I am aware you find it difficult to accept the claims of religious-minded people. I must sympathize with you in discounting the myths inherent in these claims, particularly in view of the fact that in the National Council of Churches alone there are 247 different sects or denominations, each claiming to be the true Christian religion.

But are you sure of your grounds in dismissing My Creative Spirit of Love along with the unbelievable features of these various religions? Surely, you can separate myths from facts. Is it not a fact that a Power greater than man's created the Universe, created humans, and sustains both? You would not claim that you created yourself. Nor that you keep your heart beating. Nor that you keep open the lines of communication between your brain and the rest of your body so that you are enabled to think straight, talk straight, work straight.

As a person of extraordinary brain power, why don't you use your talent to research the scientific facts about the nature of man, leaving aside the claims made by structured religions? Surely, you have some questions in your mind as to those particular cases where you have not been able to help your patients gain better understanding of themselves. Have you ever given thought to how the Supreme Intelligence feels about being disregarded by you and other psychiatrists, mostly because you find the claims of established religions to be unacceptable? Does this warrant your ignoring the simple truths about the Supreme Intelligence so manifest all about you and within you?

Can you explain why psychiatrists apparently have made no research into Alcoholics Anonymous to learn how this group of laymen have helped over a million men and women recover their sobriety after many years of drunkenness and loss of control?

Is this lack of interest on the part of psychiatrists due to the fact that Alcoholics Anonymous promotes among the victims of alcohol a belief in a Supreme Intelligence, infinitely above man's, including psychiatrists?

As a matter of learning the truth, can not psychiatrists learn from The Twelve Steps of Alcoholics Anonymous? Take just the first three steps which have helped more than a million people overcome drunkenness without medicine, or psychiatric treatments: The first step: "We admitted we were powerless over alcohol—that our lives had become unmanageable."

You surely would not take issue with that confession. The second step: "Came to believe that a Power greater than ourselves could restore us to sanity." This may give you a little trouble, but should it, really? The third step: "Made a decision to turn our will and our lives over to the care of God *as we understood Him.*" Now this step introduces God, but does it introduce religion? Quite the contrary, does it not leave up to each person his own understanding of God? Surely, psychiatrists admit there is some Creative Intelligence, call it by whatever name you choose. You would not quarrel with the First President's statement: "One cannot reason without arriving at a Supreme Intelligence."

And can you quarrel with a movement—even though non-scientific—that has helped more than a million people overcome such a powerful addiction as alcoholism?

You base much of your thinking on what Sigmund Freud has set out for you to believe and practice. But has not enough time elapsed since the publication of his views to prove that something is lacking in his teachings? Otherwise would so many psychiatrists be visiting other psychiatrists for treatment of mental concerns of their own?

Freud bases his reasoning largely on the irresistible urges of sex, claiming that this is responsible for most of man's problems. As the Creator of humans, I am responsible for having implanted the sex urge in them, and I am aware of its force and power. May I ask why you don't pay much attention to the words and reasoning of Gustav Carl Jung, a truly understanding psychiatrist?

If you gave consideration to Dr. Jung's view of psychiatry, you would not ignore the part that My Creative Spirit of Love plays in man's everyday affairs. I doubt that you would have approved of the action of psychiatry's most powerful organization in going on record to the effect that homosexuality is not a disease and therefore not in need of treatment. As the Creator of sex, I had planned for heterosexuality between man and woman (indeed, between one certain man and one certain woman). The pronouncement of the psychiatric organization, in essence establishing that homosexuality is as normal as heterosexuality, is an irresponsible affront to Me, who created humans and planned for the peopling of My world thru heterosexuality. This act of the psychiatric organization asserts the wisdom of psychiatrists is above that of the Supreme Intelligence.

Many understanding psychiatrists will rise in protest of this kind of egotism, evinced by the pronouncement, which may in the end contribute to the signing of the deathknell of psychiatry as currently practiced. What the psychiatric association has done is to deny there is a plan to life and that I ever planned for true love to exist between man and woman. They are putting their stamp of approval on any method of satisfying the sex urge.

Psychiatry is making it easy for those uncertain men and women who were not taught self-knowledge, to forsake the natural belief in a Supreme Being, and to disregard all the evidence about them and within them of My part in their life. Psychiatry now has assumed responsibility for leading these uncertain people into a way of life that can never yield them true happiness. It is only a matter of time when these unfortunate people's unspeakable anguish caused by their perverted use of sex will lead them to acts of desperation, even to doing away with themselves.

This grave error stems from the failure of psychiatry to include the Creative Spirit of Love in the work of psychiatry. Professors of psychiatry have elected to disregard My wisdom and capacity to heal. They have been persuaded by Freud to throw Me out along with religion. How can you reason thus? I created the earth several billion years before men created religions. Because religions have some unbelievable aspects is no reason to completely reject the Creator and dismiss My part in life as "the religious sentiment." This is like unto a person living in poverty unaware that a priceless estate awaits his claim.

It is but fair to acknowledge that Freud was close to the truth in his belief that children figure somewhere in most psychiatric problems. But when Freud advanced the theory that the way to be cured of one's present worries is to go back in one's mind to the time when one was a child, he made a simple truth complex. The simple truth was—and still is—that I created humans because I wanted to live in Partnership with each, in the loving relationship of parent and child.

A child comes fresh from the Creator, and it should be simple, with the right kind of teaching, to keep the child close to Me. With the teaching of self-knowledge, the child would have learned to seek My guidance in all things. I counted on this truth being self-evident. The greatest of teachers sought to make this clear: "You must become as a little child . . . You must be born again . . . A little child shall lead them."

But perhaps therein lay its greatest weakness. It was too simple. Freud probably felt that My plan was too simple to be accepted by his brother psychiatrists. Or was it that he figured he would gain more followers among psychiatrists through the method of turning a patient's mind back to when he was a child, exploring for some resentment which had its origin then.

Because of Freud's unshakable faith in his own wisdom, I was not able to reach him. This famous professor of psychiatry seemed content with just part of the truth, leaving out the most vital part—the wisdom of his Maker.

I was, however, able to get through to one of Freud's pupils, Carl Gustav Jung, whose insight into the truth of man's nature proved infinitely deeper and more dependable than Freud's. Jung sought to make clear in his book The Undiscovered Self, the true dual nature of man: part-self, part-God. Where Freud scorned My presence in man as a mere "religious sentiment" of no particular importance in psychiatry, Jung realized that My partnership with man was the whole reason for man's existence. Jung forthrightly stated that the purpose of life was to reach oneness with one's Creator-Partner.

Jung stated clearly in his book:

> "The individual who is not anchored in God can offer no resistance on his own resources to the physical and moral blandishments of the world. For he needs the evidence of inner, transcendent experience which alone can protect him from the otherwise inevitable submersion in the mass."

Jung was supported in his belief by other wise men. H. G. Wells, the eminent historian, speaks to every psychiatrist as well as to every human being:

"Until man has found God, and has been found by God, he begins at no beginning and works to no end. Nothing in the Universe or in man's life falls into place except with God."

Another great historian and psychologist, Arnold Toynbee, wrote:

"God has created man to be God's free partner in the work of creation."

And one of the Founding Fathers, Benjamin Franklin, one of the most practical of men and many-sided, concurs with both Jung and Wells as well as Toynbee: "If a creature is made by God, it must depend upon God, and receive all its power from God."

Not one of these believed he was stating anything of a religious nature. What each said made sense to him, and it should to all psychiatrists. The psychiatrist of the future will not relegate My Creative Spirit of Love to the area of religion, but rather will help his patients to understand their own nature. By so doing, the psychiatrist will be working with Me to heal his patients, gaining their respect and affection. Moreover, the psychiatrist will gain for himself greater inner peace and love for his brother-man.

Much illness is caused by man's struggling little ego in conflict with his higher self—his self-part vs. his God-part. In a sense this conflict is between what one finds himself to be and what he aspires to be. For thousands of years past, the priest and the doctor were one and the same person. Should this not have continued?

For a man to be whole, the goal is the integration of

his potentialities, including his physical, mental, emotional and spiritual essence. Man has a central core, a center of awareness, pure and unchangeable, distinct from the physical and mental turmoil of his outer life. This center core is his God-part.

A psychiatrist who has spiritual understanding tends to meditate with his patients, gaining from this practice an intuitive perception of their problems. His medical knowledge, his natural gift for healing, his sense of humor, and above all the love that emanates from him all contribute to the success of his treatment. He learns that living thus with his patients is a very important factor.

Such a psychiatrist approaches his patient with the belief that life is a gift of God which has to be respected, and that his own life is an opportunity for service to others. He looks at each patient not only in the light of biology and psychology but also as a mystery. It is this mystery within each person that is the real person, as distinguished from the various identities which serve as his mask. When the psychiatrist finds an unattractive individual unlovely or full of hate, he is able to look thru these apparent characteristics to the true person beneath—the God-part. Such a psychiatrist sees three parties involved in every marriage: the husband, the wife and My Creative Spirit of Love, called God.

A psychiatrist with spiritual understanding recognizes the need for interpersonal relationships in which people respect each other's dignity. The example of such a relationship can be found in the very personal encounter of marriage. Modern science has profaned much in life that once was secret and sacred, but the wholeness, the oneness in marriage can still have a truly sacred character, since society has devised no structure for such a highly personal matter. Marriage can bring a couple to the supreme experience of unity. Sexual union should be not unlike spiritual union. What is important in this relationship is the meaning of the sexual act to each of the two individuals involved, not the act itself.

A psychiatrist with spiritual understanding sees three factors as important in the shaping of human life: heredity and environment, naturally, but more important than these, an interior force which propels each individual towards certain experiences and fulfillments. This force accounts for the uniqueness of each person, which he needs to discover within himself, seeking it especially in an inner stillness.

The psychiatrist of the future will work in partnership with Me in treating his patients and also in every phase of his own life. For, as psychiatrist Jung stated: "The individual who is not anchored in God can offer no resistance on his own resources to the physical and moral blandishments of the world."

If God Spoke to the Politician Might it be Something Like This:

> What you are about to read is simply the imagining of one who has learned when he sincerely strives to become "an agent and instrument of Divine Providence" (Lincoln's words) his Partner will guide him, speak thru him and work thru him. The author believes this holds true for you, too.

Has there ever been a time in the history of the U.S.A. when respect for the politician dropped to a lower point than in the year of 1974—a situation most unfair to many honest and capable politicians sincerely seeking to render true public service?

This distressing lack of respect came to a head in the campaign for the Presidency in 1972. The American people were far ahead of their political leaders. They sensed their beloved country was decaying from within. The various Jesus movements by youth pointed the way back to Lincoln's admonition "We have forgotten God."

Where the two Presidential candidates were concentrating on their personal ambitions—one to become the President, the other to remain so, many Americans were fervently hoping for another Lincoln. They felt the country needed a new kind of leadership, which would bring about a change in the American standard of success. A change from the symbol of money, power, position, fame to that of service to mankind.

Their greatest disappointment—in which I shared—was in the candidate who had raised their hopes he might lead the way back to the ideals of the Founding Fathers. This man, a Senator from South Dakota, had overcome great odds to become the candidate of his party. He had inspired many youth in the country to volunteer their aid, confident their man was being guided by the God-part of man's nature.

Disappointment began to make itself felt when the candidate made his speech of acceptance of the Democratic nomination. It turned out to be a purely political speech, devoid of inspiration that would lead people back to God. It was as if, having secured the nomination, he credited his own wisdom and that of his political advisers with having brought it about. Of all people, how could he have left Me out of his thanks?

I am not sitting in judgment on him, realizing he is a victim of an education that leaves Me, the Creator of the Universe out of the everyday affairs of life including politics. This led him to succumb to those political advisers who insisted "You can't talk about God in a political campaign. You will be charged with mixing religion and politics—a fatal blunder. Stick to political bread and butter issues. Attack your opponent. Give him hell like Truman did. But whatever you do, leave God out of it."

The candidate's advisers were practical politicians, influenced by PTCH (Precedent, Tradition, Custom,

Habit) but the people, particularly the youth of the country were hoping for a return to Lincoln's way: "I have been driven many times to my knees by the overwhelming conviction that I had nowhere else to go; my own wisdom and that all around me seemed insufficient for the day."

The Democratic candidate should have been among those calling for a re-examination of PTCH. A public opinion poll indicated this was in order. When the American people were asked what one thing they wanted most out of a list of important current subjects, their first choice was "getting people to believe in God."

This should have been no surprise to either of the two candidates, particularly to the Democratic candidate. Despite the materialistic way of life all about them, should they not have known that I, the Creative Spirit of Love, had implanted in each human being a hunger for all the noble things the spirit of Love engenders?

Surely, the Democratic candidate, a man of character and compassion, was aware of this. Even if he was going to lose—and all the polls indicated he would lose by a large margin—why not go down gloriously for a great cause, fighting Lincoln's battle to get the American people back to God and thus save the nation? Lincoln, in a statement of eleven words, had shown the way: "We must disenthrall ourselves and then we will save our nation." To disenthrall is to be freed from slavery to self. Better than their leaders, the American people sensed the American way of life promoted slavery to self. Forgotten was the advice of the Master Teacher: "First seek the will of God and all other things will be added to you."

But the desire of the Democratic candidate's self-part to win was too irresistible to place his trust in My guidance. This led him to accept his advisers' counsel that he demand the resignation of his own appointed Vice-Presidential candidate, after it was disclosed that this unfortunate man had occasion in the past to consult a psychiatrist. Why, the American way of life in itself promotes consulting psychiatrists. Why dishonor a man permanently for having consulted a psychiatrist? But the practical politicians had their way. My guidance went for naught. The constant battle I had planned between man's self-part and his God-part had been won by the self-part of man's nature. The hopes of many people that there would be new spiritual overtones to the 1972 campaign were dashed. There would be no call to return to the God of Lincoln in order to save the nation. The practical politicians had succeeded in convincing the Democratic candidate it would be fatal to even remind the people of Lincoln's Proclamation "calling for a day of national humiliation, fasting and prayer," (based on the theme: "we have forgotten God.")

The polls showed that 98% of the American people expressed a belief in God. Every President, every elected Government official takes an oath which concludes "So help me God." Is this not a plea for God's help? Every U.S.A. coin and paper money (of whatever denomination) bear the words "In God we trust". Your national anthem carries these words. Why should politicians be reluctant to speak of your belief in God? Surely, it is not because you feel that I, your God, the Creative Spirit of Love, should be confined to the area of structured religion. May I remind you, Mr. Politician, I created the earth. Men created religions. I created the earth several billion years before men created religions. Who has the authority to confine Me, the Creator of the Universe, to the realm of man-made religions? In what area of your life, Mr. Politician, do I not play a vital part? Can you even think straight unless My Creative Spirit pumps blood from your heart to your brain? Can you even talk straight unless I keep open the lines of communication between your brain and your lips? Do you, of your own will, keep your heart beating? When you sleep at night, who breathes for you? Are there not countless things I do for you each moment that have nothing to do with "religion" as you understand religion?

How can knowledgeable and intelligent men become so blind as to confine Me to "religion"? As a politician, should you not follow Lincoln's way of breaking with PTCH in this regard. Lincoln dared to challenge Precedent, Tradition, Custom, Habit, at a time when he was apologizing for not being a "religious" man. The truth is that Lincoln lived closer to Me, his Creator and Sustainer than any person since Christ. Lincoln knew that I was always present with him, and he sought My guidance in all things. Can you as a politician do better?

The Democratic candidate for President in 1972 evidently believed he was getting better guidance from his political advisers than I could give him. But did not the Republican candidate seeking re-election also trust his own wisdom in preference to the wisdom that comes only from God? Did he not from the day he was inaugurated the first time, leave Me out of his planning to get re-elected? Was it My guidance or that of his self-part that led him to the unnecessary overkill that brought about Watergate?

Had not your 37th President been given ample proof that he had been looked after? Only six years before, following his defeat for Governor of California, he publicly acknowledged that he was done politically. Yet within those six years, things worked out, enabling him to become President of the U.S.A. In order to do this, his opponents, the Democrats had to war among themselves. They did this to the extent that permitted him to win by the narrow margin of less than 1% of the popular vote.

Was this not the kind of thing to make him aware that some Power besides his own had worked in his favor? This was the type of situation that provides a testing point for a man. Either he realizes that he has been the beneficiary of a higher power or he takes unto himself credit for having waged a skillful campaign, taking advantage of his opponent's errors, indeed contributing to them.

But I was not prepared to give up on your 37th President. There were moments early in his administration when there were more than glimpses of a desire to become a truly great President and win the support of the American people and the people of the world. This aroused hopes even among his sternest critics that the holding of the office of President was impressing him with its prestige and potentialities. Some may have actually discerned he was choosing the God-part of his nature over his self-part. This was really the greatest crisis in the life of the man who wrote of six other great crises in his life.

Why then, did he give in to the urging of his self-part? Why did he decide to leave Me out of his consideration and plans? The practical side of his nature seemed to tell him the most important thing to do was to insure his re-election four years hence.

Every political fight he had engaged in up to that time had been a close one, and he was determined that the next one he would win by a great margin. He was convinced he could not leave this to anyone but himself. He concluded the thing needed to insure his re-election was money—lots of money. Therefore he had hardly begun his first term when he was planning how to raise money for his second. This seemed to be an obsession with him. If there was any choice in his mind between his self-part and his God-part, his self-part was an easy winner. Indeed, it was as if I did not figure at all in man's daily events, only on a Sunday morn from 11 to 12 noon.

A man had to be practical, you know. So, to make sure I was not completely ignored, he paid his respects to Me each Sunday morning with church services at the White House. But this was not what I wanted and it surely was not good for your 37th President. His own experience of having become President when things had looked so impossible a few years before should have caused him to have more trust in the God-part of his nature.

I do not force things on My children, even on the

President of the United States. I want to live in partnership with each of them, not compel them to do My will. I count on their intelligence supplying the understanding that I am part of their nature. I do not ask them to believe in predestination—that regardless of what they personally do, certain events are bound to transpire. This is not in My plan. My plan is Partnership. Predestination would exclude man from Partnership with Me. This would be wrong just as man's leaving Me out of his everyday life is wrong and futile. Working in partnership yields a joy to man he can never achieve on his own.

This is the beauty of the Partnership of Man and Maker. It would be a perfect Partnership because the two of us would work together perfectly. Each would recognize the contribution the other is making. The plan called for teaching each child from its beginning that My Creative Spirit of Love which formed its frame and built its brain never departs from it, but remains with the child in eternal partnership. The child would readily accept that it is My power that keeps his heart beating, digests and transforms the food he enjoys eating into blood, bone, muscle, brain, and promotes his growth, physically, mentally and spiritually. Importantly, the child would learn that I need him as he needs Me. In this way, he would also learn to seek My guidance in all things. Thus he would experience the great joy that comes from man's yielding his will to Mine and realizing the unequalled peace of mind only the perfect partnership can yield.

All of you should look into your present system of

education. Your 37th President is but one of the victims of that faulty system. The education he received from the beginning thru college and law school left out of its teaching the most important of all knowledge—self-knowledge. In addition, in his particular case, the religion he claimed affiliation with failed to get across to him the real essence of Quaker belief: that there is "that of God in every man—the Inner Light." The Inner Light in every man is My Creative Spirit of Love. The Inner Light bespeaks the Partnership of Man and Maker.

Despite your 37th President's remarkable intelligence and unusual self-discipline, he was persuaded to rely on the self-part of his nature. Thus he depended on his own wisdom instead of My guidance. Is this any way to run our Partnership? It is not the way I planned for humans to live.

So that in the case of both candidates, each left Me out of consideration. Each believed he had brought about his nomination on his own skill and hard work. This was not the case. Nor does it make sense.

The landslide victory for Nixon was clearly foreseen. Both men disappointed Me—though in different ways. The Democratic candidate by persisting in "politics as usual" despite the polls showing this was folly; the Republican candidate by not following up what should have been obvious to him—that he should show his gratitude by seeking My guidance in the conduct of the highest office in the land.

Why am I addressing Myself to politicians in this

manner? Because it leads Me to the greatest politician of all time—your 16th President who lived the Partnership Life of Man and Maker. It is not too happy a commentary on the American people that it took a Russian writer, Tolstoy, after years of research into Lincoln's life, to describe Lincoln as "a Christ in miniature." Tolstoy did not consider he was making a "religious" observation. He regarded both Christ and Lincoln as practical men—the most practical of men. Tolstoy regarded Me as the Creative Spirit of Love.

Lincoln who had no specific religion endeavored to live Christ's way of life—perfect partnership with the Creative Spirit of Love. Lincoln came to believe that Christ lived so selflessly that to all intents and purposes it was I thinking thru him, speaking thru him, working thru him. Lincoln did not seek to be exalted, nor did Christ before him. Both were meek before Me, conscious that it was My Creative Spirit of Love which was the source of their strength and wisdom.

If I appear to be sitting in judgment on both 1972 candidates, it is because I have a point to make with all politicians. With the example of Lincoln before you, showing how he sought My wisdom above his own, seeking My will above his own, why did these two candidates rely so completely on their own and their advisers' wisdom, ignoring Me as a current, living force? Could Lincoln have stated the case more clearly:

"I should be the veriest shallow and self-conceited blockhead upon the footstool, if in my discharge

of the duties that are put upon me in this place,
I should hope to get along without the wisdom that
comes from God, and not from man."

These two candidates both professed to believe in Me.
Were they afraid the American people would not understand a sincere appeal to God? Consider how well people, even abroad, accepted Lincoln's acknowledged dependence on God. The London Times, commenting on
Lincoln's Second Inaugural address, said:

> "It is the most remarkable thing of the sort ever
> pronounced by a President of the United States
> from the first day until now. Its Alpha and Omega
> is Almighty God, the God of Justice and the Fa-
> ther of mercies, who is working out the purpose
> of His love."

Let Me remind you: "Know thyself!" "With all thy
getting, get understanding." Because education does
not teach self-understanding, I, your Creator and Sustainer, have been relegated to the religious realm, iso-
lated from all other phases of your life. I, whose purpose
in creating you was to live in Partnership with you.
What a mockery! If professional educators insist there
is no way to teach children the truth about their nature
without introducing religion, why do not you as a politician show them the way?

The Founding Fathers knew the way. They were all
determined to keep religion separate from the state, but
they all had an unshakable belief in God. Your first
President, George Washington said: "One cannot rea-

son without arriving at a Supreme Intelligence." Benjamin Franklin stated: "If a creature is made by God, it must depend upon God and receive all its power from Him." Your 3rd President Thomas Jefferson wrote: "The God who gave us life gave us liberty at the same time." Surely, these men believed it was possible to teach children the close relation of man and Maker, without in any way introducing structured religion.

I realize a politician is so surrounded by materialism that it is not easy to keep Me in remembrance. If you had a hand in growing things as does a farmer, it would be more natural for you to keep aware of our Partnership.

As a rule, politicians are more formally educated than farmers, but you can learn some things from farmers about your own Partnership with Me that would improve your health and give you added peace of mind. In his work of growing food, the farmer knows I operate as his Partner. He depends on Me as I depend on him. His faith in Me may not be a structured faith. It is real, down-to-earth, bedrock. No one has to remind the farmer that it is I who created the seed, the soil, the sun, the rain and the air. The farmer counts on My arranging for these elements to work together in harmony and love. Otherwise, he cannot produce. The farmer knows he is not the grower. He knows that I, the Creative Spirit of Love, am the grower. When I speak of farmers, I do not mean the large corporations and conglomerates that have taken over much of the farming interests for the sole purpose of making money. I mean the real farmers—those who rise early in the morning to take care of their animals and to work the soil to produce grains, fruits and vegetables, whose hands caress the earth with reverence and gratitude and are rewarded by seeing the growth I promote thru the contribution of My seed, soil, sun, rain and air. If only the processors of the foods these farmers grow would realize that these natural foods contain the very elements needed for the health and growth of all animals—dumb and human— they would be more careful to insure that the minerals and vitamins and all the elements are maintained thru the process. It was understandable how years ago before transportation and fresh frozen facilities were available, that the natural foods would spoil on the shelves of food stores, but now with almost instant transportation facilities and splendid preservation thru modern freezing methods, these foods can be maintained close to their natural state. This can mean the difference between vigorous health and illness due to mineral and vitamin deficiency.

A politician has much to learn from a farmer. His simple belief in Me may seem based on blind faith but is it really?

The farmer may not think of it as such, but ours is a perfect partnership—the Creative Spirit of Love in action. What joy this Partnership affords us both. We love one another and we love the things we produce together, knowing that people in different walks of life will enjoy and be sustained by our handiwork. One of the things a politician can learn from a farmer is the art of being honest with himself, something which comes naturally to a farmer. Your inadequate education causes you to be too wrapped up in self to realize you are living in a Universe of law and order. Not man-made laws but My Laws. The fields you see as you drive in the country are fields of Life and Love. Some call them L-fields because they are a manifestation of My laws of Life and Love. Without these laws you could not exist for a moment. These laws compel an acorn to grow into an oak tree—and only an oak tree; they compel an apple seed to grow into an apple tree, not a pear or cherry tree. This shows the existence of law and order. Anything that compels growth and development in such an organized way is in itself irrefutable evidence of law and order.

Each human being is created and literally held together by My definable laws. You must feel sorry for those supposedly wise folks who declare with solemn finality that there is nothing new to be discovered in any particular field of study. For such an authority will soon be made to look foolish by some new discovery of My plan that humans were created to live in Partnership with Me.

If you were asked why you chose to become a politi-cian, you would probably answer, as one honest with himself, with one of two reasons: 1) personal ambition, which is the self-part of your nature; 2) to be of the greatest service to your brother-man, which is your God-part in action.

In the case of Lincoln, I was able to imbue him with a sense of My will. His natural humility was such that he did not deem himself qualified to lead the nation, particularly in the light of the oncoming war between the North and the South. How many Americans know the extent to which Lincoln's humility carried him in his efforts to avoid becoming President? I had to use Mary Todd as an agent and instrument to bring it about. Lincoln failed to put in appearance for his scheduled marriage to Mary Todd, because he knew she had determined to become the First Lady and she saw in Lincoln the means of achieving her ambition.

Lincoln believed he could talk with Me, and it was only after we had several talks together that I was able to convince him it was My will that he dedicate himself to saving the Union. He married Mary Todd, recognizing I was working my will thru Mary Todd's use of her skill and influence to make him a candidate. As a politician, would you yield your will to Mine? It has been well said "To thine own self be true, and it follows as day the night, thou canst not then be false to any man."

True, but a vital question remains. To which self shall you be true? To your self-part or to your God-part? This is the simple but vital point many professional educators have chosen to disregard. And because it has been ignored, you and your children are off to a wrong start in life, causing needless suffering and misunderstanding, producing millions of little wars in everyday living, which lead to bigger wars between nations.

You must learn from the beginning that it was not in My plan for your self-part to be all of your nature. Your self-part is too self-centered, too selfish to permit it to be all of your nature. My own Creative Spirit of Love which built your body and brain remains with you, serving as your God-part, the higher part of your nature. If you will diligently search your brain, you will find that My Creative Spirit does things in your body that you cannot do for yourself. Can you question there are two separate forces at work in you—one yours, the other Mine? One is your self-part, the other is your God-part. This is the way I planned it, and the purpose of life is for you to reach oneness with Me. So the question is, to which self should you be true?

As a politician, seeking to be honest with yourself, you know how this question should be answered. Your education may have failed to teach you self-knowledge, but earnest self-examination will give you a common sense answer.

I am aware that your constituents have not had a politician speak to them along these lines, but the time is ripe for it and you may discover most of them have been waiting to be reminded of Lincoln's admonition that I have been forgotten. What people will be looking for when you say or do something is the God-part of your nature at work. They may be listening to you but they will be hoping to hear Me speaking thru you. They may be looking at you but they will be looking for your God-part, not your self-part.

The people may not be as knowledgeable as their political representatives, but they are almost always closer to Me and therefore to the truth. They sense that something must be done and soon to counteract the decay that has been going on in your country for many years. The people and especially your youth know there must be a better way of life than the one handed down from one generation to another. They may or may not be thinking in religious terms but they are seeking God, just as I, their Creator-Partner am seeking them. They naturally believe that I planned for the U.S.A. to be "the last best hope of earth," and they would willingly give their lives to save America.

When they elect you as their representative, they are hoping it is not just *you* they are voting for, but your *Partner.* The American people want the real thing, not anything phony. If you truly believe Lincoln was right in telling the American people "we have forgotten God," your God-part will supply the courage for you to say so. You may be surprised to learn your constituents prefer this to "politics as usual."

With this new understanding, you will re-arrange your priorities. The first priority is not inflation, taxes, energy, jobs, or the like, important as they are. The first priority is to arrest your country's decay. To do this, you must first bring Me, your Creator-Partner, back into the picture.

When politicians understand their true nature, they will then seek My wisdom and it will follow as day the night that they will do what is right regarding inflation, taxes, energy, jobs, etc. When you try to settle these things first without establishing the first priority, it will mean the country will have to tackle these problems all over again as has been the case in the past, time after time.

Lincoln saw this clearly back in 1863, and it prompted him to issue a Proclamation calling for a day of "national humiliation, fasting and prayer." In this Proclamation, President Lincoln said:

"We have been the recipients of the choicest bounties of Heaven. We have been preserved these many years in peace and prosperity. We have grown in numbers, wealth and power as no other nation has ever grown, but we have forgotten God. We have forgotten the gracious hand which preserved us in peace, and multiplied and enriched and strengthened us; and we have vainly imagined in the deceitfulness of our hearts, that all these blessings were produced by some superior wisdom of our own. Intoxicated with unbroken success, we have become too self-sufficient . . . too proud to pray to the God that made us . . ."

The politicians of Lincoln's day disregarded his Proclamation calling for a day of National Repentance and Prayer. They saw no political advantage in admitting publicly that the nation was showing signs of decay.

A more recent President, seemingly conscious of the inner decay taking place in the U.S.A. warned the people:

"I think of what happened to Greece and Rome and see what is left—only the pillars. What has happened, of course, is that great civilizations of the past, as they have become wealthy, as they have lost their will to live, to improve, then they have become subject to the decadence that eventually destroys the civilization. *The United States is now approaching that period.*"

Who uttered this warning? It came from your 37th President, Richard Nixon, one year before his overwhelming re-election of 1972. For President Nixon to make such a statement required courage and vision. The question may be asked: "If the President knew your country was in such grave danger, why was something not done to point the country back in the proper direction?"

It is natural to inquire why your 37th President did not follow up his warning to the American people that their beloved country was decaying from within. Could it be that he did not want to offend his wealthy friends who were content with the status quo and who resisted any new approach that might interfere with their money-gathering?

Or was it that he sincerely believed that the comparatively few rich are better able to look after the interests of the country? Many genuinely believe this, though your 3rd President, Thomas Jefferson, did not. He said: "I have great confidence in the common sense of mankind in general . . . I am not among those who fear the people. They—and not the rich—are our dependence for continued freedom."

It could well have been that your 37th President's ambition to make sure of his re-election persuaded him that he could introduce this matter of America's decay *after* he was re-elected. And who knows that he would have done just that, were it not for the Watergate affair? Surely, he wanted to go down in history as one of your great Presidents. Is it not a possibility that he had planned to take steps to overcome the decay that had been going on in your country ever since Lincoln warned of it in 1863? Could it not be that your 37th President had plans to lead the U.S.A. into higher fields of man's relationship to his Maker and to his fellow-man, but that same weakness which led his self-part to the colossal blunder of Watergate prevented his rising to higher aspirations? Might this not be the true explanation for the attempted cover-up?

If you will, for the moment at least, follow Lincoln's practice of seeking My wisdom rather than your own, you may realize that I *truly* have been working My will at Watergate. In the Partnership life, it is not I who does the punishing. Man punishes himself. Watergate should tell everyone who seeks to learn the truth that this is a classic fallacy being exposed for the fraud it is. <u>The fraud is that money and power beget happiness and a successful life.</u> Ask yourself, is this why I created you? Does it make sense that I would have forsaken the peace and serenity that pervaded the earth before I created humans? And to do so in order that humans may engage in a race for money and power?

If you can get yourself loose from the way of life handed you by the generations that came before you, and seek the truth as to why I created humans, you must come up with something better and more believable than the way of life humans have accepted as the way to live. I created you to live in Partnership with Me, and to keep well and vigorous to past 100. Yet you seem to have accepted a way of life that starts to tear you down long before your early fifties and cuts your life span down to an average of less than 70.

Your youth realizes that this way of life doesn't make sense, even though they may not yet know the right way to live. <u>Why can't you see the fallacy of it and do something about it?</u> I'm not talking religion, in the structured sense, although the true meaning of religion is man's relation to his Maker. If you do not learn from Watergate that the pursuit of money and power is not what I created you for, you may keep getting yourself elected, but you will not make your life worthwhile. You will not be making use of your Partnership with Me, which is like saying you are a failure.

I would caution the critics of your 37th President against sitting in judgment on him. They would do well to ask themselves how did they get their own higher ideals? Were these not a direct gift from Me? Did they have to fight hard battles overcoming the self-part of their nature? Do they understand and appreciate that it was My God-part of their nature that has helped them conquer their self-part? The very fact that they find it hard to be compassionate toward Richard Nixon might indicate that their own self-part has not been entirely subdued.

Lincoln never sat in judgment on his fellow-beings. Too conscious of his own weaknesses ("I am weak, poor, sinful" he wrote) Lincoln's attitude even toward those who were trying to undermine him as President was one of compassion and understanding.

The need for another Lincoln can be pointed up by a comparison of the ways your 16th President and your 37th acted towards those who disagreed with them. Where your 37th President had an Enemy list towards whom he planned bitter actions of hostility, your 16th President, guided by Me as in almost everything he said and did, showed love and understanding. A beautiful example of this shows up in Lincoln's response to his friend Horace Greeley, whose editorial in the New York Tribune of August 20, 1863 was titled "The Prayer of Twenty Millions." Greeley's editorial was addressed to Lincoln and expressed dissatisfaction with the policy Lincoln was pursuing "with regard to the slaves of rebels." Greeley's attack was offensive in tone, but where ordinary men follow their own wisdom and self-centered ways, Lincoln's dependence on My wisdom rather than his own shone thru his response.

With subtle humor and gentle treatment, Lincoln took Greeley's self-righteousness down a peg. Referring to the editorial, your 16th President said: "If there be in it any statements, or assumptions of fact, which I know to be erroneous, I do not, now and here, controvert them. If there be in it any inferences which I may believe to be falsely drawn, I do not, now and here, argue against them. If there be perceptible in it an impatient and dictatorial tone, I waive it in deference to an old friend, whose heart I have always supposed to be right."

This response should be a classic example, demonstrating why your 16th President always sought My wisdom rather than his own. For he followed the above statement with what was surely a matured statement of national policy: "I would save the Union. I would save it in the shortest way under the Constitution." While there was no doubt about Lincoln's "personal wish that all men everywhere should be free" he had also an *official* duty. Lincoln explained that while the official responsibility did not modify his personal wish, it necessarily took precedence over it. Consider how amazingly unambiguous his explanation reads as Lincoln gave it, and ask yourself could mortal man with his own wisdom have so simply and brilliantly responded with a complete absence of confusion to Greeley's judgmental mood with one which was radically different? Only because Lincoln sought My wisdom, as My agent and instrument, did he make it possible for Me to speak thru him: "My paramount object in this struggle is to save the Union, and is *not* either to save or to destroy slavery. If I could save the Union without freeing *any* slave I would do it; and if I could save it by freeing *all* the slaves I would do it; and if I could save it by freeing some and leaving others alone I would also do that." This policy was not applauded by extremists on either side, but the Union was saved!

It was only when the safety of the Union was assured that Lincoln issued the Emancipation Proclamation freeing all the slaves. To save the Union at this time when your nation is decaying from within is why I am addressing myself to you politicians now. That is why I am searching for another Lincoln. That is why this nation needs another Lincoln. You need someone who is conscious all the time of My presence within him and who will continually ask himself as did Lincoln, "What is God driving at?"

From a practical standpoint, how can you as a politician ignore My part in your nature? In your ability to speak and influence many people, don't you ever give a thought to the Creative Power that gave you this talent and the ability to put words together that prove persuasive?

Consider what happened to the elder Senator Robert LaFollette in the Presidential campaign of 1912. This great and good man was on his way to become his party's candidate for President. He was making a very important speech to the country's leading newspaper editors. These influential men were greatly impressed with Senator LaFollette's brilliant presentation when, suddenly his clear, intelligible words turned to babble. What came from his lips didn't make sense. He rambled on repetitively, and extravagantly, for 2½ hours, far beyond his scheduled time.

What had happened? Something that could happen to you, Mr. Politician. Indeed, have I not on occasions given you warnings of such a possibility? What public speaker has not experienced moments when his words became tangled as he uttered them, causing him embarrassment and possibly even concern? Fortunately, you were able to straighten things out and continue with your speech. But could you explain what had happened?

Could it not be that your Creator and Sustainer was trying to make you aware that the Power which kept open the lines of communication between the brain I gave you and the lips I built for you was My Power, not yours? You are the beneficiary of this Power, not the author or creator. Why not, as one who wants to be honest with himself, acknowledge this and be eternally grateful for My presence and partnership and guidance? May it not be that I had hoped Senator LaFollette's tragic experience, which ended his political career, would serve the purpose of bringing closer to Me not only all politicians but those who count on their ability to speak persuasively?

Unless you reflect soberly on this question, you may continue to believe you are the one who keeps these lines of communication open. But the fact is you can no more do this than you can keep your heart beating. It is I, your Creator and Sustainer, who does these things for you. This is part of My responsibility in our Partnership.

Your education may have failed to spell out for you the many proofs of our Partnership, but I have given you a brain, and you know this brain has helped get you where you are. Let your brain dwell on My part in your life. It may convince you to get your self-part out of My way. Lincoln operated this way. He did not delude himself as to who is boss of the Partnership. "We are all agents and instruments of Divine Providence." There is no other way you can be a true success, Mr. Politician. Your own wisdom is not enough to solve the complex problems of society. When you let My wisdom flow into your mind, accompanied by My love and power, you will understand why Lincoln said "I do not consider that I have ever accomplished anything without God." If you still feel that too much mention of God opens you to the charge of talking religion, perhaps the best way to meet this is head on. Come right out and say that God transcends religion.

I suggest you take time to read (and re-read) the words of Lincoln (p. 350) and consider that his expressions of belief in Me were those of a man who did not consider himself religious. Indeed, your 16th President had no specific religion, never having joined a church. He lamented:

> "I have often wished that I was a more devout man than I am. Nevertheless, amid the greatest difficulties of my administration, when I could see no other resort, I could place my whole reliance in God, knowing that all would go well, and that He would decide for the right."

Is this not the greatest profession of faith any person can make? I am suggesting that every politician, every one in administrative work, every one who has difficulties of any nature, commit to memory the words of Lincoln: ". . . when I could see no other resort, I could place my whole reliance in God, knowing that all would go well, and that He would decide for the right."

Mr. Politician, is this not the kind of understanding you would want every American child to get from his education? Does it not teach true self-knowledge? Should you not do all you can to have self-knowledge taught in public schools? Why permit visionless people to deter you from pursuing the true way to save your beloved nation? Educators who protest that to permit God's name to be mentioned in public schools is to introduce religion and to violate the Constitution need to do a little re-examination of PTCH.

As a politician holding a position of responsibility, you may deem it too risky to follow the Master Teacher's advice when you have to make an important speech: "Give no thought to what you should say. It will be given you at the moment."

Christ was assuring you that I, your Creator-Partner, would speak thru you and that your audience will react accordingly. They will be inspired. Their respect and confidence in you will increase tremendously.

But this presupposes you genuinely believe that I am your Creator-Partner. Even if you so believe yet feel it would be safer to prepare your talk in advance, let us do it together. Your listeners will intuitively understand that I am speaking thru you, and conclude you can be trusted and should be supported. The people who believe in Me will also believe in the politician who shows he believes in Me.

I urge that you beware of falling for the accepted fallacy that money is the answer to everything. Some politicians seem to have made money their God. I suggest an enterprising reporter can render a great service to the country by researching a few hundred wealthy people, investigating the measure of their increased happiness, if any, over that possessed before they achieved their wealth.

What this research will reveal is that the safest area for true happiness is in the moderate zone where one has the security of at least food, shelter and clothing. The line of happiness which accompanies your line of progress towards security stops when your ambition takes you beyond security into the realm of luxury.

The line of happiness does not just stop there. It takes a downturn. Why should this be? Because of My Law which says: "Too much of anything is not good for man." Think about that in every phase of your life. You need money in your way of life. Too much, however, almost always will create a rift in the family, either between husband and wife or between parents and children. If you have no close relatives, too much money will create a rift between you and your brother-man, unless you devote some of your wealth to helping him.

Your self-part will probably disagree, insisting that in your case, you would know how to handle your increased wealth. But I know it is not in the nature of your self-part to handle excess money in a way to promote your true happiness. The temporary pleasures that come from self-indulgence soon evaporate. But money you spend in helping your brother-man never ceases to give you lasting happiness.

What I am trying to convey to you is that your own highest happiness will not come from gathering more money for yourself but in helping others. You might take a leaf out of Ben Franklin's book. He retired from the business of making money for himself when he was still in his forties, explaining that he had achieved a measure of security and sought greater happiness in another way: "I can only show my gratitude to my Creator for these mercies by a readiness to help His other children and my brethren."

Franklin lived long enough to give a living demonstration of the joy that comes from deeds of love for one's brother-man. Approaching eighty years of age, he reminded the representatives of the 13 colonies who were struggling to form a union, using their own best wisdom in the process: "I have lived a long time, sirs, and the longer I live the more convincing proofs I have that God rules in the affairs of men."

I am mindful that the way of life which encompasses you on all sides today inhibits your capacity to see God in everything. Only the God-part of your nature can give you the spiritual maturity to wake up mentally and emotionally. As long as the self-part of man's nature is in control, how can one escape from the old limited pattern of thinking, from the old anxieties and fears that people accept as normal? Greed becomes normal. It is your self-part in action.

When you come to know the truth, that the Creative Spirit of Love which created you incarnated itself as part of your being, and serves as your ever-present Partner, there is no limitation to what you can do. And you also come upon the joy that the Master Teacher was talking about: "I have come that you may have life and have it more abundantly . . . My joy I would give you—not joy as the world knows joy" (born of riches, power, fame)—but the kind of joy only your Creator-Partner can give you. This is really the peace beyond understanding. Alongside this inner unspeakable peace, money is impotent. It is a fraud to lead people to believe otherwise.

The guidance I tried to get to the 1972 Democratic candidate that the U.S.A. was in danger of decay and the time was ripe to call the people back to God went unheeded. "One has to be practical," was the answer. But the money proved unavailing. He carried only one of the fifty states. An overwhelming defeat, a landslide!

Had this good man stuck to his original belief that the people were ready for a return to the ideals of the

Founding Fathers and Lincoln, and this meant a recognition of the presence of God in each person, he would not have needed money for TV, radio and newspaper advertising. His unique campaign would in itself make news. The media would have looked him up. "We have forgotten God" is really news as the theme for a Presidential candidate. Youth all over the country would have rallied to him, enthusiastically offering their services. But sadly, when he was persuaded to become "practical" and to adhere to "politics as usual" the youth deserted him.

How much more effective is sincere unsolicited word of mouth praise than commercial advertising! The latter is spending money to tell people how great you are, where the former is people telling their friends, "This is a man that can be trusted." Even the best advertising minds acknowledge there is no more potent form of advertising than sincere word of mouth praise. This kind of goodwill is really your God-part in action. It is irresistible. It speaks love. If you don't feel goodwill in your heart for all My children, don't try to tell Me you love Me, your God and Creator-Partner.

You may fool yourself and even some others, but you can't fool Me. Christ laid it on the line for such people: "How can you claim to love God whom you cannot see when you don't love your brother-man whom you can see?" Goodwill is love and love is God. No one who hates another human is a true believer in God. As the Creative Spirit of Love, I have implanted in you and in each of My children, a hunger for love. Money cannot buy or satisfy this hunger, nor can money interfere long with the Spirit of Love. Love cannot be defeated. Mr. Politician, take note!

Mr. Politican, should you not be helping your constituents gain a new understanding of an important aspect of life which seems to have been lost sight of in the pursuit of possessions? This has to do with the general belief that if a person is clever enough, he can get away with taking advantage of someone else. It is only fair that everyone should learn that no one, no matter how clever, can get away with any wrongdoing—big or little. Not that the Law will catch up with you—that is the laws of men. It is My Law of Compensation that makes it impossible for anyone to get away with the slightest wrongdoing.

My Law of Compensation is no man-made law in which shrewd lawyers can find loopholes. There are no loopholes in My laws. I want all my children to get that straight, because of education's failure to teach that my Creative Spirit of Love is part of their nature, and would guide them away from wrong doing.

If people had been taught this truth, they would know why no wrongdoing can pay off. The explanation is simple, and is well known to all who know of My presence within them. Along with the pleasure one gets from the wrong, there grows the punishment for it. The two are inseparable, because the two—crime and punishment—grow out of the same stem. As stated by one of My partners (Ralph Waldo Emerson), "Punishment is a fruit that unsuspected ripens within the flower of the pleasure which concealed it." In other words, it is impossible to sever the two—crime and punishment —any more than you can sever cause and effect, means and ends, seed and fruit. If you were taught to follow My wisdom rather than your own, you would know that the effect already blooms in the cause, the end pre-exists in the means, the fruit in the seed.

No matter what the nature of your wrongdoing, no matter how great the pleasure it brings you, the punishment rides along with the wrong and there is no way to escape it. Men may call this circumstance retribution but whatever it is called, you should know that no one committing a wrong can get away with it.

Let Me add that while the retribution is inseparable from the wrong, it may be spread over a long time and thus may not become distinct until after many years. Nor need the punishment be associated closely with the actual wrongdoing. It may leave the offender with his wealth or position intact but wound him in a much more vulnerable spot. He or his most dearly loved one may be stricken and suffer for a long time. There is no limitation on the kind of punishment. The more heinous the wrong, the more grievous the punishment. The offender brings this on himself. It is not I doing the punishing. He is the one.

There is no use deluding oneself that he will be smart enough to get away with it. Both pleasure and punishment are part of the one stem. If you choose to do the wrong, you are electing to take the punishment. You may ask, is there no forgiveness? Indeed there is, but only after the Law of Compensation has taken effect. And then only if you have earned forgiveness and sincerely seek above all else, to work your Partnership with Me.

The Law of Compensation is not aimed to punish as much as it is to set things straight. Consider how this law operated in the Watergate case. The aim was not to punish all who had a hand in the wrong as much as to save the U.S.A., to set things right in your country. Let your mind review the situation. It is not My way to compare one of my children with another, yet there is much to be gained by studying the way of your 16th President and contrasting it with the way of your 37th President. As Creator of both these men, I gave them good minds. Some would say great minds, but the first indication of a great mind is in its realization that there is within him an infinitely greater mind than his own. It is the mind of the Creative Spirit of Love which created the Universe and all its inhabitants, and sustains each and every one.

Take note of the sincere humility of your 16th President. In the century since his assassination, all Americans have come to appreciate his true greatness. Yet in his lifetime, he openly said of himself "I am weak, poor, sinful." His first inaugural address was more about Me, his Creator-Partner, than about himself.

Contrast this with the acceptance speech of your 37th President, in which he used the word "proud" at least five times. The favorite poem of your 16th President was "O, Why Should the Spirit of Mortal Be Proud?" Lincoln was surely not amongst those Americans who "vainly imagined in the deceitfulness of their own hearts that all America's blessings were produced by some superior wisdom and virtue of their own."

What your country has needed is a politician who understands as did Lincoln and the Founding Fathers before him that their own wisdom is insufficient for the day and they must always seek divine guidance from the Supreme Intelligence.

Your Creator is always seeking such a man. The one I will find is too humble to consider himself the makings of a Lincoln. Indeed, if he possessed that much self-confidence, he would not be the one I am seeking. Lincoln's faith was in Me, his Creator-Partner, not in the self-part of his nature. There is a vast distinction. Faith in Me as your Creator-Partner begets faith in yourself as My agent and instrument. Lincoln made his belief clear: "We are all agents and instruments of divine Providence." Often he stated, "Without the assistance of the Divine Being, I cannot succeed. With that assistance I cannot fail."

Has not the time come for all politicians to place their country's welfare above their own and thus follow Lincoln's way of seeking My wisdom above the wisdom of man? Surely, you Americans must disenthrall yourselves if you want to save your nation. If your nation continues to decay from within, you will lose the liberty you love. "Nations die by suicide. The sign of it is the decay of thought," warned My Partner, Emerson.

Proof of your nation's decay can be seen all about you. In drug and alcohol addiction, in the mad pursuit of money, in the distrust and hatred and prejudice so common it has become accepted as a way of life. Yet there is great hope in your youth. They know there is something wrong with the American way of life. They may not know what direction to take to reverse the decay they observe. Here is where you as a politician who wants to save his country can work with youth who want to rescue their country.

The way back to God should be a believable way based on common sense.

The Boys Scouts and the Girls Scouts proved you can lead people back to God without invoking structured religion. Millions of children of all denominations of religion, of all skin colors and ethnic backgrounds have demonstrated their love of God and country and yet established religion is carefully restricted from entering and causing divisiveness.

One of the greatest groups ever brought together is Alcoholics Anonymous. Their Twelve Steps lead the way back to God. Yet organized religion is carefully restricted from this group, though its members come from many different religions and backgrounds.

There is much that established religion can learn from this. Religion must be transformed into a way of life, if people are to be united in their belief in God. I did not create my children with the thought they should become Protestants, Catholics, Jews, or any other religion. I created them out of my Spirit of Love so that I may live in Partnership with them.

Would anyone dare to say I approve of the prejudice and persecution and warfare going on in My name and in the name of Christ? Let Me again state, particularly for the "religious" people who profess to believe in Me that if there is not love in their hearts for their brother-man, they approach Me in vain. Religion must be more than a talky business. It must come from a heartfelt love for your brother-man. Man-made creeds and rituals have proved helpful to some people, but without love for one's fellow-man, they can prove divisive. Christ made clear that without works of love, professions of belief can be hypocritical. In his wisdom and love, Christ reduced the Ten Commandments to two: love of God and love of man. When children learn that the Creative Spirit of Love is within each human, they will strive for happiness by giving rather than getting. In such selflessness, they will save your beloved nation.

* * *

The time for a change is upon you. Your people are ripe this time for a call to free themselves from slavery to self. They will surely respond if their leaders show the way. When the people respond in America, people from all over the world will take note and demand for themselves the new way of life Americans are living.

How much better to reach the common people of Russia and China, for instance, than to deal with their crafty and unreliable leaders whom you know from past experience cannot be trusted to keep agreements! When the people of China and Russia learn of the new America, they will rebel against dictatorship, in their desire to adopt the American new way of life.

There is going to be a new America. And to bring it about there is going to be a new breed of politicians.

They will follow in the steps of your 16th President, who openly acknowledged:

> "Without the assistance of the Divine Being I cannot succeed. With that assistance I cannot fail. Trusting in Him who can go with me, and remain with you, and be everywhere for good, let us confidently hope that all will yet be well."

The politician of the future will not have to seek the office. The people will seek him. Personal ambition is the self-part of man in action. What your country needs is the person seeking to respond to God's will. As Creator of the Universe, I am determined that the U.S.A. shall show the rest of the world an example of how to live in partnership with Me, insuring peace, happiness, prosperity. In this I need the help of the right kind of politician.

* * *

If God Spoke to the One
in Search of Healing
Might it be Something Like This:

What you are about to read is simply the imagining of one who has learned when he sincerely strives to become "an agent and instrument of Divine Providence" (Lincoln's words) his Partner will guide him, speak thru him and work thru him. The author believes this holds true for you, too.

You want to be whole. I planned for you to be whole, for all My children to be whole. Why then is there so much illness? Specifically, why are *you* ailing? I must confess part of the answer is in My determination that humans be free to make their own decisions. If freedom means anything, it means being free to do wrong things as well as right things.

One of the wrong things some humans have chosen to do is to deliberately disregard Me in their everyday affairs. Some pay Me respect on a Sunday morning, but I want to live in constant Partnership with each of My children, to guide them to their highest happiness. Indeed, this is why I decided to create humans. I planned for each to have a sturdy body, a sound mind, and a constant awareness of the presence of My Spirit within them, as their Creator-Partner.

To insure that My children realized that this was My plan, the right kind of education was essential. Children would learn early in life why and how they were born, how My Spirit spent nine months with them building each a body with a brain. They would then understand there were two separate though integrated powers at work in them. One was Mine, their Creator; the other was their own. The purpose of life is for these two separate powers to become ONE.

If this truth were made part of their education, so that all the way from the beginning to their college graduation, self-knowledge was their most important study, the children would be aware of My Partnership with each. But something arose to interfere with this plan. It is ironic that this something was created by men with the best of intentions. Its object was to make people aware of Me and My part in their lives. Instead of using Education to bring this about, they chose Religion.

Now, simple religion is man's relation to his Maker, a way of life. But some people did not think this was enough, so they went in for structured religion. This introduced rules and regulations, setting out how people were to sing praises to Me and worship Me. This served to change wholeness to holiness. It also presumed that I wanted My children to worship Me when what I really wanted was their love and Partnership. It was not long before the very name by which people called Me—God, carried a completely religious connotation. This had the unfortunate effect of taking Me out of their everyday affairs and confining Me to a segment of life which they called religion. The effect was to destroy or at least seriously interfere with My plan for education to give children understanding of My part in their nature. Because My name—God—was so closely identified with structured religion, professional educators became timid about using God to educate children to their true nature. The result is I am left out of education, and children are led to believe their self-part is the only part of their nature. The guidance I planned to give My children to keep well physically has reached only a few.

People unwittingly use only their own wisdom in matters of health and obviously this is not enough. If you want to know why you are ailing, the answer is those who came before you left Me out of their everyday affairs. They did this not intentionally but out of a lack of understanding. The way to help yourself become whole is to recognize that My Creative Spirit of Love which built your body and mind never departed from you but remains to keep you going and to serve as your Creator-Partner. This will be the beginning. But then you must work at it. You must work our Partnership. The fundamental rule governing our Partnership is "God guiding, man doing."

I am aware that you want to become whole promptly. This is natural. You would like to have Me undo in an instant what has been years in the making. It is possible I will do this. I have done it in the past for others. Why then, do I not do it for all My children? You know the answer to that if you have children of your own. How would this help to prevent future illnesses? Is not the proper step to get people to learn the truth about their nature and Mine?

Yet, you naturally want to know why you can't be healed as some others have been in a miraculous sort of way. What if your greater happiness as well as your best contribution to your fellow-man is in the way you are accepting your misfortune? If people see in you one who has tried one's best to become whole, without avail, and whose attitude then is one of complete acceptance of God's will, you are giving many people faith and inspiration, and belief in My Partnership with them.

Look about you, and you may find people who are suffering far greater illness and incapacity than you. Observe how they are rising above the self-part of their nature and letting their God-part take over. Then take note of how these people are beloved and respected. They are doing My will. They are working their Partnership with Me. In the doing, they have found a happiness and an inner peace that they could achieve in no other way.

You may ask further questions about the particular ones that have been healed in mysterious ways, like the laying on of hands, or the result of prayer. Why were these selected? The answer might be that I am hoping for things from them. "To whom much hath been given, of him shall much be required." I count on these fortunate people helping My other children to a better understanding of their nature. I want each of My children to know My plan to live in Partnership with them. If these recovered ones fail to do what I expect of them, they not only fail Me and their fellow-man, they fail themselves. The healing that came so miraculously may depart as instantly. This will leave things worse than they were before. My blessings are never for one person alone. My blessings are to get My children to help My other children, and thus they all find greater happiness.

I owe it to you to explain how and why you have become a victim of ill health. I do not lay this at your door. It is due to the way of life that leaves Me out of My children's everyday affairs. Let Me explain. Long before I decided to create humans on the earth, I had created dumb animals. I gave them simple tastes, so they were content to eat grasses, leaves, grains, and some fruits and nuts. As an experiment, I made some animals carnivorous, but I planned for animals to live mostly on natural growing grasses and grains.

After more than a billion years of experiments with animals, I decided to create humans because I wanted to live in Partnership with them. I gave them each a brain capable of almost unlimited development. I also gave them freedom to go their own way, even to ignoring Me, their Creator, if they chose to do so. To make life more enjoyable I endowed them with taste buds which enabled them to relish countless kinds of foods. With their greater intelligence, it was to be assumed they would soon learn that the experience of eating was not only a delightful pastime, but was the means I was using to sustain their bodies, promote their growth and enable them to keep whole and healthy.

In order for humans to arrive at this understanding, however, they would first have to acquire some knowledge of themselves. They would have to learn why they are here and what is the purpose of life. Was it not to be expected that in their education would be included mention of My part in their nature? After all, I had created them, I brought about their growth from infancy to maturity. It is My Creative Spirit of Love that keeps their hearts beating and does the many other things in their bodies which they can't do for themselves. For some reason hard to understand, they used their freedom to disregard Me, their Creator and Partner. They left Me out of Education and consigned Me to Religion. This permitted them to follow the wishes of their self-part: to gather money, to acquire power, position, fame. This meant disregarding My part in their nature.

But how does all this affect your health? The answer is that their disregard of the part I take in their everyday lives includes a disregard of the blessings of food and sunshine and sleep and fresh, invigorating air. They took all these for granted. Indeed, they did worse. They began to tamper with the natural foods I created. In doing so, they removed from natural foods much of the life-giving elements needed for health and vigor. This meant people were eating foods that had been robbed of invaluable mineral salts and vitamins.

What was the purpose of food processors in this? The refining of the whole grains (to make white bread, for instance) was done either out of complete ignorance—which you may accept or disbelieve—or for commercial reasons. When My natural foods become ripe, they do not last long. However, if the life-giving elements are removed, the remainder of the food can keep on the shelves of food stores for quite some time without spoiling. The question remains: how much good is this kind of food doing you?

Nothing in their education—nothing even in the physician's medical training—includes the teaching of nutrition. What most physicians know today about nutrition, they have picked up on their own and for this they deserve thanks and patronage.

Then consider air. People take air as much for granted as they do Me, their Creator-Partner and Sustainer. Yet, if air were removed from them, they would perish almost instantly. Why then, do they stand by and allow this invaluable sustainer of life to become polluted to such an extent as to adversely affect their lives, in some cases to actually shorten their life span? What other answer is there than that money has become more important than health?

Then there is the simple matter of sleep. It had been My plan for sleep to be the great restorer. Sleep would re-charge your battery, as it were. But because humans were not taught My part and contribution to their everyday lives, they found a better use for night than Mine. They invented a new way to live. They called it night life. This way of life provided artificial ways of escaping from themselves. Unfortunately, this way of life did not provide sleep—in fact, it seriously interfered with sleep. They got around this by resorting to different kinds of pills, drugs and concoctions to become unconscious so as to escape from themselves. It is a question whether this kind of "sleep" helps restore the body in the slightest. It does provide a temporary escape from self.

Is it any wonder that people soon begin to show signs

of body deterioration? Is it any wonder their children begin to inherit certain deficiencies which hamper Me in My plans for their health and wholeness? From the beginning, I was determined that every child was entitled to a proper start in life. So great was My insistence on giving each child his due that, on occasions, I had no choice but to deplete the mother's life-giving elements in order to supply the proper material needed to build the baby's body. This was sadly a case of robbing the mother in order to assure her baby of a proper start in life.

Then, there is the matter of water. I dotted the earth's surface with natural springs—pure, wholesome, refreshing water. Man, following the wisdom of his self-part, congregates in cities to such an extent they are compelled to use rivers for their drinking water. In the pursuit of possessions, men build factories which pollute the rivers. Then they use chemicals to clean up the water so that they do not become infected with disease.

This discourages many people from drinking water, as they find the taste, the smell and the very idea of drinking cleaned-up water that had been polluted with human sewage and factory wastes most repugnant. This promotes the use of soft drinks that have been sweetened with refined sugar or coal tar derivatives.

It is good to observe that many people are giving sober thought to escaping city life and getting a place out where My natural gifts for health and peace of mind assure them of better health and longer life. They sacrifice money in so doing, but is it really a sacrifice giving up money for better health?

Now, you may be getting some idea of the difficulty in restoring you to health and wholeness. It may have taken a long time reaching your present state of deficiency of life-giving materials. Added to this, you yourself would know if the use of drugs and alcohol have had a part in making your condition worse.

You may also be getting some idea of what you are asking for in praying for immediate relief and healing. But something can be done for you and, as your Partner, I am determined to bring it about. However, as My partner, you will have to co-operate. The first thing I need is your sincere belief in My presence in you as your Creator-Partner. I do not ask this in blind faith. Rather, I want you to use the brain I have built for you. I want you to re-examine some of the things your education has persuaded you to take for granted. Just examining everything in your life from the time you arise in the morning until you go to sleep at night, will supply you with positive proof that I have a part in every phase of your everyday life.

What should that mean to you? Surely, that your own best interests would be served by turning your will over to Me. I suggest you read and re-read the third of the Twelve Steps of A. A.: "Made a decision to turn our will and our lives over to the care of God *as we understood Him.*" Nor should this be considered a sacrifice. Is it ever a sacrifice giving up the lesser for the greater?

You will receive the benefit of My guidance in more matters than rebuilding your health. My Creative Spirit of Love will guide you in everything. And to your surprise and delight, you will discover how much inner peace and joy help in health. Breathe out ego, breathe in God, My friend and partner. You are not alone. Let us work together, giving out love to all we meet. You will feel better each day. You will sleep better each night. You will be getting My constant blessings. Peace! To learn of Christ's miracle healings, take note of the following:

1. Christ firmly believed the spirit of GOD is in every person.
2. He believed the Spirit creates the physical.
3. He believed the Spirit works with the physical.
4. He believed the Spirit controls and dominates the physical.
5. Whenever he found a sufferer who believed as he did on these points, a healing took place.
6. This required faith on the part of the sufferer. Sincere unshakable faith on all these points.
7. Christ knew this was all there was to it. It was no miracle to him. He expected it. He knew it was God working thru him.
8. If you can believe the spirit of God is in you, if you seek to have God's spirit dominate you completely, miracles can take place in you.
9. They need not be tremendous miracles. They can be little things in the body, brought about by the Spirit working with the physical.
10. But faith is the necessary ingredient, although occasionally it seems that God will bring about a miracle for My own purposes, perhaps to force a transformation in a person's understanding.

11. To one whose faith in the presence of God has become unshakable and who sincerely strives to be dominated completely by his Creator-Partner, miracles will occur every day of his life.

12. It is a result of God's Spirit working with your Spirit, to the benefit of your physical, mental and spiritual being.

13. God created you to be God's free Partner in the work of creation. Life begins when this understanding takes complete hold of you.

14. All that this requires of you is a complete surrender of your little self. To turn your life and your will over to God, as you understand Me.

15. God created breathing a two-way exercise to remind you of My presence. With every breath, "Breathe out Ego, breathe in GOD."

16. True faith includes the art of consent—to consent to what God sends your way—trusting in My purpose for you. I want to use you to inspire others by your faith and courage.

If God Spoke to the Parents of a Newborn Child Might it be Something Like This:

> What you are about to read is simply the imagining of one who has learned when he sincerely strives to become "an agent and instrument of Divine Providence" (Lincoln's words) his Partner will guide him, speak thru him and work thru him. The author believes this holds true for you, too.

Is there anything more wonderful than a new-born child? Is there a greater miracle anywhere? And yet, is there anything more taken for granted? How many prospective mothers are aware of the significance of being pregnant? How would you feel about wearing a tiny insignia indicating: "Careful! Creator at work"? If there is any time when you should be aware of our Partnership it is when I am at work within you building your baby. Because most everyone about you takes pregnancy for granted, leaving Me out of it altogether, you probably leave Me out of consideration too. But think a minute. Think of the building process going on in your body without your contributing to it in any way. Your only contribution, and this goes for both father and mother of the child to be born, lasted but a few minutes. And it was not work; it was pleasure; and if you allowed Me to participate it should have been ecstasy.

A miracle has just happened in the lives of you both, but most likely everyone around you will pass it by with the comment, "They just had a baby." In your hearts, you may both feel that what happened to you is indeed a miracle, but because your way of life leaves Me out of the everyday affairs of life, you have been trained to accept your newborn child as a casual event. Also, you unwittingly deprive your child of the kind of upbringing it is entitled to, and which I, its Creator, planned for the child.

When I have completed my task of building the child and am easing this new creation out of your body, another miracle occurs and I would like to believe you count Me in on this. For I am the Creative Spirit of Love, and I am causing to flame in your heart the spirit of love for this new creation of Mine which you naturally regard as your child. This feeling of love—this closeness you feel to your new-born babe—do you realize I am responsible for it? You wouldn't take credit for this feeling of love? You can't help yourself. I instilled it in you—this is part of My Creative Spirit of Love. You may not have given this much thought before, but you should now. You want to feel this close to your child all the time from its first day on. Why should this not be so? Why must children draw apart from their parents as they grow up? Why should not this kind of selfless love that a mother feels for her new-born child last? Indeed, why should it not grow as the child grows? I who planned for the child to grow also planned for the love between parents and a child to grow. Why then, is this so seldom the case?

The answer is really simple. The Partnership of Man and Maker has been ignored. Had your parents been taught, as children, that My Creative Spirit of Love which spent nine months in them building them a body with a brain, never departs from them but remains with them in loving Partnership, they in turn would have made sure you were so taught.

Why were you not so taught? Because professional educators were intimidated to hold that any mention of My part in a person's life would be regarded as introducing religion into education. This is like confining Me to a pigeonhole earmarked religion. Does this make sense that the Creator of the Universe should be so confined?

The result is that no one dare refer to the Creator in the public schools, and children do not learn the truth of their nature. They do not learn there is a higher part to their nature than the self-part. They grow up not knowing that My Creative Spirit of Love is the higher part of their nature.

Ask yourself, "How about love? Is it an accident?" "Did it just happen?" If you have ever asked yourself why there is so much trouble in the world, it is because most people do not know they have a higher self—My Creative Spirit of Love. They did not learn that by virtue of My presence within them, as their Creator-Partner, they need not be guided by their little self. It is the little self in people, when allowed to have its way, that causes most of the world's troubles. The little self does not know much about selfless love. This means your self-part does not know the answer to anything. For the answer to all things is love.

Without love, nothing works. When you hear someone propose a solution to a problem, if love is not present in the proposal, beware! Love must be in the proposal because Love is the answer. Any other proposal, regardless of how wise the person offering it, will not work. Nothing works without love. That's how and why I planned the Partnership of man and Maker. I created the earth out of love. I created you out of love. I needed your love. I want it now. I want you to know that the only way you can enjoy life is thru selfless love. Your self-part thinks it can enjoy life by getting things. More and more possessions. It won't work. It has never worked. Oh, some people may think it works. It seems to work for a while. But it cannot work for long because My plan is to the contrary.

I knew the risk I was taking in giving man both a brain of such potential development and freedom to ignore My presence, but I knew men would eventually discover the truth of their nature. Also that peace and love would eventually conquer the little self and persuade this self-centered entity that its own highest happiness demands a complete surrender to the higher self within. Having given man freedom, I feel I should wait on him to make the great discovery of his partnership with Me. I considered the matter for several billions of years after creating dumb animals before creating human beings. I knew it would be tough going for many centuries. But My love was so great, My desire to live in partnership with you so irresistible, that finally, a few thousand years ago, I created man.

Some scientists, put off by structured religions, state as a fact that man evolved from dumb animals. Is this their way of denying the existence of a Supreme Being? Are evolutionists trying to make the point that man evolved on his own? From an ape? If man did evolve from animals, would it not be because this was in My plan? The difference between dumb animals and human beings is so vast, why is it not clear to the evolutionists that it would be much easier for Me to create human beings "from scratch" rather than to wait the millions of years it would require for man to evolve from an ape? Or is it that they limit My power to that of man and therefore doubt My ability to create? How would man get a brain of such tremendous potential development, if I did not plan it that way and create him with it? It all comes back to the failure of education to teach children the truth of their nature. Children would learn from the beginning something of the Creative Spirit which formed the earth and the universe, with its billions of galaxies each containing billions of planets and stars, trillions of light years apart.

The influence of PTCH may cause you to tremble at the thought of daring to break with Precedent, Tradition, Custom, Habit. But with My presence and Partnership, all things are possible, and you will prove a help to your fellow-man in ways you never dreamed of. Regardless of what others may say or think, you have just had a miracle happen to you. Show that you believe it and others will do likewise because it is the truth and because it makes sense. I created your child to live in partnership with Me, to give it the benefit of My love, wisdom and power. Once you understand this is true for your child, you will be persuaded it is also true for both of you.

PTCH would have you believe nothing can be done to combat present conditions. "This has been going on for years" is their argument. Let not this sort of fatalism impress you. You surely have learned from your past experiences and from the way I have often rescued you in the past, that when people work with Me, nothing is impossible.

People need but look at a newborn child. PTCH takes this new creation for granted. That's the way it has always been regarded and that's the way PTCH would keep it. But you and I can get people to see the truth when they look at this newborn child. We will set people to thinking this child is not a creation of man's or woman's. Only God can create humans. People will think again: Someone has to keep the child's heart beating and cause the child to grow. Someone has to transform the food the child eats into blood, bone, muscle, brain. Who is that Someone if not the Creative Spirit of Love?

Now, these simple truths don't require an enforced belief to impress them on your mind. They are simple everyday events. Every few seconds I cause a child to be born. I see that the food each eats is transformed into blood, bone, muscle, brain, etc. I bring about their physical growth. I see that their brain grows and I keep open the lines of communication so that as they grow they can think and speak and work, using the other parts of the body I made for them. Now, why should these things be hard to understand?

Let Me say again you two have just had a miracle happen to you. Your newborn child is that miracle. The fact that most people are blind to this truth is no reason for you to follow suit.

What did not exist a few months ago is now a live human. This is a miracle. To see the child grow each day for years to come is another miracle. Treat your child like the miracle it is. Help it to understand that I, who created it, will remain with it forever, living in partnership, guiding it to its highest happiness. The miracle that is this child will lead you both to make a miracle of your lives.

If God Spoke to the Athlete Might it be Something Like This:

What you are about to read is simply the imagining of one who has learned when he sincerely strives to become "an agent and instrument of Divine Providence" (Lincoln's words) his Partner will guide him, speak thru him and work thru him. The author believes this holds true for you, too.

My athletic partner, and I include all types of athletes in every field of sport, from heavyweight fighting champions to ping pong, and particularly the one who plays for money, and who may have lost the art of getting fun out of the game, I have something to say to you and I am assuming you want Me to give it to you straight.

I will not say a word you can't believe. Not even a pep talk like that your coach or trainer might give you. Just some reminders of truths you have known a long time but may have since lost awhile. May I first ask if you know how you got your exceptional skill? I know you worked hard to get it. I know you must have made sacrifices. For this you deserve great credit, and if you choose to leave Me out of having a hand in instilling in you the desire to excel, I will not raise an issue about this.

Do you ever ask yourself how you got the potential

for athletic skill in the first place? Who gave you that splendid body? Who gave you a mind to go with that fine body? How did you go about making your body and mind so well co-ordinated and agile in reaction? Who gave you a flair for the game, the instinct to do the right thing at the right time?

I'm not denying what credit is due you. What I am hoping for is to get you to realize that our Partnership —yours and mine—is a classic example of what a perfect Partnership could be. A perfect partnership exists where each partner is aware of the contribution of the other. A perfect partnership is where each partner knows the part he must play in the partnership, and the need to be fair and square to his partner. He must want to show appreciation of the part his partner plays in the success of the partnership, and to do so with love and humility.

Sadly, your education and training did not encourage you to seek answers to these questions. The chances are that as a child, you were not taught there was at work in you a Power infinitely greater than your own and that this higher power was serving as your Creator-Partner. Had you been so taught, there might be no need for questions like Mine to arise now.

When you achieve the rank of one of the great athletes of your day, it is surprising and disappointing that not one of the well recognized sportswriters mentions the part your Partner played in your achievements and in getting you where you are. It is as if everyone believes your Creator went off and left you on your own. How could I leave you on your own? Who would keep your heart beating? Not to speak of all the other things I do in your body to bring about such a beautiful specimen of a human being?

This kind of inadequate thinking stems from a faulty education. It comes from a failure to understand what the Master Partner sought to get across: "It isn't I who do these things. It is The Father within me. He tells me what to say and what to do."

As an athlete, you know you can have a spell when everything goes right for you and you seem unbeatable. If it's baseball, you go errorless and bat over 300. At basketball, no matter from where you take a shot at the basket, there's a swish. At football, you snare a pass that looked impossible to even get your hands on. At tennis, your returns just stay in bounds and are unreturnable. At golf, you see a line between your ball and the cup from any part of the green.

Surely, you have had spells like that. Have you ever given thought to the possibility that maybe you're being looked after? Or have you just assumed you had brought these plays off all by yourself? Well, if you can stand being entirely honest with yourself, let Me try to explain these streaks of excellence and what they may signify. The truth may reveal why, after you have had a run of victories, you suddenly lose the touch or the feel. Try as you may, you just can't recover the skill that gave you that run of perfection.

If you believe you have a Creator-Partner, who is doing things in your body which you can't possibly do for yourself, you have no trouble in realizing that your good streak was really your perfect partnership in action. It is really a simple fact that you and I are working our Partnership in perfect love and harmony. You have a feeling of being guided to take the steps you take, anticipating what should be done. And when you go off your game, it may very well be that I find it necessary to bring you to a realization of My part in your life.

For believe it or not, I work My will in athletics as I do in every aspect of life. I constantly seek the kind of partners whose aim is to attain liberation from the self. To achieve this purpose, I may give you a streak of good fortune, and then test you with a streak of ill fortune. If you are one who leaves Me out of consideration of your skill and prowess, and I can't get to you with a run of victories and defeats, it is proof that our Partnership is not working well. My aim is to have you realize My presence within you in order to change your whole attitude toward life and toward your fellow-man. Can there be any other explanation for a streak of good and bad fortune?

When I say I work My will, My aim is not to punish or set you off your game. Rather, My will is to work our Partnership. This means I must at times work things out to balance affairs in your life, all in your interest. Frustrations serve a real purpose in establishing our Partnership.

Because I respect your freedom and your right to choose, I cannot force understanding upon you, but I reserve the right to use whatever means I deem best to get you to understand your true nature. Sometimes My way is tough on you. Everything seems to break badly for you. It may be that on these occasions I am trying to do more than just get you out of a slump. I am trying to get our Partnership working right. If this means I first have to knock your self-confidence into a cocked hat, that's what will happen. But please remember that what I do is not to punish, but to bring us closer together.

How many times do you start a game not feeling too well physically or mentally or emotionally? If you knew there was a secret you could make use of to put you in really good condition for the game, wouldn't you want to know it? I am giving it to you now. It has to do with My part in your playing. If you persist in closing your mind to My part in your life, then I cannot do much for you. If you will open your mind to one simple fact affirmed scientifically by your Atomic Energy Commission, you may change your whole attitude about My part in your everyday life, including every movement you make in the games you play.

This one simple fact is that the physical body with which you won and lost games last year is no longer with you. In that one year I built you a new body. I do this every year for each of My human creatures. In a recent report, the Atomic Energy Commission after tracing isotopes in the human body stated that "in a year approximately 98% of the atoms in us now will be replaced by other atoms that we take in our air, food and drink."

This scientific fact should never have remained a secret but it seems to have been pretty much neglected. For it spells out My Partnership with you. This new body was not made by you. I made it. It is I, your

Creator-Partner who transforms the food you eat, the water, milk and fruit juices you drink, and the air you breathe into blood, bone, muscle, brain, to replenish your worn-out body parts and build you a new body. Why does your education ignore this scientifically proven fact? Because professional educators are guided more by PTCH (Precedent, Tradition, Custom, Habit) than they are by Me.

Let Me tell you now how to take immediate advantage of the secret I mentioned, as you are about to start your contest. The revelation is a six-second exercise— the simplest, most natural and the greatest of all exercises. You start this six-second exercise by heaving a great breath out, almost like a bull snorting. As you do this, you think to yourself: "Out self." With the slower incoming breath, you think "In Partner." Or if you like, "Out ego, in God."

With its finish, you repeat the six-second exercise. Slow it down or speed it up, as you wish. There is magic in it. And there is no end to it or to the good coming from it. Doubtless, there will be pauses as you forget to exercise, but you can always come back to it.

It is My plan that you must breathe in order to live. The six-second exercise adds a unique and compelling dimension to breathing. No matter where you are, no matter what you are doing, you have to breathe to keep alive. As you were not properly taught about our Partnership, you probably leave it to Me to breathe for you. The six-second exercise will give you a decided plus. It will help restore your strength, it will inspire your thinking, it will uplift your spirit.

In making breathing a two-way process, I wanted to provide an answer to the natural question: "If God is my ever-present Partner, why was not a way provided to make me always conscious of God's presence within me?" Breathing is the way that was provided for this purpose. Air is as invisible as God, yet you have no trouble believing in air. Why should it be difficult to believe in the Creator of air? How can you fail to believe in the Creative Spirit of Love which formed your frame and brain, and which sustains you each moment with the breath of life?

You will discover thru actual practice the miracles that come naturally in the wake of the six-second exercise, and when you do, you are not to keep this secret. You are to show your love for your brother-man by passing on to him this natural way to work his Partnership with Me. The great good it will do for him will come back to you in many ways.

In the hope that all athletes will gain in understanding of My love of infinite variety, I want to call attention to the growing athletic accomplishments of My black partners, to keep match with their steady improvements in all other fields. Because of the prominence of athletics in your life and the lives of all My children, I have planned to compensate for the ignominies heaped upon black people by adding to their athletic skill in your most prominent sports: football, basketball, baseball, boxing and track, in such a way as to call attention to their superiority. Due to the failure of education to teach that I am the Creator-Partner of *all* people, regardless of skin color or ethnic background or nationality or any difference whatsoever, I have implanted in My black partners a greater sensitivity and awareness of My presence within them.

Most black athletes are aware of My part in their athletic accomplishments. They do not hesitate to acknowledge My part in their success. They tell Me and they sing praises of gratitude to Me. Their spirituals tell often of My presence within them. I might inject here that the most effective black leaders know that the best way to achieve better black-white relations is for the blacks to so live the Partnership Life that My white children will learn from them. What better way to remind My white children of their own Partnership with Me?

Moreover, the highly successful black athletes who are earning large sums of money have an opportunity to help their fellow-man instead of spending the money in self-indulgences or a large expensive home for themselves. What an example this should be for *all* My children who have acquired money, to show their gratitude by acts of kindness to their brother-man and My other children.

There are some splendid associations of athletes which strive to emphasize religion in athletics. How helpful to get athletes to understand the natural advantages coming from recognizing their Partnership with Me. Their sincere unselfish efforts are doing much to transform formal religion into a way of life. This was the mission of the Master Partner, who gave his life to teach the Partnership life of Man and Maker. Jesus lived so selflessly that he achieved perfect partnership with Me. By perfect partnership, I mean he became One with Me. This enabled him to take the misfortunes, frustrations and adversities which all humans are subject to. He overcame them by letting go and letting God take over. He attained liberation from the self so completely that it was really God thinking thru him, speaking thru him, working thru him. He knew it was I working thru him and with the greatest humility he said so. He has these encouraging words for you: "The things I do, you, too can do."

Remember this, particularly when you have had a bad day or a series of bad days. When that forward pass is right in your hands and your little self looks up too quickly to get going; when the bases are loaded and you strike out; or in basketball you miss an easy layup; or a "gimme" putt slides by the hole; or any one of a dozen things that can go wrong in a game, happens to you. Do you ever wonder how this sort of thing happens? It is generally attributed to carelessness or taking your eyes off the ball or whatever. How many give a thought to the possibility that I was working out My will? Lincoln always did. He constantly asked himself "What is God driving at?"

You may not think I would interest Myself in such trivial things, that I'm far too holy to be concerned with a tennis ball, a baseball, a football or a basketball. Why do you think I arranged for you to play topnotch athletics unless I wanted to have a hand in it as your everpresent Partner, sharing the excitement with you, the ecstasy of winning, the agony of defeat? To count Me out of any phase of your everyday activities is to belittle yourself.

Every athlete, like every other person, experiences

times of frustration and adversity. Like the others, he suffers because of them. He has his times of doubts when his skill seems to have deserted him. These periods of suffering and unhappiness are added to by some thoughtless people who, in their self-disappointment at being denied the victory they came to see, start to boo the athlete who is disappointing them. Strangely, they do not seem to realize that they cannot feel as bad as the athlete they thoughtlessly are booing. The act of booing an athlete for an error is really the self-part of man in action. The probabilities are that these "boo-birds" never indulged in athletics themselves. No self-respecting athlete ever boos another athlete. His own experiences when he had bad days inhibits him from booing another athlete.

Sportswriters who should be familiar with the difficulties athletes have in staying on top of their game would render a real service not only to the athlete but to all fans by educating the "boo-birds." Is it either an intelligent or adequate argument to hold to the position that the fan pays for admission to the game and is entitled to boo? Booing surely does not promote good sportmanship, and good sportsmanship is a part of good character. It may be natural for the spirits of fans to rise and fall with victory and defeat. But where does My part of a person's nature figure if his self-part is encouraged to boo an athlete who is doing his best to bring him victory?

It is natural to want to win, but learning how to lose is also part of life. There is such a thing as playing for the joy of it—win or lose. The "boo-bird" wants so much to win that the fun has gone out of the game for him. Wanting too much to win may be taking the fun out of the game not only in professional sports where athletes play for a living. This lack of sportsmanship is invading college and high school—yes, even kid games. There is an insistence: "Winning is not the most important thing—it's the only thing." This is stupid and false. It's great to win, of course, but it is not everything. It's more important that you are aware it is your little self who wants so much to win. It's more important that you understand that your opponent has feelings, too. A proper understanding of these things would help people get more fun out of playing and out of life.

Athletes and fans alike should learn to take their lickings like a man. Today, one can readily get the impression that some people take pride in being poor sports. How can anyone defend the practice of some fans booing a member of their own team or the whole team or the coach? This is raising the self-part of one's nature to where it is everything, and My part is nothing.

There was a time when people engaged in sports for the fun, the sheer exhilaration, exercise and healthful benefits derived from the sport. Today, sports has become big business. Millions of people are engaged in it as an occupation to make money. Money may be the principal objective, but there is also the desire to win, which in a very large measure, is tied to the making of money.

How far should the desire to win take hold of an athlete? Should it encourage him to risk permanent injury—to play even in pain, with torn and strained ligaments and cartilage, broken bones, hamstring muscles? In order for an athlete to continue playing, is it o.k. to inject him with steroids and painkillers of various kinds? Can one not go too far in a belief "there is no substitute for victory?"

Is this because victory means more money? Does the extra money make it right for an athlete to continue playing while enduring physical pain that might result in permanent damage? Has victory become your magnificent obsession? Has the desire for victory taken hold of some athletes to the point where they are willing to compete while under hypnosis, turning themselves into zombies, instilled with an overpowering concentration and desire to win?

How many people understand that the desire to win at all costs is a classic case of man's self-part excluding My part in his life altogether? There is no way that such an attitude can be made to work for a person's good. Oh, you may win the game. You may make big money, but there is no way the net result will give you the happiness you seek. There can be no lasting happiness without My participation. Your self-part simply does not have what it takes to insure lasting happiness. Athletic history is filled with the names and records of men and women who achieved fame and money, only within a short time to be forgotten, and the anguish they suffer is all the greater, because they had once reached close to the top.

Some modern youth, seeing the dangers of being caught up in the money-and-popularity whirls of competitive school athletics, have gone to the other extreme and rejected all forms of exercise. This, too, is unfortunate; they are missing out on the joy and vigor of the body which I gave them.

To arise early in the morning, to do some jogging, and perhaps a dip in an outside pool promotes vigor and a form of Spartanism. Very little expense is attached to this form of athletic training, but the rewards are great and it serves to bring us closer together, reminding you of the simple things in life which I have arranged for all My children.

There are other simple forms of athletic exercise: yoga, dancing, swimming, running, gymnastic variations—these are forms of movement which I've made possible for your body to perform. There is a tendency on the part of most of My children to take these body movements for granted, but when you see a handicapped person glory in a victorious struggle to take one step or lift an arm, you should appreciate the physical capacities you who possess a sound body have been blessed with. The potential for movement varies as much as people's personalities, proving My love for variety.

Some exercises can be done alone, such as running, swimming, yoga. Then there are team games and dancing which are made for fellowship with others. Some sports like wrestling and judo serve as an outlet for physical contact without need for spurring aggressive instincts. It is possible that quarrels could be settled thus in a fair way, as some primitive peoples have done.

Running, walking and yoga can be practiced by people of all ages, rich or poor. These solitary exercises offer an opportunity for you to meditate on the rhythms of breathing and body movement which I have instilled in you and in the universe.

As you practice, you can feel your body growing stronger, becoming a more efficient channel for My power. As you breathe out, you exhale the waste which has accumulated in your earthly system, to make way for the cleansing and energy of My Spirit. At the same time, you can breathe out the self-part of you and breathe in the God-part. As an athlete who recognizes power when he runs across it, you will give more thought to the power of the Creative Spirit of Love, which built the universe and all the inhabitants thereof, and has the power to sustain all living things therein. When you consider that all these attributes of power are within you as part of your nature, you wonder why anyone would choose his own power, his own wisdom, when the power and wisdom of his Creator-Partner is available to him. You realize why Lincoln had that same wonder:

> "I should be the veriest shallow and self-conceited blockhead upon the footstool, if in my discharge of the duties that are put upon me in this place, I should hope to get along without the wisdom that comes from God and not from man."

The value of exercise to good health and longevity is well recognized. Yet, too often exercise is made to seem like a chore, something you do apart from the rest of your work or play. But in the Partnership Life, exercise becomes a natural and essential event. The self-discipline that exercise requires comes easy when you turn to your Creator-Partner to join with you.

When you learn the truth of your nature, you and I working together can re-make America, and even the world. As an athlete, people hold you in great respect. Indeed, some people tend to worship an outstanding athlete even more than they do Me, the Creator of the Universe. Your good sense will tell you that this kind of situation does not last very long. Fame is fleeting and talent slips with age.

However, there is a way you can be remembered for a long time for what you have done to save America. A good athlete can help as much or possibly more than a good intellectual, a prominent politician, a successful writer. While you are still in your prime and in the public eye—or on the way there—you can so live that when people look at you, they will see not you so much as your Partner at work in you.

When they learn from your way of life that they, too, have the same Creator-Partner you have, they will move to get this Power to work for them. You will then experience the joy and peace of mind the Master Partner was speaking of. You will then be achieving the purpose for which I created you.

Every athlete knows what momentum does for him. But do you know what momentum *is?* Momentum is My Spirit at work in you or in your competitor. I am better able to help when you breathe out your self-part and breathe in your God-part.

If God Spoke to Clergymen
Might it be Something Like This:

What you are about to read is simply the imagining of one who has learned when he sincerely strives to become "an agent and instrument of Divine Providence" (Lincoln's words) his Partner will guide him, speak thru him and work thru him. The author believes this holds true for you, too.

If you believe in the one God, Creator of the Universe and of all living things therein, I plead with you to take note of the condition of this earth, and to move without delay to avert its self-destruction.

At the time I created humans, giving them 1) a brain of unlimited potential and 2) freedom to disregard Me, their Creator, I realized that what now confronts humanity on earth was a distinct possibility.

Why then, did I proceed with the creation of humans? Because of My nature. I am the Creative Spirit of Love and My heart was filled with love for the humans with whom I wanted to live in Partnership. Besides, nothing is impossible for the Creative Spirit of Love.

I believed then and I believe now, that once humans learned that My reason for creating them was to live in Partnership with them, and that if this self-knowledge was made a part of education, humans would not pursue their own self-centered will, but instead would seek the will of the God-part of their nature.

It is now a race for survival and time is running against man. Can you believe—and I realize how difficult it is for the minds of humans to grasp this awful truth—that one man can press a button with the result the earth would be destroyed? *What progress man has made in the art of destruction!*

Is this not a sad commentary on our failure—yours and Mine—to make religion meaningful in the lives of humans? Where have we failed? And what can we do about it? For we must do something. Living on the brink of the earth's self-destruction calls for an immediate re-appraisal of all religious effort. Time for complacency and stubborn adherence to past customs is over. Clearly, whatever we have been doing, it is not enough. Prayers by the millions have not been enough. Religious practices and preachments have not been enough. One man, by the simple press of a button can bring about the earth's destruction.

Regardless of your faith in God, can your mind comprehend this awful possibility—more like a probability? *Your mind had better* do so. And don't put it all up to Me. True, I could have prevented this possibility, but this would have meant taking away man's free will. Without free will, there would be no Partnership of Man and Maker. The joy and perfection of the Partnership is in man yielding his will to Mine.

The teaching of this simple concept of the Partnership of Man and Maker—for which Jesus willingly gave his life—has been the responsibility of men of the cloth. What have you done with it? Have you placed your emphasis on other matters your seminaries taught you were more important? What could be more important than helping people to understand that My Creative Spirit is within them as a part of their nature? The things that have split Christianity into hundreds of different sects and denominations—are these more important than the simple belief of Christ that My Spirit is within each human, a living Partner in his everyday affairs?

No matter what you may have previously thought, the picture of that one man with his finger on the button should be enough to force you to do some *re-thinking. And some re-doing.* And to do these with all deliberate speed. You may be counting on My holding back that man's finger on the button? But for how long? And for what reason? What hope do you offer of a change? Are you not rather content with your position? And that of your church? Would you willingly abandon your position and prestige to bring about a complete surrender of your will to Mine?

Please take note, this is no time for temporizing. Consider how Christ reacted when he knew that, if he persisted in telling the people My Spirit was within each of them, he would die on the morrow. Harken unto his last words to Me: "Father, the hour is come . . . I pray that they all may be *One;* as Thou, Father, *art in Me and I in Thee,* that they also may be One in us; *that the world may believe Thou hast* sent me. And the glory which Thou gavest me I have given them; that they may be *One,* even as we are *One . . . I in them and Thou in me, that they may be made perfect in One."*

Oneness with God—the Partnership Life in action was the prayer with which Christ went to his death. How far are you, as a man or woman of the cloth, willing to go to teach people that My Creative Spirit of Love is within each of them, serving as their Creator-Partner?

If you are wavering, I suggest you look at the pictures of Hiroshima and Nagasaki. Then consider these bombs will be dwarfed into insignificance compared to the power responding to that man's touch.

What must you do first? I will endeavor to move your heart to make a complete surrender of self. This means a surrender of things you have held to in the past —ideas, notions, practices. They have not been enough. Had they been, that man's finger on the button would not be threatening. No mid-way measures, please! Nothing will work but a complete surrender of the self-part of your nature to your God-part. Our Partnership —yours and Mine—works very simply: God guiding, man doing. Christ showed the way: "Of myself I can do nothing. It is the Father within me. He tells me what to say and what to do."

I am saying to you just what I said to Christ, but it will work only if you work our Partnership together. Whatever else you do, if you are not working your Partnership with Me in your every thought, word and deed, it will not be enough. This means religion must have a renaissance. It must become a way of life—not a matter of form with words and rituals.

You will be guided to the one natural ritual I created

for you to remind yourself of our Partnership. This natural ritual is also life's most natural and greatest exercise: With every breath, you are to breathe out self, breathe in God. BREATHE OUT EGO, BREATHE IN GOD.

This natural exercise will help liberate you from the self, for by its very nature, the self is self-centered and selfish. When you empty yourself of self, I am able to fill you with My love, wisdom and power. You will know better what Christ meant when he spoke of his joy—not joy the way people think of it, things for the self—but the deeper joy of selfless living, "the more abundant life."

This is why I created the simple ritual of breathing out ego, breathing in God. To give you joy and an abundant life. This is the way of life the renaissance of religion will bring to men. And this must be done without delay. That finger is still on the button. And more and more fingers are finding their ways to more and more buttons. Nations—large and small—are learning about nuclear power.

This makes the situation more hopeless, doesn't it? But remember, with My Creative Spirit of Love everything is possible. I created the Universe, of which the earth is one of the smallest spheres. I can save your earth, but this requires your surrender of self. Are you willing? Let Me confide to you how the earth will be saved. When religion in America becomes Christ's way of life—the Partnership Life—this will instantly be reflected in the attitude of people to people. "Love one another." Christ's words, "You must become as a little child . . . You must be born again" will become meaningful. Children will be taught from the very beginning that My Spirit of Love remains with them their whole life long, to guide them in all they do. Each child will know his Partnership with Me is the most important thing in his life. Soon, your way of life will bring about a complete change in America. The God-part of each human will control his self-part. Love will replace hate.

The purpose of life will no longer be to gather things for self—money, power, fame—but for each human to work his Partnership with Me. The result will be a new America—neither excess wealth, nor poverty. There will be better health and longer life. People will no longer depend on *things* to give them joy. My Spirit will give them joy and peace of mind. When the peoples of other nations see this new America, they will want this way of life for their own. The people of Communistic nations will demand from their dictators they be given freedom to live the Partnership Life. They will be real friends of the American people, not enemies seeking to destroy you.

There will no longer be need for nuclear bombs. The finger will no longer be on the button. And you will have accomplished the true purpose of religion: everyday living in Partnership with God—the hearts of people filled with peace and joy.

Are you up to this? Are you moved to make a complete surrender to Me? Is there any other choice? That finger is still on the button—many fingers now. We can remove them—you and I working our Partnership.

I must repeat, in this final word to you as a theologian

what may seem stern, but I feel must be said. You do no service to Christ or to your fellow-man or to ME, your Maker, if you allow structured religion to come between any of My children and Me. My Creative Spirit of Love cannot be confined to religion, no matter of what organization. People must learn from the very beginning that I figure in every part of their lives from the time I first join the cell, which I use to build their bodies, until the time they die. I transcend religion, regardless of what structure. I am the Creator-Partner of each and every one of My children. To teach this truth to all humans should be the most important job of religion. This truth will make for unity among all My children. "Seek you first the Spirit of God within you and all other things will be added unto you."

Start now, with your very next breath!

* * *

If God Spoke to the Patriot Might it be Something Like This:

> What you are about to read is simply the imagining of one who has learned when he sincerely strives to become "an agent and instrument of Divine Providence" (Lincoln's words) his Partner will guide him, speak thru him and work thru him. The author believes this holds true for you, too.

I commend you for your love of country. I commend you for being on guard against anything that would subvert the freedom of the American people. There is much merit in your feeling that America was set aside to show the rest of the nations on earth how to live in mutual respect and love. Lincoln spoke aright when he said that America is "the last best hope of earth." But I trust you know the circumstances under which Lincoln made this statement.

He had been accused of carrying on the Civil War solely to free the slaves. Lincoln refuted this accusation because his real purpose was to save the Union. He explained:

> "My enemies pretend that I am now carrying on the war for the purpose of abolition. So long as I am President it shall be carried on for the sole purpose of restoring the Union."

Lincoln knew from our many talks together that I chose him to become President in order that the Union be preserved. I counted on the U. S. A., by its new way of life, saving the earth. While Lincoln's first responsibility was to save the Union, he believed the way to do this was to free the slaves. This would assure freedom to the free. In his second annual message, Lincoln said:

> "We say we are for the Union. The world will not forget that we say this. We know how to save the Union. The world knows that we do know how to save it. We, even we here, hold the power and bear the responsibility. In giving freedom to the slave we assure freedom to the free—honorable alike in what we give and what we preserve. We shall nobly save or meanly lose the last best hope of earth. Other means may succeed; this could not fail. The way is plain, peaceful, generous, just—a way which if followed the world will forever applaud and God must forever bless."

You don't hear much about God blessing the United States. Do you, as a patriot, ever think that I am blessing the United States? Do you, in any way, associate Me with your patriotism? Or do you feel that the only safe way is thru armed military might?

I am not finding fault with preparedness. Indeed, I might go further than some patriots in keeping the United States prepared for any eventuality. Quite possibly, you may not think much of My way of keeping the nation prepared. For I would suggest you bring up American children with a much more Spartan way of life. As a patriot, are you not concerned that the youth in America are being brought up too soft? Are not the conveniences too plentiful? Are they not living too much of a push-button existence?

Have you thought of joining with other patriots to promote earlier morning rising, to engage in physical exercise of various types, ending up possibly with a dip in an outside pool? And then sitting down to a hearty breakfast of natural foods, devoid of artificial sweeteners and refined flour? Would you not soon have a race of vigorous healthy young men and women? Might this not lead to friendly discussions about the part that I, their Creator-Partner, play in their daily lives? Would this not bring about a nation of men and women prepared for any emergency? Would not this be a better way to train young men than teaching them how to kill and maim? And if some sudden threat were to appear on the horizon, would not such a group of young men be very quickly prepared to repel enemies who would threaten the safety of the country?

Would not these better trained young men and women have a greater respect and love for their country? Would they not enthusiastically and wholeheartedly rise to the country's defense should any nation pose a threat to the country's freedom? Remember how your soldiers felt about your last war? How they hated it, how they distrusted their commanders and the leadership of your country? How a very great number of them evaded the draft and chose to give up their citizenship? Your system can make young men serve as soldiers but can you make them love their country?

How about your own patriotism? You wouldn't want anyone to say you fight for your country because the law requires you to. You would rather say you fight because you love your country. Why not, then make conditions such that the young men and women of America love their country?

If you start early and see that children are taught in education the truth about their nature and the part their Creator plays in it, you will soon have a country they will come to love and willingly fight for, yes, even die for. Surely, true patriotism means love of country. I love America. To me, it is more than "the last best hope of earth." I have blessed America with a safe location, friendly neighbors to the north and south, a fertile soil, a moderate climate, oceans on both their east and west, everything to be self-sustaining.

As a patriot, surely you must have asked yourself why I have done this. What could have been My purpose? Put in your language, America was My "ace in the the hole." If nations elsewhere were led by men who ignored My presence and were content to let the self-part of their nature control their thinking, there would still be America to eventually become a Mecca for the rest of the world to study, admire, respect and love. In this great melting-pot of different races and colors would emerge a new way of life, taught from the beginning of education thru the post graduate college class, so that each student understood his own nature and the nature of all humans. Believing that I, his Maker, created him to live in partnership with Me, he would believe too that I am also the Creator-Partner of all humans, so that he would resist fighting his brother-man, except in self-defense.

Do you know the Founding Fathers had this kind of faith in Me? Theirs was a simple faith. Having had recent experience in their home country of England, they were determined that in forming the new country—the United States of America—they would not permit the slightest measure of control to be in the hands of any structured religion. Therefore, their Constitution ruled that church and state should be kept separate.

But this separation did not in any way interfere with their own personal faith in Me. By commonsense reasoning and not by blind faith, they acknowledged a deep and reverent belief in God. Washington, your first President, stated "One cannot reason without arriving at a Supreme Intelligence." Jefferson: "The God who gave us life, gave us liberty at the same time." From Franklin: "If a creature is made by God, it must depend upon God, and receive all its power from Him."

I commend you again for your determination to keep America free. But tell me, by freedom do you mean being free to accumulate all the money you can? The trouble with this concept is that excess money does not make good on its promise for greater happiness. You may not know it, but there's a law against a person having too much money. It's not a man-made law. It's My law. I have a law—been there from the beginning of time—that too much of anything is not good for man.

You see its operation in the sun. You need the sun, but too much results in a sunstroke or heat prostration.

You see this law operating in the rain. You need the rain, but too much brings a flood. Take food. You need food, but too much brings distress and needless weight and often serious illness. So it is with too much of anything, particularly too much money.

You can check this with a little research among your friends and some back history. You often find that too much money causes a rift between husband and wife, between parents and children. Too much money spoils almost everyone and everything. It robs you of the joy a few simple things used to bring you.

If you truly love your country and want to preserve its freedom, give thought to the threat imposed by a standard of success which extols the acquisition of money, the love of power and fame. Are these all not desires springing from the self-part of man, rather than from his God-part? Or do you think I created man to engage in a race with all men for money, power, fame?

I'm sure that as a patriot, you favor laws against gambling. Probably, you approve laws making gambling a crime. Have you thought that perhaps unwittingly you have helped make legal the greatest gambling joint of all? Indeed, you may be doing business with it at this time. Is not the Stock Exchange a legal gambling joint? Is it not because some people are gambling that certain stocks sell for 25 points above or below what they sold for the day before? Has the value of the company changed that much in one day? Or is it simply that some people think the stock will bring more or less in the near future? Surely, there is a need for an exchange where people may buy or sell securities. But this is a different thing from the gambling that is now a steady procedure at the stock exchanges.

And while I am aware that gambling in itself provides a thrill, it is the lust for money that is the great fallacy. Too much money just does not work for your greater happiness. It can't. My law prohibits it. And don't think you are smart enough to get around this law. You'll be blowing in the wind. If you want a real thrill, use the excess money above your real needs for the good of others. Then you'll find true happiness.

As a sincere patriot, you should remind yourself that the noted historian and philosopher, Arnold J. Toynbee, pointed out that "19 of 21 civilizations died from within and not by conquest. It happened slowly, in the quiet and the dark when no one was aware." Ask yourself if it is possible this kind of decay is going on now in your beloved land. As a patriot, let me call your attention to the risk of your beloved country suffering a frightful disaster in the near future. Most Americans do not understand their true nature, and so they are being persuaded by their self-part that a successful life means acquiring enormous power. The result of this misconception of a successful life is that control of your largest industries is gravitating to a comparatively small number of people. To a democracy this represents a grave danger, "where one man, one vote" is the rule. Conglomerates undoubtedly have certain advantages over smaller individually owned stores in that they will be able to offer products at lower prices because of larger volume. That is the money side of the picture.

But how about the loss of personal relationship with

the corner grocer, the druggist, hardware and other small business people? Can money replace this? Is money to be exalted as the most important and desirable thing in life? If it is, it can be the ruin of your beloved country.

Bigness has its appeal but human relationships help make life worthwhile. Why sell your happiness for money? Look about you and you may find some of the most unhappy people are those with more money than they know what to do with. This danger of bigness is extending to your banks, which are a necessary part of modern life. As a patriot, are you not concerned about the way control of large corporation stockholdings is being concentrated in the hands of a small number of institutionalized investors, of which banks are leaders? Do you not regard this as a threat to the nation?

It would be a true form of patriotism to inquire as to whether this concentration of power in the hands of a few hundred men does not represent a genuine danger to the "one man, one vote" principle.

I know how deeply you believe in armed preparedness for the defense of your beloved country. In the course of events as you have known them, this has been a "must." But is there not another and better way that has been kept from you by PTCH (Precedent, Tradition, Custom, Habit)?

Why not consider the possibility of a new way brought about by modern communication? If this country were to educate its children from the beginning as to their true nature, so that your people understood and loved one another, sharing as did the Early Christians, so that poverty was eliminated, there would be no way to keep this information from the great mass of people in Communistic nations. Might not these people come to admire and respect the people of the United States so as to rebel against attempts to harm Americans?

Might these people even insist that military preparedness for war be changed so that the military leaders as well as the political leaders will be at the front of any military engagement? With nuclear bombs being the deciding factor, old style warfare may soon be a thing of the past. The way of the future lies in prevention. Prevention of war, prevention of ill health and disease, prevention of strikes in business.

To you, my patriotic son, I suggest you break the bonds in which PTCH has been holding you and bring about a new form of patriotism to your beloved country. A patriotism where materialism is dethroned, and love of people and love of country and love of God are one.

One more point, My Patriot Partner, and this has to do with enforced integration vs. practice of the Partnership of Man and Maker. Well-meaning people who are for enforced integration to give justice to the blacks are missing the point. Your beloved country is in danger because your people leave Me out of your set attitude toward people of skin colors other than white. I would like to ask every prejudiced person:

"Are you taking credit for the color of your skin? How did you arrange to get yourself born in the first place, and in your favorite skin color? Do you honestly believe your country will be safer and better protected if there is prejudice where I planned love? What kind of patriotism is it to blind oneself to the danger of a country divided against itself?"

Your patriotism can be made much more effective if you let Me into the act. I can make good use of you in our mutual desire to safeguard and protect the nation. Lincoln's advice is still sound: "We must disenthrall ourselves and then we will save our nation." To free yourself from slavery to self is true patriotism.

* * *

If God Spoke
to Women Liberators
Might it be Something Like This:

> What you are about to read is simply the imagining of one who has learned when he sincerely strives to become "an agent and instrument of Divine Providence" (Lincoln's words) his Partner will guide him, speak thru him and work thru him. The author believes this holds true for you, too.

You have a right to the same privileges men expect and demand. As your Creator, it was not My plan to make you less worthy in any respect than man. Different, yes, in many respects, but no less worthy. Indeed, as far as intelligence and know-how are concerned, you surely need not be satisfied with being equal to man, particularly when it comes to self-knowledge. Consider what man's lack of self-knowledge has brought to the world: millions of private little wars in everyday living, big wars between nations, leading to two world wars (the last of which killed 50 million people) and leaving you faced with the imminent possibility of a third and probably final world war.

You have every right to feel you and women generally could do no worse. Moreover, the way man has greedily and stupidly used up much of the life-giving materials I have provided for him in the bowels of the earth and on the earth's surface, is nothing to excite admiration.

You were not given less intelligence than man and you may have a greater sense of understanding. In your demands for fair and equal treatment with men, however, care should be exercised that you are not demanding to be considered physically man's equal. Obviously, I created you different physically and for good purpose.

Truly, this was no accident any more than humans are an accident. You and man are integral parts of the Cosmos. You and man have a definite purpose in My plan—to reach Oneness with Me, your Maker. There is the one plan for both man and woman, but this does not make you alike physically. Nor does it make sense to try to change the physical differences I have established between man and woman. Indeed, these differences should draw men and women together. My plan is for you as one certain woman to be drawn to one certain man; for the two of you to fall in love, to marry and raise a family. This calls for physical differences but spiritual unity. What draws you to this one certain man physically is a different physical attraction from what draws him to you. True, I have implanted in you as I have in the man you love, an irresistible desire to become one flesh. The urge I planted in your womb to be penetrated by your lover is the same urge I planted in him to do the penetrating.

You must understand that this is My plan, conceived and formulated by My Creative Spirit of Love. Before your coming on earth, I had made a similar arrangement with dumb animals, but with a vast difference. With animals, the urge for intercourse was a purely physical one. The spirit of love was not a factor. My plan was for propagation only. At certain periods, the physical urge in animals (called "in heat") told them it was time to mate. The male mounted the female and after a brief period of friction, ejaculated sperm, one or more of which united with ovum or ova in the female body to form a cell or cells from which I proceeded to build reproductions of the two animals and thus continue and multiply the species. This was the plan for animals and it has worked as planned.

But with humans, an infinitely nobler dimension was added. My Creative Spirit of Love was that dimension. Humans were not limited to intercourse for physical and reproductive purposes only. The Creative Spirit of Love planned intercourse for humans also as a natural and exalted climax to the loving union of a certain man with a certain woman. This opened the way for loving touches and caresses leading to the natural union of one flesh planned by My Creative Spirit of Love. Obviously, this called for two different physical bodies, one to eject the male sperm, the other to receive it. I planned the female human body to be so attractive to the male that when he found the one woman he loved, the desire to touch, to kiss, to caress her was naturally irresistible. I planned the male human body to prove so attractive to the female that when she found the one man she loved, she longed to be approached and taken possession of by him. To provide the greatest pleasure, My

Spirit of Love gave each of the five senses added delight in association with the act of becoming one flesh.

Would you, as a female, have Me change in any way the beauty of face and form that delights a male? Would you have Me change the lovely curve of the breast that is one of the female charms? The female breast serves more than an appeal to the man's eye and sense of touch. As a female, you may not appreciate what it means to a man as he gazes upon his newborn child nursing at its mother's breast. Would you, as an advocate of the Women's Liberation movement, do away with nursing an infant? It seems that this practice is becoming obsolete as it is.

Where you can be of great service is in refreshing man's mind about My part in his everyday affairs. This is where your movement can help save the country and the world. Men today are conducting the Government business, education and all facets of life, as if there is no higher intelligence than man's, as if there is no God. Why does not the Women's Liberation Movement do something about that?

As far as can be observed, your movement is also leaving My Creative Spirit of Love out of your considerations. You demand to be given the same privileges as men. But surely, your movement does not see eye to eye with those who seek to violate My plans for normal heterosexual relationship between men and women. Would not the Women's Liberation Movement oppose the claims of some women that as long as some misguided men have been persuaded it is proper to engage in homosexuality, women have the right to engage in Lesbian activities?

Your movement would also oppose, I hope, the practice of bisexuality, a lifestyle that permits sexual interests in both men and women? Experts in sexual studies state that in recent years there has been a definite increase in bisexuality among women. A prominent California psychiatrist stated the change among women has been "partly for political reasons—a feminine-liberating thing as they dissociate themselves from the extraordinary dependency they've had on men all these years."

The pathetic thing about this is that some physicians consider bisexuality as "normal and healthy." A prominent psychiatrist, affiliated with a Medical School stated "I think we're all born potentially bisexual." This attitude toward bisexuality, homosexuality and Lesbian practice represents the ultimate in leaving My Creative Spirit out of consideration. This holds Me up to ridicule. This view no longer regards Me as a God of Supreme Intelligence who planned to live in Partnership with each of My human creatures. I have been cast aside out of disbelief and out of man's (and woman's) intense egotism. The one who sustains you from moment to moment in countless ways, you dare to regard with ignominy and ridicule. This very night your soul might be required of you!

If, indeed, the Women's Liberation Movement sincerely desires to be of help to women, I will show you how to correct the errors of man's leadership. The world would not be in its present mess if children had been taught that the Creative Spirit which gave them life never departs from them but remains with them in eternal Partnership. The Women's Liberation Movement could do no greater service to the people of this country than to use its influence to have the teaching of self-knowledge included in education.

Many of the things you aspire to accomplish by the Women's Liberation movement will come naturally, if you give children the understanding of their nature. Let children learn early that the Creative Power which created them also sustains them, keeping their hearts beating and in countless other ways. Let the child learn some of the many things going on within its body and mind that can be done only by the Creative Spirit which built its body and mind. The child will readily accept and understand the physical differences between boys and girls, and the Creator's plan in arranging this.

The so-called experts who condone homosexuality, Lesbianism and bisexuality—even to the point of having them made legal between consenting parties—show a pathetic lack of understanding of true human nature or they would not be treating the symptoms instead of the cause. They do not seem to understand that I do not create anyone a homosexual, a Lesbian or a bisexual. This would be counter to My plan of life and love. How then do people become that way? The answer is simple: They become that way as a result of an education that leaves Me out of their everyday lives. This tragic omission makes God too distant, somewhere far off in outer space, to possibly be interested in their cares and concerns.

The very purpose for which I created humans—to live in Partnership with Me—is virtually ignored in their education. This is the reason there is so much misunderstanding, hatred, prejudice and war in your world. This is why sex is misunderstood and perverted. This is why women have been taken advantage of. But the way out is not to create more misunderstanding. The way out is to learn your true nature. To know yourself. To know that My Spirit is within you, as part of your nature. The way out is to reassert the purpose for which I created you—for man and woman alike to strive for Oneness with Me, the Creative Spirit of Love. I planned that man would enjoy treating women with deference and respect. It is not My plan for man to assert his superiority over women.

The Women's Liberation Movement can do much more for all mankind, not just women, if they work with love to see that children are taught self-understanding. The Spirit of Love and understanding will win for you much greater rewards than what you are fighting for. Men will learn from you how to get the self out of their way. You will help all people to achieve "liberation from the self."

No condoning by psychiatrists or psychologists, no man-made laws can give homosexuals, Lesbians or bisexuals the inner peace and self-respect so essential to happiness. What will accomplish this for them is the knowledge that My Creative Spirit of Love is part of their nature. I am just as much their Partner as I am of the most admired man or woman. But if these unfortunate people do not know that My Spirit is within them, they look for escapisms, in the effort to be comforted.

Surely, they should not be blamed for never having learned the self-knowledge which would have spared them this grief. Education must take the responsibility for this failure. This is a job for the Women's Liberation Movement. You must not fail Me. You must not fail future women, men and children.

If God Spoke to the Person Considering Suicide Might it be Something Like This:

What you are about to read is simply the imagining of one who has learned when he sincerely strives to become "an agent and instrument of Divine Providence" (Lincoln's words) his Partner will guide him, speak thru him and work thru him. The author believes this holds true for you, too.

My dear Partner: I will not talk religion to you. You are in much too desperate a frame of mind to listen to preaching of any kind. I will talk common sense with you, and I hope you will believe I speak with love and understanding.

You have been betrayed—unwittingly but nevertheless betrayed—by your elders. In speaking to you, I also hope to reach them. For there are many like you, thinking about giving up the life I gave them. Each day, around the world some 10,000 of My children attempt suicide. About 10%—one out of ten—succeed. One thousand suicides every day!

Why should so many humans with a brain to appreciate life's blessings find life unendurable? It is easy to blame your present civilization, which sparks the emotional states of alienation, isolation and loneliness, espe-

cially in large cities. There are the breakdowns in relationships between people, and the kind of life-crises
generated by accidents, serious illness, and physical
handicaps. But consider the victories of many like the
deaf, dumb and blind Helen Keller; of Beethoven who
continued to compose music after losing his hearing at
the peak of his career; of the Russian pilot Meresjev
who lost both legs in World War II, learned to walk
on artificial legs and to fly again. These people did not
count Me out and resort to suicide.

It is also easy to blame Me. Many conclude that I
erred in giving man a deadly combination: 1) a powerful
brain and 2) freedom to follow his own self-centered
will. Perhaps this combination was too potent for My
children, and if one were to judge the events of history
since man was created, it is easy to come to that conclusion. Still, I do not regret creating you. I know you will
come to believe I am your everlasting Partner.

So, first before you decide to do away with yourself,
seeking escape in oblivion, I ask you to consider the
possibility that this one life you're living now is *not* all
there is. You have had dreams in your sleep. You may
have dreams again. What human can state with finality
that these dreams have no origin in a previous existence? Why can some five-year-olds produce music with
an expertness many trained grownups cannot equal?
"Out of the mouths of babes shall pour forth wisdom."
Could such talent and insight be a carry-over from
previous lives?

And what about the children born with such severe
mental and physical handicaps that they cannot care for
themselves or express thought and feeling? Don't you

feel these unfortunates may get another chance? Do you think it fair of Me, their Creator, to say to them: "Sorry, but that's all there is." Or do you believe it is impossible for Me to incarnate their spirit in another human body? Humans have a tendency to limit Me to what they can do. Nobody, of course, has a right to assume My plan of life includes reincarnation. You must trust and have faith that your Creator-Partner will do what is right and necessary, since I have planned to be in Partnership with you for eternity.

But keep in mind My capabilities are infinite. I have created billions of galaxies, each containing billions of planets and stars, each larger than the earth, some of them trillions of light years apart. Come now, you know it doesn't make sense to limit Me to the things *you* can do. You probably don't know that your Atomic Energy Commission confirmed that I make you a new body every year—replacing billions of cells to do so. If I can give you a new body each year, I can also give you a new state of mind.

Chances are, if you had been taught the simple truth which Christ gave his life to teach, you wouldn't be in the state of mind you are now. I did not send Christ on earth to talk religion. He never mentioned the word religion. He came to tell you of your Partnership with Me: "The Spirit of God is within you." He urged you to seek God's guidance in all you do. Jesus wanted you to know there was a higher power at work in you than your own. You were entitled to know the truth of your own nature, that there are two separate though integrated forces at work in you.

The first is My Power—the Creative Spirit. You were

nothing until I created you. I was the first Power at work in you, joining a certain sperm with a certain ovum to form a certain cell. You know it's a scientific fact that I spent nine months at work in you building you a body with a brain to learn and understand the truth. At the end of the nine-month building period, it was My creative spirit that ushered your body from your mother's womb onto the outer earth.

But you were not sent out alone. YOU ARE NEVER ALONE. You are the second power in our Partnership. I planned to be with you every step of the way. This truth should have been taught you in education. I have to be with you all the time. Not alone to keep you going physically but, as you will shortly learn, for even more important reasons: to achieve the purpose for which I created you.

Before telling the truths which your education tragically omitted, I should make sure you understand something of My nature. I am not a physical being. I am not "The Man Upstairs." I am not a man with a white beard, sitting on a throne in outer space waiting to sit in judgment on you when you die. These are things I am not.

What am I then? I am the Creative Spirit of Love. My Spirit creates the physical. My Spirit controls the physical. How is it possible for an invisible Spirit to create and control the physical? I will give you the answer and it is important that you understand it, else you may not believe it. My Spirit works in love and harmony. Truly, I am Love in action. LOVE is GOD. Let Me prove it to you.

Take a simple thing—a tree. The tree you see standing firm and strong depends on Me to keep it going and growing. But to do this, I need the seed, the soil, the sun, the rain and the air. All of these must work in love and harmony to keep the tree going and growing. If any one of these contributing factors did not do its part with love and harmony, the tree would not flourish. The physical contributions of each of these factors are not in themselves enough to keep the tree prospering. There is a secret ingredient: Love. It must be a selfless love. It must be seeking to give, rather than to get.

This is true of everything that grows. It is true of you, too. It has been true of you from the beginning. Scientists have established that if you were given as a child everything you needed in the way of physical wants— food, clothing, shelter—but no real love, you would be handicapped from the start. That may well be the trouble in your particular case. You may think it too late for anything to change your situation. But this attitude ignores Me and the power I have. Nothing is impossible for Me. You must remember I am the Creative Spirit of Love. And Love can do anything.

Let Me set out a few simple truths that should make you believe I am with you, as your eternal Partner. I am constantly doing things for you which you cannot do for yourself and which no one else can do for you:

1. I keep your heart beating.

2. I breathe for you during your sleep, the breath of life, without which you would instantly perish.

3. I transform the food you enjoy eating into blood, bone, muscle, brain, etc.

4. I operate the sewage system of your body so as to eliminate poisonous waste.

5. I keep the billions of cells in your body going their proper way.

6. I build you a new body each year.

7. I keep open the lines of communication between your brain and the rest of your body so that you may think straight, talk straight, work straight.

I could go on but these should be sufficient to make you realize that My Spirit is indeed a part of you, and that it makes sense to acknowledge this condition and to live in partnership with Me. The Partnership of Man and Maker is the most vital truth you can learn. Live it and you will completely transform your life.

When I created you, My desire, as is true of all My children, was to work in partnership with you. Look back in your mind to a year before you were born. You were nothing. You did not exist until I decided to create you. To do this, I selected you out of a possible billion other combinations. I wanted you then. I want you now. Let us (you and I) not be too concerned about what others think of you. You can be an abject failure in their eyes. In mine, you are still My partner, and I am not giving up hope our Partnership will yet get going and give happiness to My other children and in so doing, to you.

What you have become is not so much your fault as it is proof of the failure of education. What good is an education that teaches a child all forms of knowledge except the most important—knowledge of its own nature? You were not taught your true nature. Had you been taught that I was a part of your nature, I am certain our Partnership would not have misfired.

How, then, can we make our Partnership effective? First, try to forget everything you know, everything you have learned about people. Forget yourself most of all.

You say you can't forget yourself and that's the reason you are about to destroy yourself. I, your Maker and Partner, assure you that you *can* forget yourself. I have prepared a way for all My children to forget the self. For the self is your worst enemy. The self lures you to become its slave.

President Lincoln, who had no specific religion yet lived in close Partnership with Me, urged his fellow-Americans to free themselves from slavery to self: "We must disenthrall ourselves (to free oneself from slavery to self) and then we will save our nation." The great scientist, Albert Einstein, gave his fellow-Americans a standard for a human being to aspire to: "The true value of a human being is determined primarily by the measure and the sense in which he has attained *liberation from the self.*"

The purpose of life—the reason I created you—requires that you strive to achieve liberation from the self. Unless you strive for this, our Partnership cannot get off the ground. How can we (you and I) become one, which is the purpose of life, if you let the self of you have its way?

I'll show you the simple way I've arranged for you to forget the self. The way is as simple as breathing. In truth, it *is* breathing. I've divided the act of breathing into two parts: out and in. My purpose was not just to get rid of poisonous carbon dioxide and waste in your body, and to breathe in pure air.

Above that, I planned breathing as a means of getting the self out of the way and letting Me, your Partner, work My will thru you—work My love and wisdom and power thru you to make others happy. For it is in making others happy that you will find your own happiness. I could have made breathing as independent of you as I made the beating of the heart. I chose to make breathing an act of our Partnership, you and I working together toward Oneness.

So start now, My child and partner. With each outgoing breath, think to yourself "Out, ego." With each incoming breath, think: "In, God." Breathe out ego, breathe in God. You know you have to breathe in order to live. Make breathing truly worthwhile. Start our Partnership going. No matter if you'll forget about it time and again, as you probably will. Start it up again. Thousands of your brothers and sisters who forgot time and again resumed trying and today are experiencing an inner peace and joy which transformed their lives.

A person filled with self cannot perceive objects clearly. But at times flowers will bloom on what seems to be a completely dead vine. There comes a time when one awakens to one's true self. Your true self is not the self considering suicide. Your true self is My part of you. It is My nature to constantly create. True, created things disappear with time. It is natural for things to change and disappear and re-appear. But when you yield your will to Mine, you are no longer bothered by appearing and disappearing, or life and death. Impermanence is accompanied by continuity. In the Partnership life of man and Maker, enlightenment is everlasting, unending.

But what of your problems? What about the burdens in your life that led you to contemplate total escape? I will speak directly to this. First, it may surprise you to learn that many people, at one time or another, give at least a thought to escaping from life because something seems unbearable. The number who go thru with the notion is very small, but the fact that so many give it even a passing thought is proof in itself that most people do not know that I created them to live in Partnership with Me.

Take the case of alcoholics. Almost without exception, every alcoholic—the one who has lost control of his desire for alcohol—has had moments when suicide was considered. In itself, the use of alcohol (and drugs) indicates an attempt to block out life's problems. Alcoholism is often associated with loss of job, loss of money, loss of mate, loss of health, loss of self-respect, loss of hope. All these losses stem from one cause: People have left Me, their Creator-Partner, out of their everyday affairs. No doubt, well-meaning friends have tried to save them thru different man-made ways, but often without avail.

Because I realized the first need was to get alcoholics to understand My part in their nature, I planned a move that would do just this. This move involved getting two certain drunkards to meet. One of these was a successful medical man; the other a successful investment banker, but both were powerless over alcohol.

While they were individually helpless, I caused them to discover they could help one another where they could not help themselves. They helped one another by separately and jointly turning their will and their lives over to Me, the Creator-Partner of each. This was a perfect demonstration of getting the self out of the way, of helping someone else and thus achieving one's own happiness. This was the beginning of Alcoholics Anonymous, with its Twelve Steps which every one of My human creatures will benefit from. These 12 Steps refer openly and positively to My part in the lives of humans. (Page 387).

This posed a stumbling block because the name God by which people call Me has acquired an almost exclusively religious connotation. Seeking My guidance, the two co-founders of Alcoholics Anonymous sought a way out of the problem. I inspired these two sincere seekers to add four simple words following God, so that it read "God as we understood Him." The addition of these four words offers proof that sometimes the gravest problem can be solved in a simple way, if My human partners seek My wisdom. These four words have proved of invaluable assistance in transforming about a million drunkards in different parts of the world into what may well prove one of the most unique and powerful forces for good existing on earth.

"God as we understood Him" left it up to each individual drunkard to decide what God meant to him. No sectarian religion has been allowed to infiltrate into Alcoholics Anonymous. No person, no institution, no organization is permitted to come between the individual and his Creator-Partner to tell him how he must worship God. If you doubt that the use of this simple phrase "God as we understood Him" is really meaningful to many people, consider two public opinion polls recently taken. The first asked "Do you believe in God?" and 98% answered "Yes." The second asked: "Does your church (and your religion) have influence in your life?," and to this only 25% answered "Yes."

Although I credit A.A. with having put this idea to uniquely effective use, it is really not new. Students of philosophy will recognize it as a modern adaptation of an idea promoted long ago, and used today by various non-sectarian groups of mystics (those who concern themselves with the mysteries of life and the universe). These people do not require that all accept a single fixed concept of God. Even in their prayers and rituals in which all may join, they use the expression "God of my heart" which means precisely "God as I understand Him." Among these people, there is a common acceptance of the concept that there exists a Higher Power or Supreme Intelligence that controls the Universe. It matters not what one may call this Power or how one may perceive this Power. Most people—even those who profess not to believe in Me or those who assert I am dead—call this Power: God. You may find it more acceptable to use "God as I understand Him" or "God of my heart." The important thing is to know that I AM a part of your nature.

When you have moments of doubt of My presence within you, consider what happens in your body when an accident—minor or major—befalls you. At My command, every cell and organ in your body start immediately to repair the damage. If you could see with your eyes the perfect harmony with which millions of cells and bloodvessels rush to the specific injured spot and start to heal it, you would surely believe what you see: the Creative Spirit of Love in action. You would not limit Me as some people seem, to the part of Conscience. This is but one of the virtues but by no means the sum total of the virtues which My presence offers you.

I promised I would not talk religion to you and I do not propose to do so. Anyone contemplating suicide has probably lost faith in structured religion, but can you find fault with the attitude of members of A.A. as expressed in the 12 Steps? After all, I did not create religions. Formal religions are man-made. The very existence of several hundred different religious sects and denominations shows divisiveness.

People who believe in Jesus should know he believed in My presence within him as well as within you: "The Spirit of God is within you." He urged that you seek God within you and follow God's will rather than your own, promising "all other things would be added unto you." I sent Christ as a layman to convince people of My Partnership with each of My children. Christ made clear he considered it as much a commandment to love your fellow-man as it was to love God: "How can you claim to love God whom you cannot see when you don't love your fellow-man whom you can see?"

It is in helping their fellow-man that members of A. A. prove their faith in Me, their Creator-Partner. Each member gains greater strength and faith by helping other alcoholics stay sober. They willingly respond to calls even at night to help another member. How many members of religious denominations would be willing to leave their homes on a winter night in all kinds of weather, responding to the plea of another alcoholic: "I need help. I'm about to take a drink and you know what that means. I won't be able to stop."

But to you, having weaknesses really serves as an asset. This helps you identify with others who have problems. I have made an example of Alcoholics Anonymous. Remember, I sent Christ on earth as a humble carpenter. I show My love for you and all My children through a group of lowly drunkards.

Your despairing state of mind carries a silver lining—the opportunity to see the truth that you refused to admit while you still had some measure of success or happiness—that by yourself you are powerless, but working your Partnership with Me and surrendering your will to My Spirit, enables you to rise above the most agonizing situation.

You know now the truth that will make you free. Soon, you will be finding your happiness thru acts of devotion and love for your brother-man. You will help him to understand his partnership with Me. The happiness you give him will soon find its way back to you. You may not have to do much talking. What will convince others will be the way you will be living—the kind of person you are. They will see this new person and wonder about it. What they see in your face and eyes and manner, they will want for themselves. You will be helping them. LOVE will be doing its work.

Others will learn from you that there must be something more to life than the way they have been living. As for you, no one can make you miserable as long as you know I am with you. Together, we will understand the person or persons who were contributing to your unhappiness and misery. By forgetting the self, you will start with My help to love this person or persons. Probably, they need help as much as you, or they wouldn't be making you suffer.

You and I must work our Partnership so that Love can work its way thru you. When you get your little self out of the way, My love and power and wisdom and joy will flow thru you, flooding you with inspiration and happiness. This is My plan for our Partnership and no person or group can stop it.

Breathe out ego, breathe in God. This will start you in remembrance of our Partnership. It works!

If God Spoke to the Musician Might it be Something Like This:

> What you are about to read is simply the imagining of one who has learned when he sincerely strives to become "an agent and instrument of Divine Providence" (Lincoln's words) his Partner will guide him, speak thru him and work thru him. The author believes this holds true for you, too.

Is there any means of communication between human beings that is equal to music? Music is indeed the universal language. Music is love and harmony. It speaks a language that all can understand, because it is the language of love. Disharmony is the result of a lack of harmony and love.

When you make music or teach music, it would be helpful if you convinced all that music is God speaking the universal language, and that My Spirit is within each person as part of one's very nature. I need not belabor you as to the part I play in music. As a musician, you know music is God's voice speaking in a loving language to all His children.

When you teach children music, whether it be the simple singing of songs together or how to play an instrument, you are also teaching them that music is the language of love. You are teaching that music is proof of the presence of My spirit within them and all about them, in the very air they breathe which carries the sound of music so all may hear and receive My love.

I have said that music inspires. I planned music so that I could talk to my children in a universal language. All great musicians have acknowledged My part in their work. Mozart told of how while walking thru the forest, a complete symphony came to him, so that all he had to do was to write it down. This is the meaning of inspired. When you refer to something as being uninspired, you are saying it is the work of the little self. My Spirit has been left out of it. Inspired things arise only from our Partnership in action. You know you have your greatest joy when you are living up to your part in our Partnership. No joy can equal that which you feel when you get yourself out of My way or better yet, become, in the words of Lincoln, an "agent and instrument of divine Providence." This is pure rapture, pure ecstasy. Beethoven described it, "It is the acme of bliss to approach the throne of Diety and thence to diffuse its rays among mankind."

There are many spoken languages—several thousand different languages. I am continually astonished that so few people give any thought to how so many languages came to be. They do not see My hand in this at all, just as they count Me out of virtually everything in their daily lives. Musicians should have a better understanding of My part in language because they realize that there could be no music without My contributions and handiwork. I created the different sounds from the very lowest to the very highest on the scale. While nonmusicians may just assume the 2000 spoken languages were created by the various ethnic groups speaking them, most musicians are inclined to go along with Lincoln who openly stated that I created each language:

"The inclination to exchange thoughts with one another is probably an original impulse of our nature. . . . To carry on such communications, some instrumentality is indispensable. Accordingly, speech—articulate sounds rattled off the tongue—was used by our first parents. . . . From this, it would appear that speech was not an invention of man, but rather the direct gift of his Creator."

Those who doubt this and believe men did invent their own languages might try getting a group of the most intelligent people in a room and challenge them to form a new language, without using a single word of any known language to help them form the new language. In a very short time, these brilliant people might go mad.

What was My purpose in forming so many different peoples and providing them with so many different languages? The answer is that the Creative Spirit of love has a love for infinite variety. I love the different skin colors, the different races and the different ethnic groups. There is one thing which I cannot be credited with. That is the various, differing religious groups, each claiming to be My handiwork. Religions are the works of men. Some day, religions will be transformed into a way of life based on Christ's assurance of My Spirit in man and our Partnership.

Then there will be peace and love, not divisiveness

and hatred and war. Churches will be filled with people filled with peace and love for their brother-man. The air will be filled with music and joy. This is the greatness of music. It brings with it, by its very nature, love and peace. Music brings inspiration into the lives of people.

When you sing, let Me sing thru you. When you play your musical instrument, let Me play thru you. Let us join together to produce inspired music. Your listeners will feel inspired as indeed they always are when listening to the glorious sounds of love coming thru. Music helps people to carry over this love into all their relations with other human beings. Music is indisputable proof of my Partnership with you. Let music sing thru your every thought, word and deed. You will bring joy to your brother-man and this joy will come back to you many fold.

* * *

If God Spoke to the One Who Wants to Grow Younger Might it be Something Like This:

What you are about to read is simply the imagining of one who has learned when he sincerely strives to become "an agent and instrument of Divine Providence" (Lincoln's words) his Partner will guide him, speak thru him and work thru him. The author believes this holds true for you, too.

If you are earnest in your desire to grow younger, bear these points in mind:

1. Keep before you the simple truth that you were given life by the Creative Spirit you call God. Your brain and your entire body were formed and are being sustained by My Creative Spirit.

2. Present with you all the time, it is My Creative Spirit that keeps your heart beating and does the countless things for you which you cannot do for yourself, including keeping open the lines of communication between your brain and the rest of you, so that you may think straight, talk straight and act straight.

3. The wisdom, power, love and joy of My Creative Spirit are available to you all the time. For

you not to make conscious use of these blessings is like living in poverty unaware that a priceless estate awaits your claim.

4. When you get your little self out of My way, these blessings are free to enter. They start reversing the trend. You begin growing younger. This will be noticeable to you and to others. With your Partner, all things are possible.

5. To get your self out of God's way; to make your self an "agent and instrument of divine Providence," make sure that with every breath you take, out and in, you begin the simple practice of breathing out ego, breathing in God. (Each day, read a page or two about this practice in the book "You Are Greater Than You Know.")

6. Your Partner will guide you in your treatment of every person you meet. Each will observe the radiance in your face, reflecting the presence of your Partner. Because you have found your place in God, some will surely feel inspired and helped.

7. The body your Creator-Partner made for you deserves care and respect. Recently, the Atomic Energy Commission reported after tracing isotopes in the human body that "in a year approximately 98% of the atoms in us now will be replaced by other atoms that we take in our air, food and drink." When you open yourself to your Partner's guidance, you will choose foods as close to their natural state as possible. Your Creator-Partner has placed in these foods the very elements needed to replenish your body, to insure its health and vigor.

8. In all things, your desire will be to have your Part-

ner rule your life, confident that the Supreme Intelligence knows what is best for you.

9. The world around you will lose much of its influence and control over you. People about you may continue to crack in their mid-forties and early fifties, but with your new understanding you will grow younger.

10. Make this your motto:
    MIND OVER MATTER. SPIRIT OVER BOTH.

The reason many men in their mid-forties and early fifties are cracking today is because they are trying to stand alone. The man who *knows* the truth of Lincoln's statement "God is the silent partner of all great enterprises" is free of the pressure, tension and strain that cause breakdowns, ulcers and coronaries.

It is a simple, provable fact that you depend constantly and unceasingly on your Creator-Partner to maintain the life My Creative Spirit has given you.

It is true also that My Creative Spirit depends upon you to carry out My plan of life: the unity of man and Maker. It is a perfect Partnership Plan.

All your troubles spring from ignoring, knowingly or unknowingly, this great Power within you. Your physical and mental ailments are almost always the result of failure to observe your Creator-Partner's simple, natural laws for body and mind.

* * * *

This is not to say that you are to sit back and wait for your Partner to do everything. Your Partner needs you as you need Him. Your place, however, is as servant, not master.

Through your Partner's guidance and inspiration, you are enabled to do more work and do it better than when you delude yourself you are doing the work alone.

It's a question of whose will rules. In its simplest terms, life asks: "Who is your boss, Ego or God?"

Your troubles arise when self (ego) takes over. Always, there is a dark spot in your sunshine. It is the shadow of your self.

The fallacy that man is an individual, going through life without the comforting presence of his Creator-Partner, may be responsible for the alarming situation of one in every five Americans suffering from some mental disorder at one time or another.

It is the ego part of you that worries and envies and becomes unhappy—never your Creator-Partner. When you let your Partner guide you, you learn how to take adversity and suffering. These do not defeat but ennoble you.

When faced with problems defying all your efforts to solve, you learn to consent to what you must bear. Thus you leave frustration behind and come atop your problems.

* * * *

DO YOUR PART IN OUR PARTNERSHIP AND YOU WILL FEEL YOUNGER

1. Your part in our Partnership is to stop kidding yourself you are going thru life alone. Give some thought to the countless things your Partner is doing within your body at this very moment—things you cannot do for yourself.

2. Take time to analyze whether you or your Partner should be boss of our Partnership. Whose wisdom is greater? Whose power? Whose vision?

3. Consider what a persuasive fallacy the way of life handed down to you really is. It has led many to allocate to me just one hour's attention on a Sunday morn. This permits many to spend their time pursuing money, power, fame. It does this at the expense of ulcers, strokes and heart attacks. It is this way of life that has increased the rate of crime, divorce, mental and physical breakdowns. Does it make sense for anyone to leave His Maker and Sustainer out of his everyday affairs? NO ONE STANDS ALONE!

4. If you sincerely want to feel younger—and infinitely happier—you have to be honest with yourself. Acknowledge My part in your everyday life. Did I not create you? Do I not keep your heart beating?

5. Choose this day who is to be boss of our Partnership. If you seriously decide I am to head up our Partnership, I suggest you practice the six-second exercise of breathing out ego, breathing in God. No matter how often you forget, go back to it. You will feel younger tomorrow than you do today.

"Whilst we converse with what is above us, we do not grow old but grow young. When these waves of God flow into me, these moments confer a sort of omnipresence and omnipotence." (Emerson)

If God Spoke to TV Network Owners Might it be Something Like This:

> What you are about to read is simply the imagining of one who has learned when he sincerely strives to become "an agent and instrument of Divine Providence" (Lincoln's words) his Partner will guide him, speak thru him and work thru him. The author believes this holds true for you, too.

Not too many decades ago, I directed the minds of some electronic engineers to discover TV. You would probably choose the word "invent" instead of "discover," but the truth is there are no inventions. Discoveries, yes, because man only discovers what I have planned for him to discover. There are countless things yet for man to discover, but because education does not teach or even mention the part I play in everyday life, men will insist on calling these things inventions.

But the point is that the advent of TV offered man the most marvelous medium the world has yet seen, not alone for entertaining but—and this was My greater purpose—for informing and enlightening humanity. By now, it should be obvious that the possibilities for TV are almost endless.

As a TV network owner, you are without doubt aware of the tremendous opportunities TV offers, but may I inquire whether your thoughts in this connection do not bear mostly on the money TV can make? I say this with sadness more than with criticism, as I know you are the victim of an education that leaves Me out of your everyday affairs. So, you become a money-gatherer, in the belief that this is the accepted success standard in the U.S.A., and naturally you want to be considered a success. In addition, you have been persuaded that the more money you accumulate, the happier you will be.

This latter is a proven fallacy. But there is something regarding TV more vital to Me as the Creator of the Universe and all humans therein than man's stupid pursuit of money and power. This has to do with the effect that some of your programs are having on the minds of children. Anyone who watches TV for any part of the night must be aware, in view of the rising crime rate, that TV is actually teaching crime to new recruits.

You cannot be blind to this situation, and yet you continue on with TV programs that threaten to speed your country's decay. I know at heart you are a true patriot, and you do not love money that much as to willingly contribute to your country's downfall. It may be that you feel compelled to compete with other networks, and this is why you continue on with shows dealing with crime. Or is it that you are convinced that the claims TV is helping make the nation one of runaway criminality are grossly exaggerated?

If you can accept that Lincoln was right in his belief he could talk with Me, I would like to communicate to you the immeasurable gratification that would be yours if you took an active hand in making TV of educational value to the people of your country. Their greatest need is self-knowledge, to understand that My Spirit of Love is within them serving as their Creator-Partner. There are some good educational TV programs that help character-building for both young and grownups, but none of them have come right out to explain the part their Creator takes in every facet of their lives. Their reluctance to do this springs from the fear that to even refer to God or the Creator is to invite criticism for introducing religion.

You are too intelligent to fall for the fallacy that the Creator of the Universe can be confined to an area of man's making known as "religion." TV is the best instrument for teaching the everyday contributions I make to each human's life, physically, mentally, emotionally and spiritually, without introducing structured religion. Without this information, no person can truly understand his own nature. And if he does not understand himself, how can he understand other humans?

The way TV is used in America, instead of educating your children to understand themselves, you are helping to make children mostly non-readers, and making grownups a nation of self-centered and materialistically-minded people. Learning about one's own nature can be exciting, even fascinating, and in America, it can be even life-saving. You will have less complaints about commercials. Indeed, commercials can be improved and made more believable in the light of better self-knowledge.

If your answer to the above is that you will suffer a great loss of audience if you did not have exciting and dramatic stories to show them on TV, let Me remind you there is no more exciting or thrilling battle in life than the ones that take place between a man's self-part and his God-part. There can be no more fascinating struggle than the contest of man with himself, his divine spark against his ancient human frailties. You need but direct the minds of your script writers to this inner contest that counts and you will find your audiences nodding their heads with approval "I had to battle that out myself."

Many of your TV shows have to do with criminals who end up in jail. This is supposed to contribute a moral uplift. The fact remains that virtually all persons confined to prison are there primarily because they were never taught the truth of their nature. Even now, if efforts were made by understanding people to teach the prisoners self-knowledge in practical ways, they will be found receptive to the premise there is another part to their nature than their self-part which got them into trouble. In a large Eastern hospital for the criminally insane, tests with hardened criminals showed that when practical proof was submitted that every person has both 1) a self-part (which by its very nature is self-centered and selfish) and 2) a God-part (which is really the Creative Spirit of Love that gave them life and sustains them from moment to moment), a transformation takes place. Some of them have actually acknowledged "If I had learned this about myself earlier, I might have ended up differently."

Even in jail, it is not too late to help prisoners to the new recognition of the spiritual energy within them and all about them—simple truths which they had never been taught before. Because I, their Creator, am left out of their lives, supposedly wise Governors and Mayors spend increasing sums of money to apprehend criminals and even still larger sums to confine them to prisons. Surely, you must realize the answer obviously lies in prevention, and prevention in turn comes from learning the truth of one's nature. This must begin with children, as early as possible.

You have it in your hands, Mr. TV Network Owner, to bring about a real reduction in crime and violence as well as hatred and self-centeredness. You can help make your streets safer to walk at night. Your own heart will be filled with inner peace and tranquility. As you love your country, let your mind dwell on the many proofs of My presence within you. You may then decide to use the greatest medium yet known to man—TV—to help your brother-man learn I created him to live in Partnership with Me.

If God Spoke to You About Sex Might it be Something Like This:

> What you are about to read is simply the imagining of one who has learned when he sincerely strives to become "an agent and instrument of Divine Providence" (Lincoln's words) his Partner will guide him, speak thru him and work thru him. The author believes this holds true for you, too.

You would not, I trust, look upon a frank discussion of sex as an exercise in pornography. If, however, you would, I must assume you feel compelled to take a strong stand against pornography as evil and harmful.

My well-meaning friend, tell me please, what is pornography? I have a great interest in this because, as you will remember, I created sex. Naturally, as pornography has to do with sex, if sex is made to look evil, then there is something evil about Me.

So, I ask again what is pornography? Is it the showing of a nude body? Or pictures of a nude body? You wouldn't call the showing of a newborn boy or girl pornography, would you? If you agree this would not be pornography, when does it become so? At age 5? Age 10? Age 15? Or is it age 20 and over?

If a newborn nude body is not pornographic at birth, what makes it at age 20? Is it the growth that has taken place? Does this make it pornographic? This interests me, because, as you will again remember, it is I who arranges the growth of every human, as I do for dumb animals. You do not consider the showing of a nude grown animal as pornography. You do not consider the showing of two animals mating as pornography, or do you?

When there is open discussion in the newsprint about a great race horse giving up racing to be put up for hire at stud, do you regard this as pornography? If you are broader-minded about this, how about the public viewing of this horse mating with a mare? Would you say this was pornography? How else would the person paying a high price for the privilege of having his mare foaled by this famous racing horse know he was getting what he was paying for? And if you o.k. this, would you deny others the right to view the mating process?

Let me ask you, my well-meaning friend, is this not all natural? Is not intercourse between human beings as natural as with animals?

Is it hard for you to understand that when I created the first animals, I had to formulate some plan for them to multiply? Otherwise, I would be put to the necessity of actually starting from scratch with each animal created. That was one reason for the two sexes. That is how reproduction answered the question of creating more animals. In the case of dumb animals, all I had to do was to instill in each at the proper time of growth, an urge to mate with another animal of the same species but of the opposite sex. This was purely a physical instinct. There was no selectivity about it. With dumb animals, it was not a case of love. *Any* animal, *any* one of the same species but of the opposite sex would do. When the female became "in heat" she sent out a notice naturally to inform any male of the same species that he was welcome to "do what comes naturally." You wouldn't call this pornography, would you?

When it comes to the human animal, I wanted to add another dimension to the reproduction process. That something new was love—the highest form of love next to the selfless love which is the purpose for which I created human beings. With this kind of love between a certain man and a certain woman, there would be an ecstasy in every phase of the mating process which would be utterly unattainable to those who engaged in "sex" out of the purely physical and almost irresistible urge I have planted in both sexes.

Because my spirit—the Creative Spirit of Love—is part of every human's nature, is it not clear I planned a grand extra for my earthly partners above the reproductive feature of intercourse? To make sure that I was not expecting too much from humans and that it was possible for a loyal and devoted love to last between one certain man and one certain woman, I experimented with some dumb animals. If you will take time to make a little research, you will find that among certain birds and animals, there exists the most complete dedication and loyalty to one certain mate. The sex urge is reserved for one certain bird or animal. The family life is honored, respected and enjoyed. My spirit—the Spirit of Love had taken hold of these animals. I knew then, that I was not expecting too much of the human animal.

Of course, this was predicated on human beings learning that the Spirit of Love was part of their nature. Otherwise, they would respond only to the physical urge of their sex nature. Without the Creative Spirit of Love, there would be hell to pay. Any person of the opposite sex whose appearance was physically attractive would be fair game, regardless of marriage or true love. The fact that this has proved to be the case since the creation of human beings should interest you, My friend, in your sincere efforts to fight pornography.

Is there not a better way to fight pornography than to deny the truth or keep it from being sought and followed? Pornography only exists when I am left out of sex. Why not work on this? As the spirit of Love, I created sex. For human beings, I planned it to transcend the mere function of reproduction. My spirit of Love wanted to share in every phase of the sex act.

It is because I am left out of the sex act that the divorce rate is mounting to the point where there is now one divorce to between two and three marriages. A good measure of this unhappy situation is due to sex misunderstandings, which are due in turn to the omission of the spiritual part of human nature.

Have you given thought to why I have endowed humans with a far greater potential of sex enjoyment than dumb animals? Consider the great joy from the sense of touch and feel. Just the holding of hands of two people who love one another can be thrilling. When in the course of true love, the hands wander to more sensitive parts of the body the thrill is multiplied. Dumb animals have not been given the joy coming from the sense of touch and feel, except from the actual act of intercourse—a purely physical experience.

If children were taught the truth of their nature from the very beginning, they would appreciate that the Creative Spirit of love must always participate in their love for that certain one of the opposite sex. This would in great measure negate the appeal of homosexuality. From the start, their desire would be directed naturally to a certain one of the opposite sex. With this kind of understanding of their nature, homosexuality would be removed from their thoughts. Indeed, the thought would never come up. As in every aspect of life, human beings cannot leave My spirit of love out of consideration. The cure for homosexuality is not by rationalizing that all sex is pornography and therefore heterosexuality is no more proper than homosexuality. I created one to be natural. The other is unnatural and the cure is to restore Me to my proper place in the relationship of one certain man with one certain woman.

The homosexual should not be condemned. He needs help, and that means he needs love—first the selfless love that only My Creative Spirit can offer and then eventually he needs the love of someone of the opposite sex. The so-called experts who condone homosexuality —even to the point of having it made legal between consenting parties—show a distressing lack of understanding of man's true nature.

As the Creative Spirit of Love, I can assure you that no one is born a homosexual. If the teaching of self-knowledge had been included in education, the unfortunate person would have no part in this perverted practice. He would have resolved this question long before the situation had reached the point of no return.

Clearly, what the homosexual needs is not to make the practice legal, but to learn the way that will free him forever from the sense of guilt that constantly haunts him. He needs only know the truth and the truth will make him free. The truth that I who created him, building his body and brain, remain with him as his ever-present Partner.

Once, he learns that he has for a Partner the loving Spirit that built and sustains the Universe, he will gain a new confidence in himself and a self-respect that will make any departure from natural sex behavior not only unnecessary but unthinkable.

Is it not sad that the solution to this problem which causes such deep-seated and tragic misery is so simple, yet the well-meaning people in the fields of psychiatry, psychology, religion and education persist in trying to discover solutions that leave Me out of the problem?

When will these experts learn that the Creative Spirit of Love cannot be ignored or left out or confined to the realm of religion? This is My universe. I created it. I sustain it. How dare anyone who must depend on Me to keep his brain working, put a limit on My powers?

Crediting you with sincerity in your fight against pornography, I suggest you take yourself back in your mind to when you first began to feel the urges of sex. You were in your teens. How did you cope with this growing and almost irresistible urge? I have a right to ask because I put you in this position. I wanted to share in it with you. I must be compassionate in My attitude toward you. Because of the powerful urges and emotions involved, I had spent a long time before finally deciding how strong to make the sex urge in humans. This was no problem with dumb animals. I simply arranged for them to engage in sex purely for reproductive purposes.

With humans in whose nature I sought to play a part, it was quite a different matter. I could not afford to sacrifice the reproductive feature, as I did want to keep My earth peopled. But how strong should this urge be? Should I make it entirely irresistible? Or should I allow for the kind of self-restraint and control to be expected of humans with brains and understanding?

This all tied in with My belief that eventually, man would come to understand My part in his nature, and this would then resolve any sex problem just as it would all other problems. In your case, My friend and partner, how did you handle this problem as a teener? Did you handle it on your own or did you realize then I was your Partner to help out in this and all your other problems? Had your parents talked frankly about how you were born? And why you were born—which would help you accept and understand better the how of being born? Or were your parents hush-hush about this delicate matter?

Just as most parents do not teach their children of My presence in their nature, so they do not tell them why and how they were born. This must have made it tough for you as your teen years began to approach the marriageable age. When you think it over, is there anything posing a greater problem for a teener than how to handle the sex urge as it grows stronger each passing day? When someone of the opposite sex makes advances, how should a teener not properly prepared and not informed of his or her true nature react to the opportunity?

Or do you feel that even to discuss such a situation openly on the stage or screen or TV or the press is a form of pornography? Unfortunately, too often, these set out to offer pornography. But would you object to earnest, serious, frank discussions of sex? When two young people think they are in love, how much a part does the sex urge play in their belief they are in love? And how much a part does the sex urge play in how they should conduct themselves from here on before they are married?

When one is not in love, self-denial of the sex urge can be much easier than when one is very much in love. If one has learned of My part in his nature, My guidance directs him to ways to sublimate his sexual desires thru athletic or other activities and thru service to others. One thus achieves a sense of gratification not open to the one who has not learned his true nature.

But what about the couple very much in love who are able to spend much time together? Having created in each of them this urge to unite in love, is it fair for Me to demand they either marry or refrain from responding to the urges I planted in them? They may be considered too young to marry. They may not be in the financial condition to marry or there may be other valid reasons for delaying marriage.

As you go back in your mind to your teenage days,

can you come up now with some fair solution to the problem of what young people are to do about this sex urge? Young people of today are more honest with themselves than in your day. They know that something is wrong with your way of life even though they may not know what to do about it.

No doubt you regard what many of them are doing as immoral when they live with someone of the opposite sex even though not married. Is it just as immoral if they are deeply in love as when not? Anyone who has suffered thru a long engagement knows that not being able to consummate their love puts a great and unnatural strain on both parties, particularly for lovers who see each other often. How long should two lovers who for whatever valid reason must temporarily postpone their marriage plans be expected to hold in check the natural sex urge I put in them?

Perhaps you, who sincerely seek to do away with pornography may come up with a respectable plan to help youth handle their sex urges. If the problem confronting true lovers is mostly financial, you should be able to devise something better than that which encourages them to live together without marriage. You might encourage them to secure a marriage license if it carries with it the legal right to enjoy at once the relationship of man and wife. They are doing this without any legal right and they are courting trouble in their future years together.

When their legal marriage is finally consummated, no matter how earnestly they strive in future years to sympathetically understand the reasons for their earlier indulgences when unmarried, they may find it difficult to maintain the respect essential to a happy married life. Pre-marital sex experience arouses doubts and suspicions later in married life that are almost impossible to completely dispel. Would it not be better to amend the marriage license so that true lovers will live together legally instead of in defiance of the law?

The fact that both are willing to go on record as intending to marry indicates a motive higher than mere sex gratification. The legal right would preserve their individual and mutual respect and trust, enabling their eventual official marriage to get off to a proper start. This may shock you, but if it causes you to come up with a better plan, it will be worthwhile. You know that love and sex are not synonymous. And it is with true love that I am concerned. Love is more than sex but should grownups blind themselves to the virtually irresistible urge I have planted in humans to consummate the love they so strongly feel?

A year or two can be a terribly long time to keep resisting the steps which come naturally to lovers: First, the holding of hands, then the kiss, the ardent caress, the arm around the shoulder, the hand touching and fondling the breast—a prominent part of the girl's sex appeal. The Bible speaks of a woman's rapturous yearning for her loved one: "He shall lie all night betwixt my breasts." I made this longing a natural part of My plan in the relationship of man and wife. Ask yourself which of the steps that come so naturally to lovers should be resisted? Does your memory tell you how as a youth you resisted the first step or subsequent steps? How and why did you refuse to do what comes naturally? Is sex wrong because both lovers enjoy it? Does the enjoyment of sex make it evil?

If you were to ask Me about this, My response would be that the only thing wrong about it is your attitude. And this comes from not knowing that the Highest dwells within you. As a practicing Christian you should know what Jesus gave his life to teach you: "The kingdom of God is within you." As a good American, you should know that when Lincoln spoke of "the better angels of our nature" he was referring to the God-part of your nature. This would help you understand that the whole plan of sex is of your Creator-Partner's doing. It is because you leave My part out of your thinking that you come to regard sex as evil.

So, I ask you again what is the pornography you are fighting? Is it the showing of the human body? Is it discussion of the sex differences between the male and the female? If a child early in life got to see and know the differences would he or she not come to accept these as natural? If the child were taught that My Spirit of Love which created him is always with him, would he not also accept that the differences in sex and the uses of sex were part of My plan in creating him and all humans?

Are you not really fighting the wrong thing? Are you not fighting to cover up something? If you feel like fighting, why not fight to expose the natural truth about all humans? The natural truth is that the human body is My creation. I made the male body strong and muscular and virile so that when the spirit of a certain female is drawn to the spirit of a certain male, she is also drawn to him physically. In her womb, I planted the yearning to be possessed by this certain male. I planned this not solely for the purposes of reproduction, but as a climax to their sincere spiritual love for one another. The ecstasy this union affords cannot be achieved without the union of the spiritual and the physical. This is my law and there is no going around it.

I created the female body appealingly attractive—yes even provocative—so as to draw the male to her. But as in the case of the female, the first attraction for one certain man to one certain woman lies in the realm of the spirit. Otherwise the attraction is mostly physical and this can not offer enough to make it lasting. It is still possible for such a couple to become touched by the spirit within them and achieve a love that is lasting. Having embraced Me as a part of their nature, I also become a part of their love one for the other.

In your fight against pornography, let the better angels of your nature guard you against regarding the nude female form as something pornographic but rather as a beautiful and inspiring work of art. You may help men to learn their true nature so that they can gaze upon an adorable female creation without desiring to possess her, preferring to carry their stimulated emotions home to their own mate. In your fight against pornography, you may consider the hypocrisy in your laws which self-righteously punish a couple genuinely in love for consummating their love, though unmarried, while permitting another couple, because legally married, to bed with one another even when there is no love between them. To lie in each other's arms when all is spent, without a deep feeling of love and respect, breeds self-loathing and despair.

In your fight against pornography, you can help people to understand it is only for humans that I planned for lovers to face and embrace each other in the sex act. You can help them to understand when embracing their mate, they are also embracing Me, the spirit of their Maker.

Another beneficial result of your fight will be that people will be reminded that family life is a gift and blessing of their Creator-Partner. Sex life that does not consciously embrace the Creator contributes little to family life. Because education tragically fails to include the teaching of self-knowledge, children grow up conditioned to look upon sexual love as something highly attractive but possessing a furtive if not evil touch. How can you expect them on their wedding night to suddenly change to the belief that married sex will prove a most exalting experience? If their education has left them disregarding My part in all other aspects of life, how can they change when it comes to sex?

Also, young people have become more sophisticated. Thru TV and instant communications with all parts of the world, young people know a lot more about life than did their parents at their age. Everything now is more out in the open, including "the pill" and abortion. Sex is no longer the "hush-hush" mystery it may have been in your day.

This makes it all the more important that children

learn My part in their nature. These days, a far greater percentage of children engage in sex relations. It is as if sex has become a commodity, not a manifestation of a spiritual union. A boy asks a girl to go to bed with him as casually as he would ask "Let's have a coke." If one wants to be popular, one has sexual relations.

Not having learned that I am their ever-present Partner, young people become possessed with the idea of having sex for the sake of sex without being ready for it in mind or body or spirit. Had they been taught the Creator's part in every aspect of their life, they would know as they become teeners and experience the first promptings of sex that this is something I have implanted in their bodies. They will accept this growing urge toward union with the opposite sex as part of My plan to keep My earth peopled and to reward them with the ecstasy that only comes with a complete spiritual and physical union with the one they love.

There is no need being coy about this or to regard it as evil. Of all my creations and gifts for My children, which is more natural than sex? Ignorance or cover-up should not be made the basis for morality. Sex is just as natural for humans as it is for animals.

In your fight against pornography, I urge that you act preventively. The right kind of education would make a child aware that My Creative Spirit of Love is part of its nature, figuring in sex as I do in everything it does. This would instill in the growing youth a greater resistance to mere physical provocation or seduction. The youth would not then be apt to look upon one of the opposite sex as a "sometime" partner.

When children go to high school, they date for fun. When they go to college, they date in a new light, seeking perhaps serious companionship or even a prospective mate. But because of a tragic omission in education, sexual activity seems to have become the rule rather than an exception. Some who indulge seriously in sexual experience end up having to get married. In your fight against pornography, would you not urge parents who force marriage in such a condition to pause to make sure there is sincere love between the two young people involved. To marry without love being present is far worse than seeking to protect a reputation.

Self-understanding would do more than put sex in proper perspective. It would carry with it a feeling of reverence toward Me, as Creator and Partner, toward My world and all My children. It would bring a consciousness of the sacredness and beauty of sex. Self-understanding would instill in each of My children a deep feeling of gratitude for the privilege of becoming co-creators with God.

As a sincere fighter against pornography, you must realize the importance of mutual respect in the sexual relationship, and that this cannot be over-emphasized. You are, I know, aware of the dangers of permissiveness, but should you not also be mindful of the harm resulting from a constant feeling of guilt about the sex urge? The promiscuity and undisciplined indulgence you are fighting are both bad. They are bad for the individual and bad for society. But in your battle against them, you should be aware that the complete repression of sex can be equally damaging. And is this not also true of the self-reproach brought about in some sensitive persons, particularly adolescents, by even mere manifestations of the sexual impulse?

Your little self has a way of sinning with a bad conscience, as if this would make the sin more forgivable. But consideration tells you it can prove more harmful to commit a forbidden deed and then feel guilty about it, because the intense guilt provides an unconscious incentive to commit the sin again.

Finally, My partner and fighter against pornography, I must leave you with the profound assurance that to really prevent pornography the answer lies in the teaching of self-knowledge. Probably in no aspect of a person's life more than sex is the adage "Know thyself" more appropriate. For, when you know yourself, you know that your Partner is the Creative Spirit of Love. This knowledge alone is the best guard against pornography.

*   *   *   *   *

If God Spoke to the Military Might it be Something Like This:

> What you are about to read is simply the imagining of one who has learned when he sincerely strives to become "an agent and instrument of Divine Providence" (Lincoln's words) his Partner will guide him, speak thru him and work thru him. The author believes this holds true for you, too.

Suppose this very day, I gathered up about 100 boys of about ten years of age, divided them into two groups, equipped them with rocks and knives and directed them to fight—one group with the other! Wouldn't that be shocking? Why should it be shocking to you? Why should it be any more shocking than to wait a few more years when they were stronger and more certain of killing one another? And be subject to your orders rather than Mine?

Is my supposition shocking because of the tender age of the younger boys? Or is it shocking because the one ordering them into battle is their Creator rather than the military who have convinced themselves that the regrettable step they're taking is necessary in order to save the country? Would you not admit it is a sign of failure of your way of life that you, their elders can't come up with a better way of life than one which every few years has to resort to organized killing in order to save that way of life?

Suppose there was a slight change of rules about organized warfare which placed the higher military ranked men in the front of the battle line instead of occupying comfortable, safe quarters somewhere in the rear. Might there then be a better chance of coming upon another and better way of life? Might it not be that this slight change would inspire sober second-thoughts on the part of military leaders to find a better way to live? Not only in this country but all over the world. Your Commander-in-Chief at the time of the Civil War, which he fought with bitter anguish for four years because I had instructed him to preserve the Union at all costs, believed there was another and better way to save the nation. He told his people of this way but neither the people nor the military seemed to understand what Lincoln was talking about. His solution had nothing to do with fighting wars. Quite the contrary, Lincoln's idea had to do with preventing wars—all wars, small, personal and large. His solution was based on his true understanding of the nature of man, and what I had planned for man when I first created human beings. Lincoln told his people: "We must disenthrall ourselves and then we will save our nation." To disenthrall means to free oneself from slavery to self.

Wars occur because men are slaves to self. They become slaves to self because one generation hands down to the next a way of life that encourages slavery to self. Not only does your present way of life encourage slavery to self, but it makes a more sensible way of life appear ludicrous and impossible.

As a military man, would you recommend a method of battle which has been tried often before and always comes up a failure? Would you not protest that it doesn't make sense to persist with a plan of battle that is a proved failure? Would you not urge that a new way be found—one that makes sense and has a better chance of working?

With present instantaneous means of communication, who knows but that young men in other countries might be inspired to rebel against their own commanders who are urging them to war upon other young people? Call this nonsense, but youth are rebelling all over the world against the way of life being handed them by their elders. But as a military man, you will probably want to follow your own limited wisdom instead of being guided by Mine.

Think a moment. It is I who created the children of all races and nations. Can you believe I created them in order to war upon other young people in different lands? It was in My plan for children to learn to walk and talk. It was not in My plan for them to seek out other young children and fight with them. Observe young children. They naturally seek out other children to play with. I do not bring children into the world bearing prejudice toward other children. They get their prejudices from you adults. Children naturally accept other children, regardless of their skin color or ethnic background. It is you, their elders who teach them your prejudices and hatred. Even as I point the finger of guilt at you grownups, I realize the blame is not yours. You had this way of life handed down to you, and part of the way of life is to hate and kill.

But I gave you grownups brains. You have done some wonderful things with your brains. But mostly, they are things that make you money. But even that is because your elders taught you to have such great respect for money. You give me lip service but money gets the worship. With your brains, why not re-examine this way of life? Why assume there is no better way? Why assume that Jesus was a good man but that he was talking religion—not commonsense? Let me assure you that when your best minds get together and try to solve a human problem, even if they come up with a suggestion they unanimously approve, the chances are it will not be as practicable or as workable as the suggestions of Jesus.

The best suggestions of human beings if born of your present way of thinking are futile because they leave the Creative Spirit of Love out of their solution. Jesus never made that kind of error. Knowing that My Spirit of Love was within him, he submitted his own thoughts and will to me and readily set them aside if My guidance told him different. This was Jesus' way. It was the way of Lincoln. All men who have ever achieved anything worthwhile know that the deed was achieved not so much by them as thru them. When they disenthralled themselves, they became My agent and instrument, and I performed the worthwhile deed thru them, enriching them at the same time.

There are many who feel themselves so smart they need no God to lean on. Do they ever ask how they got that smart? Who gave them their brain? If, indeed, they are superior to others in their mentality, should they not mix a little gratitude with their feeling of superiority? Or do they really believe I made some men smarter than others in order that they may lord it over the others, and even use their power for their own ends? Can anyone really believe I created men so that they may fight with other men, hate other men, kill other men?

Why don't these superior men exercise their superior brain and re-examine their way of life instead of accepting it the way it was handed down to them? Let them look back into history and do a little research into what this way of life has brought to human beings. They will probably cite the great material comforts their way of life has brought. Admittedly, life has been made easier for some people in certain respects, but are they any the happier for it? Let them check with the psychiatrists, who are busier than ever (often treating other psychiatrists) trying to help people with ample material things to gain some happiness out of what they possess.

But it is when the claim is made that people are in better health and live longer than they used to that they show their ignorance of the truth. Their superior brains are led astray by the juggling of statistics, which show that people are living on an average some 15 or more years than they did at the turn of the century. On the face of it, this claim seems true, but when you look at the fine print, you learn that this longer life span is a myth; that it was obtained by the saving of infants at birth. Before better sanitary measures were put into effect in natal care and the handling of infants at birth, many children died at childbirth or in the weeks following. It is the saving of infants in early life that make the statistics look good. But for the man and woman of sixty, the life span has increased only about two years since the turn of the century. Considering all you should have learned about nutrition and proper breathing and exercise, is this anything to brag about? I planned for human beings to live in vigor and in good health to well past a century. You can establish this by examining into the life span of animals. You will find they average about seven times the length of time it takes them to reach maturity. In the case of human beings, this would mean seven times 21 years.

What does your way of life do for you in this area? It is not uncommon for "successful" men to acquire ulcers or heart attacks or even strokes in their forties and fifties. To lose their vigor long before reaching even three score and ten. What price success! What a way of life! What a way to make use of intelligence!

This brings up another point about people with unusual intelligence. Or any other special talent. Or even their physical build or attractive looks. Isn't this all My doing? Why leave Me out of your admiration? When you look at a work of art, you credit the artist for his handiwork. When you listen to a beautiful and inspiring piece of music, you give credit to the composer as well as to musician and/or orchestra and conductor. When you gaze upon an imposing structure you credit the architect. All this is as it should be. But why make an exception of Me?

In all other cases, you do not deliberately withhold credit from the author, the composer, the artist, the architect. How come when it has to do with the Creator of the Universe, your Creator and the Creator of every human being, you all remain dumb, as if the thought never occurred to you, which may very well be the case. Why should this be? Is it because the minute anyone gives Me credit or even mentions My name—God—in connection with the work, people instantly consider it a religious remark. Am I to be confined to the area of religion? Who made this decision and by what authority? Does it make sense to pigeon-hole the Creator of the Universe in a man-contrived area, even one as well-meaning as structured religion?

This may be another instance of your being controlled by PTCH—Precedent, Tradition, Custom, Habit. PTCH is something handed down from one generation to another over the years and as time passes, more and more people accept it without questioning. Is this a sign of intelligence? Perhaps a little re-examination is in order.

Let Me admit that while I created your body and caused it to grow, you do have something to do with its appearance and condition. Indeed you do. What you eat and how much you eat can have a great affect on your physical appearance and on your physical condition. The way you live—your personal way of life can have a great effect on your body and particularly on your face. One of my prophets, Abraham Lincoln observed that by the time a person has reached forty years of age, he is responsible for his face. This is what another wise man meant when he said "What you are speaks so loud I can't hear what you say."

I would like to raise another point in connection with My being left out of consideration about your everyday life. Tell Me, why do people readily admit that I did things in the past and may do things in the future after they have died. Is this a matter of hope or fear? Hope that I will deal with them kindly in what they believe will be their next life? Or fear there might be such a thing as eternal damnation? I am not going to go into these two possibilities now. What I want to pursue is the question why am I being left out of the present? Is there not ample evidence all about you and within you that I exist in the present? Indeed, that I am very much in effect in every aspect of your present life. *I AM.* You need not conjure up blind faith to prove I am. You need not invoke any religious doctrine, not even the Bible.

All you need to do is to use your commonsense. This will lead to a challenge of PTCH, but then PTCH should be able to stand up against any challenge including commonsense. If it does not, it is time to dethrone PTCH and introduce the truth.

PTCH is responsible for your present way of life which leaves Me in outer space somewhere waiting to judge you after you die. Military men are supposed to be the most practical of men. You are trained on facts. You are trained to look for all possible eventualities based on known facts and past experience. You should be among the first to challenge PTCH when it comes to whether I work only in the past or the future. You need but ask yourself two simple questions: 1) Who keeps my heart beating? 2) Who keeps open the lines of communicaiton between my brain and the rest of my body so that I may think straight, talk straight, work straight? Your answers to these simple questions will annihilate PTCH and bring about a new way of life, a way that will prevent wars.

If God Spoke to the Smoker Who Sincerely Wants to Stop Might it be Something Like This:

What you are about to read is simply the imagining of one who has learned when he sincerely strives to become "an agent and instrument of Divine Providence" (Lincoln's words) his Partner will guide him, speak thru him and work thru him. The author believes this holds true for you, too.

First, I want you to know that I, your Creator and Partner, am fully aware of the nature of the addiction you are afflicted with. What I have to say may be new to you, but that is not your fault. Your education neglects Me, which is like starting the 100 story Empire State Building on level ground without any foundation going deep into the ground to hold it firm against rocking and against collapse in the event of any unexpected strain. If we succeed together in overcoming this affliction, you may want to express your gratitude by doing all you can to have education include the teaching of self-knowledge, so that children all over the country will understand their true nature.

The very fact that you are reading this may be proof that you sincerely want to stop smoking. I am laying out a few simple truths that will help you. If I seem to speak critically at times, it is not that I want to hurt you, but rather to help you.

I am setting out for you a Six-Second Exercise, which has to do with breathing, the most natural of all exercises, yet the one most humans neglect. Humans tend to take breathing for granted, leaving it to My Creative Power which gave you life to take care of for you. I made breathing in two parts: Out and In. Out, so that you may breathe out stale, toxic waste; In, so that you may breathe in fresh, invigorating air. Also—and this is vital—so that you may breathe out ego, breathe in God. When you become an active participant in this most natural of all exercises, an immediate and amazing change takes place in you, physically, mentally, emotionally, spiritually.

This is true whether you are a heavy smoker or not. In the case of the heavy smoker, however, the change may border on the miraculous.

In the case of the average or light smoker, the results may not seem so dramatic, as these folks do not have so far to go before the desire for a smoke leaves them altogether. This is probably the most remarkable thing about the exercise. It is not will power that causes you to quit. What happens is that the desire to inhale seems to depart from you.

Nicotine is not a habit-forming drug, physicians assert. The habit of smoking is the habit. However, many people think they are addicted to the nicotine and when they try to stop smoking, the chest pains, headaches and lightheadedness sometimes experienced are blamed on withdrawal. Physicians report that the discomfort is really caused by a lack of oxygen. When smokers who have been inhaling deeply for years stop smoking, they also stop breathing. The Six-Second Exercise promotes breathing and lessens, if it does not altogether dispose of, the desire to inhale smoke.

"Nature abhors a vacuum" you have been told. The truth is that GOD loves a vacuum when you humans create it by breathing out your ego. This opens the way for God's Spirit to enter with the incoming air (both invisible to the sight) thus filling the vacuum. The first step in the Six-Second Exercise which follows is to Breathe out Ego. With Ego out, the Spirit of God flows in and you hold it there as long as you can. You will learn from your actual experience that the holding of your breath is a vital part of the exercise, as God's Love and Power and Joy and the desire to serve mankind flow in with His Spirit. You become the beneficiary of all this greatness. But if you have a breathing problem, care should be exercised in holding your breath very long.

Here is the simple Six-Second Exercise (which can steadily and profitably be practiced by smoker and non-smoker alike):

When the desire for a smoke comes upon you,

1. Breathe out Ego (heave a hearty sigh).
2. Breathe in God (let air naturally fill your lungs).
3. Hold your breath as long as as you can, but without straining, thinking:

> "With all His Love
> and Power

> and Joy
> and Service
> to Mankind
> here and everywhere
> now and forever,
> and ever and ever, etc."

Of course, you won't be able to hold your breath that long at first, but with practice you'll add more each time. You'll find, to your surprise and satisfaction that your desire for a smoke has left you. It may seem a "gimmick" but by a strange coincidence, the capital letters in

> Breathe out Ego, Breathe In God
> spell BE BIG!

The regular practice of the Six-Second Exercise will do much more for you than permitting you to cut down on (or cut out) your smoking. It does the same for over-eating and over-drinking. Substituting God for Ego changes your entire perspective. You feel a deep and tremendous sense of well-being. There are positive benefits to morale, to character, to your outlook on life and to your relations with others.

You will know that it is not you bringing about these improvements but rather My Creative Power working through you. In the Six-Second Exercise you are really doing what comes naturally, and you will experience a feeling of deep gratitude for what has transpired. Could there be a more inspiring way to keep reminded of your true nature—your real greatness?

No matter how often you may fail, come back to the Six-Second Exercise again.

Breathe out Ego; Breathe In God.

You will be doing more than helping yourself to a new life. The change others see in you will make them want what you have. Thus you will help to restore breathing to the human race and with it a constant awareness of My Creative Presence in man.

If you persist in smoking, you should know that with every breath of smoke you draw deep into your lungs, you are insulting Me, your CREATOR-PARTNER. Even worse, you are rejecting our Partnership. Consider the facts: I provide pure fresh air for you to breathe to sustain and invigorate your body. Yet you choose to draw into your lungs poisonous elements that surely harm your body and will eventually destroy it.

If you are sincere in wanting to rid yourself of this addiction, I have given you the Six-Second Exercise that will transform that incoming breath of poison into a breath of inspiration and invigoration, even rejuvenation.

If you are sincere, I promise that this exercise will not fail you. It may even transform your life. But if you are not sincere, read no further. It is one thing when you don't know that My Spirit is within you as your Partner. I can readily forgive you under such circumstances, but to know the truth and choose to disregard Me as your Partner is to mock Me. And I will not be mocked! I am your Creator and Partner. I created that body you consider yours. I sustain it from moment to moment, keeping your heart beating and in countless other ways. Call it your body if you will, you are but temporary trustee of it, and some day—perhaps much too soon—you may force Me to reclaim it.

If you will pause to think about it, you will realize that you are not the individual you have been educated to believe. You are in individual Partnership with Me, your Creator-Partner. Together, we can do great things, but only if you seek to become, in the words of one of My greatest partners, Abraham Lincoln, an "agent and instrument of Divine Providence."

Another point about smoking: it's bad enough that your way of life forces you to breathe polluted air. But when you draw cigarette smoke deep down into your lungs, this is a deliberate act of your own. Besides, how about those around you who may be allergic to smoke? Are you not as inconsiderate of them as you are of Me, your Creator-Partner?

I suggest you go into a huddle with yourself. Call it meditation or prayer or whatever. You will find Me there for I am always with you.

Forget the things the world has taught you which promote self-indulgence. These things do not give you the happiness they promise. Your self-part cannot give you happiness. Only your God-part can. Only that part of your nature which will guide you to help others. In this way alone, you will find the joy of living.

This is the way I made you. You and I are Partners. My plan for this Partnership is simple: God guiding, you doing. The present way of life in your beloved country—"the last best hope of earth" is leading it to its decay. You will help save it if you work your Partnership with Me.

When you keep practicing the Six Second Exercise, you free yourself from slavery to self. So, My Partner, breathe out ego, breathe in God. From this moment on, you will be transformed.

You and I working together can overcome any problem. Don't under-rate yourself, for then you under-rate Me, your Partner.

BREATHE OUT EGO, BREATHE IN GOD.

* * *

If God Spoke to the Members of Congress and the Supreme Court Might it be Something Like This:

What you are about to read is simply the imagining of one who has learned when he sincerely strives to become "an agent and instrument of Divine Providence" (Lincoln's words) his Partner will guide him, speak thru him and work thru him. The author believes this holds true for you, too.

If you have not been aware of My speaking to you before, you would do well to ask yourself the question President Lincoln constantly asked himself: "What is God driving at?". Your country, which you are governing is showing alarming signs of decay from within. I detect little from you whose responsibility it is to preserve the nation, that would inspire the hope you know what the basic trouble is, and that you are determined to take the necessary steps to correct the situation.

Yet the solution to the problem is simple. And it is up to you to lead your people to understand it. You can do this by the simple exchange of your wisdom for Mine. Smile at this, if you will, but if you do, you show at once the difference between your thinking and that of Abraham Lincoln—between your kind of greatness and Lincoln's. The nation is in danger perhaps because you tend to disregard My wisdom, in the high regard you have for your own. Are you wiser than Lincoln to the extent you can scorn his forthright confession:

> "I should be the veriest shallow and self-conceited blockhead upon the footstool, if in my discharge of the duties that are put upon me in this place, I should hope to get along without the wisdom that comes from God, and not from man."

This is what I mean when I say the solution to your problems is simple. You need but follow Lincoln's way: give up your own wisdom for Mine. And My first bit of advice to you (and it may be all that is necessary) is this: "DO NOT CONFINE GOD TO RELIGION." It should be clear to you that I, the Creator of the Universe cannot be confined to a man-made pigeonhole earmarked "Religion." Because this has been common practice in the U.S.A. (and most everywhere else), the signs of decay are all about you.

Think about it! I created the earth some five billion years ago. This was long before I created human beings. Indeed, scientists are only able to trace man to a few thousand years ago, though some claim there is evidence going back to as much as a million years ago. But even granting this, what is one million years compared to five billion years? Does it offer explanation of the efforts of some who should know better than to restrict God to man-made religion? It is like trying to compress the sun—an area many times larger than the earth —into the earth's space.

And yet, supposedly wise men have been trying to

do this, because they still do not seem to realize this has been the real cause of your trouble. By restricting Me to religions, children have been prevented from learning in their education the most vital knowledge anyone can learn: self-knowledge. With the teaching of self-knowledge, children would have learned that I am a part of their nature. They would know that MY Creative Spirit of Love which formed their frame and gave them a brain never departs from them but remains within them, serving as their Creator-Partner. Why were children not so taught? Because the first mention of a power in each person infinitely greater than his own brought forth the protest: "This is religion. You cannot mention God in the public schools."

By whose authority has this thoughtless, irresponsible protest been recognized? By *yours,* the governing authorities of the United States. By permitting such a travesty that keeps children ignorant of their true nature, you acquiesce in the ruling that confines Me, the Creator of the Universe (with its billions of galaxies, each containing billions of planets and stars, all bigger than the earth)—you confine Me to that man-made segment of life called religion.

Surely, it must be clear to you that this was not the intention of the Founding Fathers when they wisely established the permanent separation of Church and State. It must be as clear to you as it was to them, that it is one thing to acknowledge the existence of a Supreme Being and an entirely different thing to permit man-made structured religions to have any part or influence in the affairs of State.

To believe in a Supreme Intelligence is a matter of reason and common sense. To confine this Supreme Intelligence to the area of religion is stupid and irresponsible. To allow this to prevent children from learning the truth of their nature is defenseless and beyond reason. To maintain this position because it has been the way of the past is to accept the wisdom of PTCH (Prededent, Tradition, Custom, Habit) above My wisdom. It also delays the time when the U.S.A. will be saved from the decay consuming your beloved land.

You need a new education—one that will free your people from slavery to self. Your present education promotes self-exaltation because the child learns only of the self-part of his nature. My part, the God-part of his nature, is not permitted to be taught him. The result is that all the evils coming from giving in to the desires and ambitions of self are manifest all over the land.

Lincoln, who was always open to My wisdom, warned of this more than a century ago. In eleven words that seem to have been completely forgotten, Lincoln admonished his people: "We must disenthrall ourselves and then we will save our nation." To disenthrall, as you know, is to free oneself from slavery to self. What piece of legislation now before you can prove as meaningful in saving the U.S.A. as the simple step of teaching children that the Creative Spirit which gave them life is with them till the end, serving as their Creator-Partner, to guide them to their highest happiness?

Let the public schools be used to remind all children of the words of wisdom of the Founding Fathers:

Wahington: "One cannot reason without arriving at a Supreme Intelligence."

Franklin: "If a creature is made by God, it must depend upon God, and receive all its power from God."

Jefferson: "The God who gave us life gave us liberty at the same time."

Let the children learn more of the words of Lincoln: "I do not consider that I have ever accomplished anything without God." (Incidentally, Lincoln had no specific religion).

Let them learn of the wisdom of God thru George Washington Carver, the eminent black scientist: "It is not we little men that do the work, but our blessed Creator working through us."

And I would suggest that you, who for the time being have been entrusted with the reins of Government, harken unto the words of that great American scientist, Albert Einstein who contributed greatly to your use of nuclear power: "The true value of a human being is determined primarily by the measure and the sense in which he has attained *liberation from the self.*"

Ask yourself, My child and partner: How far have you gone to attain *"liberation from the self"*? By your fruits shall I know you. And the one fruit that will be tastiest to all the people of your beloved country and all people everywhere is to learn that I created each person to live in Partnership with Me. This is simple, factual truth and religion has no place in it. Those who profess to love ME can show their love best with works rather than words.

Does it not concern you that in your democracy or republic 624 Americans have an income of more than a million dollars a year? Are you content to have one percent of your people own 34% of the total personal wealth of the country? Do you feel entirely safe that the top 10% own 56% of the wealth?

This is not to raise the question of injustice to the many millions of Americans who live under the poverty level. It is to raise the question of how can Americans, particularly the wealthy ones, persist in the belief that the greater the possessions the greater the happiness?

This is not only an enormous fallacy, there is no basis in truth for such a belief. All these wealthy people have is wealth. They also have lots of boredom, illness, unhappiness, and constant fear that someone is scheming to take their wealth from them. So full of fear are these wealthy people they have succeeded in getting their political representatives to arrange tax breaks for the over-privileged that total about 77 billion dollars a year.

You would be doing these people a great service by plugging up these loopholes and limiting the amount of money any person can gather for himself and family. They would scream to high heaven while you are doing this, but in the end they will enjoy greater happiness, better health and a longer life span. You might have fun trying this.

If God Spoke to Youth
Might it be Something Like This:

> What you are about to read is simply the imagining of one who has learned when he sincerely strives to become "an agent and instrument of Divine Providence" (Lincoln's words) his Partner will guide him, speak thru him and work thru him. The author believes this holds true for you, too.

You are the last best hope of America, the land Lincoln declared was "the last best hope of earth." You have shown you are aware that something is not right about the way of life handed you by your parents and their contemporaries. This is not to place the responsibility at their door. Like those before them, this way of life has been handed down from one generation to another.

But why there has been no strong questioning of a way that has been getting steadily worse is something every generation must answer to. Why has so little been done to counteract the increasing rate of crime, distrust, alcohol and drug use, reckless pursuit of money in the midst of general unhappiness and lack of inner peace?

I am addressing Myself to you because the time is now here for you to do something to save the nation. You have shown your displeasure with the state of things, even though you are not sure what to do about it. If your Creator-Partner were to guide you to challenge PTCH (Precedent, Tradition, Custom, Habit) as the responsible factor in your present way of life, would you have the courage to demand that every phase of PTCH undergo a thorough re-examination? This surely does not mean that your attitude toward your elders should not be one of respect. Indeed, to properly take issue with your elders involves your sincere respect, even though you maintain an unshakable determination to not follow a way of life that breeds millions of little private wars in everyday living, and which has led to two world wars in a 25-year span and which now points the way to complete self-destruction.

Your elders will admit there is something radically wrong with a way of life that promotes distrust, cynicism, hatred and sharp practice. They may not know, however, that the seeds for this deplorable condition are planted in an educational system (on which they have prided themselves) where children are taught every other knowledge except self-knowledge.

Because you want to be honest with yourself, you want to know your true nature—your littleness, even nothingness—as well as your greatness.

Surely you believe there must be a purpose to life, and that this purpose is greater than making money and glorifying self. You will surely agree that it is a duty—and it should be a joy—for every able-bodied person to earn his own way and support his family. But does it make sense to judge a man's success in life by the amount of money he gathers or the position of power he holds or the publicity he is able to achieve?

From what you see all about you, including the signs of decay, can you accept this kind of "success" as fulfilling the purpose of life? Can it reward anyone with real and lasting satisfaction? It may be the kind of success that pleases the self-part of one's nature, but because one's self-part is self-centered and selfish, this kind of success yields no lasting satisfaction to anyone.

The teaching of self-knowledge would have revealed that your self-part is not all there is to your nature. There is the part of the Creative Spirit of Love which created you, which gave you a brain and which remains with you your whole life long to serve as your Creator-Partner. My Creative Spirit of Love figures in every aspect of your life, so it doesn't make sense to confine Me to that restricted area known as religion.

You need but let your mind dwell on your beginning and My part in it. How My invisible Spirit of Love spent nine months in you building your body, which when completed I gently eased out of your mother's womb. It was My Creative Spirit that caused you to grow in body and mind. These are simple truths that should have been taught you. Now I am counting on you to take a hand in seeing that self-knowledge is taught in education. Let me discuss with you the difference that self-knowledge would make in your attitude toward 1) your parents; 2) money; 3) sex; 4) athletics and sportsmanship; 5) alcohol and other drugs; 6) your country.

1. Your attitude toward your parents. When you become aware that you have for a Partner, the Supreme Intelligence that created and sustains the Universe and all that live therein, you no longer depend solely on your

own intelligence, which unfortunately most people do. You get your wisdom and arrive at decisions the way Abraham Lincoln did (and take note of how forcefully Lincoln related this): "I should be the veriest shallow and self-conceited blockhead upon the footstool, if in my discharge of the duties that are put upon me in this place, I should hope to get along without the wisdom that comes from God and not from man."

This dependence on your Partner's wisdom will become manifest to your parents. You need not volunteer to explain it. They will learn from you. Some people may consider this a switch, for parents to learn from their children. But this is in My plan. I count on every one learning from children, as witness: "You must become as a little child . . . You must be born again. A little child shall lead them.". . . Time and time again, I have given evidence of the miracle that is a newborn child, yet mankind still takes this miracle for granted.

When your elders see such wisdom and power and love at work in you, they will desire these virtues for themselves. Your open acknowledgment that these excellent qualities are not of your doing, but that of your Creator-Partner working thru you, will help your parents and all with whom you come in contact. Your relationship to your parents will be one of love and trust. The inner radiance born of God working thru you will shine thru your face, inspiring confidence. Egotism and self-centeredness will have no place in your being.

2. Your attitude toward money. The current attitude of people toward money is almost one of worship. They

do not seem to realize that this represents a trade-in. They have traded Me in for money. They show a much greater faith in what money can do for them than in what I am able to do for them. Now, obviously, in your way of life, money is a very important factor. Many deem it an absolutely necessary factor. Among the necessities of life are food, shelter, clothing. These all require money. Then there is education, transportation, recreation and other expenses. Money will take care of these expenses. It is your duty to earn your way and to provide material security for yourself and your loved ones. This is not an issue.

Where the mistake occurs—and it is an almost universal and grossly stupid mistake—is the commonly accepted belief that the more money one gathers for himself and family the happier they will be. The fact is that when one goes beyond material security into the realm of luxury, the line of happiness which accompanies one on the march to security takes a downturn. There is no way to prevent this. What insures that this line of happiness takes a downturn is My Law—a law which no man can circumvent. This law reads "Too much of anything is not good for man." Let Me give you a few "for instances." You need the sun. Too much sun can give you a sunstroke or heat prostration. You need the rain. Too much can bring a flood. You need food. Too much will make trouble and add extra weight. You need money. Too much creates a rift in the family—often between husband and wife, often between parents and children. There are many other ways in which too much money can prove harmful. Emerson, who had an unshakable belief in My presence and in the Partnership of man and Maker had this to say about money-gatherers: "If the gatherer gathers too much, Nature takes out of the man what she puts into his (treasure) chest; swells the estate, but kills the owner."

Because the standard of success handed you is based on the amount of money a person can gather, not many people understand or believe that the accumulation of money is not a sure-fire way to happiness, but almost surely a way to unhappiness. This means you will have a job ahead of you trying to undo this fallacy. But a little research can help out. One of your able and honest pollsters can ascertain that the happiest people are not those with excessive wealth, but those who derive an inner sense of joy and peace from acts of love and kindness for their brother-man.

3. Your attitude toward sex. In the chapter "If God Spoke to You About Sex" (page 265) you will find much of what I would say to you about this subject. When you learn the truth about your nature—that I, the Creative Spirit of Love, am truly the God-part of your nature —your whole attitude toward sex becomes crystal clear. You realize that sex is not evil. You know that the Spirit of Love which created all humans also created sex. To believe that sex is evil is to imply that I, the Creative Spirit of Love, am evil. Such a belief springs from the failure of education to teach self-knowledge.

If people would realize that the participation of My Spirit is a crucial part of the human sex adventure, they would then understand that for the highest level of ecstacy between lovers the sex experience is not only physical, but also mental, emotional, and spiritual.

When two bodies join, their spirits should also join. This makes sex very special and its misuse very harmful.

It is probable that you are not yet married. You are, however, faced with the problem of what to do with the sex urge I have implanted in you. This began to assert itself in your teens and it has posed a problem for you ever since. Unless you were given understanding of My presence with you, the problem is most difficult to overcome. Even when you learn of our Partnership, the sex urge is a challenge to control. If you find yourself in love and your love is returned, it is almost impossible to deny the urge of sex. How long should young folks in love be satisfied with saying to one another "I love you?" Of course, love and sex are not the same. Love is a much deeper emotion than sex, but as your Creator I cannot ask anyone to be blind to the powerful urge I have implanted in My human creatures to consummate the love they feel so strongly for one another.

Step by step, lovers are naturally led to become endearingly closer to one another. From the tenderness of holding hands, they naturally graduate to the kiss and ardent embrace. Is it not natural for the male lover to allow his hand to reach out to fondly caress his loved one's breast? In the very nature of her sex appeal, the female breasts make a distinct contribution.

What male grownups seem to have lost sight of in their sexy attitude about the female breast is that I made female breasts for a dual purpose. It is generally accepted that males are attracted physically to the well-formed bosom. This delights the eye as well as the touch of man, and I planned it this way.

But why lose sight of the utilitarian use of the female

breasts? Is it because it has gone out of style for a mother to nurse her baby? Any father who has watched his child fed and comforted at his wife's breast knows that no man-made preparation can really approach the benefit, the beauty and the charm the mother's breast holds for the infant.

When after long deliberation, I decided to create humans and to live in partnership with them, I made them more than mere animals. Animals engage in sex only in accordance with My plan for them to reproduce. But with humans, there is the gift of love contributed by My spirit. I am aware that, because self-knowledge is not taught in public education, most people do not learn that My spirit enters into sexual intercourse, so they proceed to indulge in this relationship solely on a physical basis. They soon discover that something is missing and this leads to looking elsewhere for satisfaction.

Many young people who, for one reason or another, cannot marry promptly, decide that the answer to their problem is to live together as though married. Is there no better answer? Even if the two later marry, doubts may then arise to plague them. No matter how earnestly man and wife strive to sympathetically understand the reasons for their earlier indulgence, it is difficult to maintain the respect essential to a happy married life. Time may lessen the ardor which led the couple to engage in pre-marital sex, but may arouse doubts and suspicions as to why they indulged.

You must understand that marriage is a commitment by two people to achieve the fullness I meant them to have. Its success is dependent on the maintenance of the

Partnership and the understanding and wisdom that come from it. There are many definitions of marriage—socially, legally, etc.—but remember, as the Creator of marriage My Creative Spirit of Love needs to be a part of every marriage. Lovers should know this.

They would do well to comply with the cultural and legal exercises that society considers marriage. But people should realize that these outward signs are not marriage, but merely a ritualistic celebration of the commitment that is made. The commitment of marriage is between the man, the woman, and My Spirit of Love. The celebration of this commitment is shared with those of their community, but that commitment is between the three of us.

Education could help to achieve a better understanding of these things by teaching children about the dual powers that make up their nature. Then as the children developed, feeling the first urges of sex, they would recognize this as the Creator's plan, and they would glory in it with utmost respect and awe. They would come to understand that their Maker's presence gives them a soul, and this soul is outraged when it is left out of the sex act.

With this understanding, young people in love would ask themselves some vital questions before applying for a marriage license. They would seek answers to such questions as these: Am I sure my loved one

1) is the kind of person I could live with after the first flush of passionate desire is gone?

2) really loves children—all God's children?

3) is the kind of person to inspire in me sacrifices for others?

4) is not too ambitious for worldly things, for worldly success, for ease, for authority over others?

5) is aware that each person has the same Universal and Public Power for his Creator-Partner?

No one can be positively certain that if these questions are answered affirmatively, this will hold up in all the difficulties married life often introduces. However, affirmative answers provide a good foundation on which to begin married life. Every marriage, in itself, is dependent on how much I have been taken into Partnership with both members of this human partnership in their individual lives. Without My Partnership, marriage, despite the alluring sex factor, becomes a great gamble.

What can be done about this? Some people will think it strange—may even be shocked—for Me to say that I find merit in a suggestion that has been made, affecting marriage license requirements. Why not amend those requirements so as to grant a couple applying for a marriage license the legal right to enjoy at once the relationship of man and wife, if for any reason marriage is not immediately feasible? The fact that both are willing to go on record as intending to marry indicates a motive higher then mere sex gratification. The legal right would preserve their individual and mutual respect and trust. Those who are shocked at such a suggestion probably forget their own experiences when young and in love. Yet, if their son or daughter were living with someone in an unmarried state, would they not appreciate an amendment to the requirements that would make the situation legal?

Why do I find merit in a suggestion of this kind? First of all, I see no reason why I should not treat sex in the same open way everything else is discussed. In fact, it is largely the failure of people to treat sex that way that is responsible for pornography, rape, extra-marital relationships, and virtually all sex violations. If self-knowledge were taught all the way through education, almost all sex violations would disappear, including homosexuality, Lesbianism, bisexuality, etc. What I am saying is that if, from the beginning, every child learned that the Creative Spirit of Love which built its body and brain remains with the child in loving partnership, virtually every problem would find its natural solution.

There would, of course, in amending the laws as suggested, be legal questions to settle; for example, the event of pregnancy, the possible desire of one or both persons to terminate the relationship, and other questions. The amended laws should fairly meet all these contingencies, and if taken advantage of they should be made a part of the record.

The fact that everything would be a matter of record should prove a saving grace, because both parties would be more cautious about taking the step too lightly. They would know that a cancellation would be revealed on the record and would have a bearing on their future. Moreover, a girl would have some protection against seduction through a promise of marriage.

Another effect of the new approach might be to narrow the cases of pre-marital sex experience to those who are sincerely in love and who plan to marry. Its greatest benefits would become evident after they are married, each retaining the mutual respect so essential to a happy married life.

Other benefits would be in cutting down the number of divorces and broken homes, insuring to more children a happier home life. The change would be from a practice now carried on in secrecy, with ultimate harmful effects, to one that is aboveboard, promoting trust and respect. The fact that the number of divorces is approaching a ratio of one out of two marriages is proof that something should be done. Marriage needs to become that special part of the Partnership Life I meant it to be.

4. Your attitude toward athletics and good sportsmanship. A proper understanding of the nature of man will bring with it a different conception of athletics and good sportsmanship. The college youth is a "natural" to help bring this about.

The first obvious fact about any form of athletics is that it is meant to give fun. Beginning with the first games children play, the objective is to have fun. In competition of all kinds of games and athletics, the first objective is fun. Of course, there is always a secondary objective: to *win*. But having fun is still the original purpose in any sport.

Is it not sad that having fun is being replaced by the desire to win? The natural desire for fun is a victim of the way of life handed down from one generation to another. The self-part of man is regarded as the whole man. And man's self-part wants to win, regardless. This was not always the case.

There was a time when games and athletics were indulged in mostly for fun. Of course the desire to win was natural, but it was always accompanied by good sportsmanship. The loser would always congratulate the winner. So, too, would the losing team, and the students thereof. The losing team would give a cheer for the winning team. The students and fans of the losing team would stand and give a cheer for the winning team and student body. This was a demonstration of admiration of a hard fighting team and student body for opponents who proved to be better on that occasion. Now, a coach is admired for saying, "I hate a good loser."

What has happened to change good sportsmen into such poor sports? Some people would answer: "The love of money. Professionalism has taken over athletics. Athletes play for money. It is no fun when you lose. It is only fun when you win, for when you win, you make more money."

Assuming there is some truth in this, the question still remains: "How come the American people place so much store by money? How did money come to be their God? What happened to the real God, the Creative Spirit of Love which created the Universe and all who live therein?" The answer seems to be the greater the love of money, the less the love of God. Can anyone really believe that I created humans so they would engage in a race for money? Does that make sense? Would that constitute a good reason for Me to create humans?

If you will read The Twelve Steps of Alcoholics Anonymous (page 387) you will find the answer to addictions of any kind is contained in their 12 Steps.

5. Your attitude toward alcohol and other drugs. Any trouble here is surely traceable to your self-part.

Particularly in the case of the college youth—even the high school student—should the truth about marijuana be faced. The tolerance afforded this supposedly harmless narcotic is now being exposed as a grave and dangerous business. Thorough research into the latest findings will reveal that marijuana is a deceptive and dangerous drug.

Marijuana lures its victims on by its first pleasant, innocuous stages. Invariably, its prolonged use leads to tragic results. The inner peace this drug is supposed to guarantee can be had only thru the practice of your partnership with Me.

6. Your attitude toward your country. By your own way of life you will show your attitude toward your country. I ask all youth to examine into

THE GREATEST COVER-UP OF ALL TIME.

You are aware of the great political COVER-UP of the 1970's which sent some noted politicians to prison. But you are probably unaware of the greatest COVER-UP of all time. This COVER-UP began shortly after I first created humans, and it is still going on.

Strangely, this is not a deliberately planned COVER-UP, but its effect, for that reason, is all the more disastrous. Brought about by the best of motives, the COVER-UP has resulted in some of man's greatest troubles. It is up to youth to throw light on this COVER-UP so that those who unknowingly promote it, may be persuaded to take the necessary steps to correct it, and thus eliminate much unhappiness and misery in your country and in other nations.

The COVER-UP I'm referring to is the one that covers Me up. It covers up My part in your everyday living. It covers up the truth of why I created you. It covers up our relationship—your partnership with Me. It cheats you out of the love, wisdom, power and the joy I would contribute to your partnership with Me.

This COVER-UP, as I stated, was not purposely planned. Quite the contrary, it was brought about and is being continued by well-meaning people who unwittingly make religion hard to believe. There are now several hundred different sects and denominations in structured religion. The effect of this divisiveness is to cover Me up so that children do not learn from their very beginning the truth of their nature, and My part in their everyday life.

The most vital truth you can learn is that I, who created you, spending nine months working in you—building you a body and brain—did not depart from you when I eased you out of your mother's womb. Far from leaving you on your own, I remain with you in eternal Partnership, doing things for you which neither you nor anyone else can do for you. Harken unto

Christ's admonition: "Fools! Did not He who made that which is without, make that which is within also?"

To teach people that My Spirit remains with them was the mission on which I sent Christ to earth. Under My guidance, he stressed: "The spirit of God is within you." He urged his people to seek within for My guidance, and all other things would then be added to them. Christ performed the mission on which I had sent him even though it cost him his life. His spirit lives on.

I am now asking youth to take up the torch of Jesus. Let Me remind you that Christ was no theologian. Nor were his disciples. What Christ taught them to deal with had to do with everyday living. You may want to work with children, with educators, with church leaders, aiming to restore Christ's simple approach. With My guidance, your work will surely bring people together in love and brotherhood.

However, I must tell you that your efforts will meet with resistance, and you may be engaged in this battle for the rest of your life. But what a thrill this courageous effort will give you! What rewards of inner peace and inspiration will be yours! Here is something to live for— even to die for! To resolve on an undertaking of such selflessness is proof you have disenthralled yourself and that you want to help others to free themselves also from slavery to self. You will work to dethrone materialism and restore My spirit of Love as God. You will save your nation. Even more, you will give other nations an America to respect, admire and emulate.

If God Spoke to the Proud
Might it be Something Like This:

> What you are about to read is simply the imagining
> of one who has learned when he sincerely strives to
> become "an agent and instrument of Divine Provi-
> dence" (Lincoln's words) his Partner will guide him,
> speak thru him and work thru him. The author be-
> lieves this holds true for you, too.

The battle of life is the transformation of the Pride of
Self into a selfless "agent and instrument of Divine
Providence."

Pride of Self resists fiercely the effort to be transformed
into a selfless channel.
It closes its eyes and ears to the Truth.
Calling itself a realist, it does the most unrealistic
things.
On the ground that pride inhabits men naturally, it
contends it is up to each man to become the most proud.
Yet secretly it hates pride of self in others.
When Pride of Self shows up in your children, you
discipline them.
Pride of Self in others doesn't make too much headway
with children, for they spot it at once as a "show-off"
—a phony.

With many adults, Pride of Self does not show itself, but stays within, lulling its possessor into a false sense of importance.

Pride of Self inhibits true love.

It has so much love for itself, there is none left for others.

What it calls love is only possessiveness. It loves that it may possess. When it desires not to possess, it loves not.

Pride of Self keeps a man living in a world all his own. None other can get close to him.

His every thought and deed are tainted with thoughts of self: "What is there in it for me?"

There is no dictator quite so powerful as Pride of Self. It is absolute. It controls one's whole being. It brooks no interference with its rule.

When it meets up with another powered by Pride of Self, it is to be supposed there would be a union.

Here are two who think alike, who behave alike in every particular.

They are both slaves of Self. Yet both consider themselves strong and free.

They seek to control other men. Other men do their bidding.

Other men defer to their judgment. Other men look up to them as great and successful.

But no one loves them.

Your present standard of success promotes not love but Pride of Self. In yourself you consider Pride of Self natural and realistic. In others you deem it insufferable.

That's why the two strong men, so much alike in all particulars, have no love for one another.

They hate one another. Each is inhibited by Pride of Self from loving anyone but himself.

Pride of Self promotes war. It promotes millions of little wars in everyday living.

The big world wars are but an outgrowth of these millions of little private wars in every day life.

The person with understanding is saved from Pride of Self. He knows that of himself he is nothing.

He knows that of all his possessions, there is nothing that has not been given him.

Life, body, brain, health, talent, these are all gifts from his Creator.

One does not have a sense of pride because of gifts. One becomes humbly grateful.

One realizes a responsibility to develop these gifts.

Not to indulge Pride of Self, not to be known as a benefactor. But simply because that is what is expected of him by the Giver of all good Gifts.

It is also a way to show his gratitude for blessings conferred. One strives to be a selfless channel for his Benefactor.

He realizes that the Giver did not end His gifts with these. He keeps giving. He keeps supplying new gifts every day.

His Benefactor IS, not WAS. He did not go off and leave His beneficiary. He is present with him all the time.

Were He to cease giving, man would soon be bereft of what had been given him before.

What man possessed yesterday would be gone today. The brain of which he was so proud yesterday would be stricken today.

The talent in which his Self took such pride would be a shambles.

His body which he figured to be so strong would sicken and grow faint.

Then filled with remorse, he would turn on Pride of Self and berate it. "You have been a snare and a delusion."

And turning to the real Power—the only Power—he would plead on fallen knees: "My God, forgive me. I was foolish enough to believe I was great in my own right. Now the truth has been forced upon me. Of myself I am nothing. Thou art all. I am now sick and forlorn. By your grace and love I can become whole."

And as your heart is full, your Creator will give you peace.

Words come to your mind even though they may not pass your lips: "O God, make me an instrument for thy peace and love. Empty me of Self. Fill me with thy Divine Self."

And I, your God, will heed your cries, though they be unuttered.

And though you fail a thousand times, and are sincere, I will help you to try again.

Now you know the truth. Now you would be free of the Pride of Self.

Now you would achieve your destiny: a partner of My great Creative Spirit of Love.

Now you know you can arrive at happiness only by being a selfless channel for the great and loving Creative Spirit. Your heart speaks:

"For Thine is the wisdom and the power and the glory, forever."

If God Spoke About the Next Life Might it be Something Like This:

> What you are about to read is simply the imagining of one who has learned when he sincerely strives to become "an agent and instrument of Divine Providence" (Lincoln's words) his Partner will guide him, speak thru him and work thru him. The author believes this holds true for you, too.

Have you lived before? Will you live again?

Only your Maker has the answer to these questions. Some people assert it is not your business to even inquire about the hereafter, but if you are truly seeking God's will, is it not proper that you explore into what might be My plan for you? If I, your Maker, in giving you life and in sustaining that life from moment to moment, planned to live in Partnership with you, do I not want you to know these vital truths and to live accordingly?

If, indeed, it is My plan for you to live in Partnership with Me, your aim should be to become ONE with God. This would involve the complete surrender of your will to Mine. For you to become ONE with Me, you have a right to ask whether so great an undertaking can possibly be achieved in just one lifetime. Such an effort does seem hopeless. What human could possibly in one lifetime achieve the selflessness of Jesus? This raises the question as to whether Jesus himself reached the Oneness of his perfect partnership with God all in one lifetime.

33 years is indeed a short time in which a human can conquer the self so completely. In his day, many of Jesus' followers believed he was the reincarnation of one of the earlier prophets. Who knows whether Jesus himself believed he had lived before? You do know that he did believe he would live again. The evidence on this point is quite specific and positive. But did this mean he would live again as before—in the same physical appearance? And what could be God's purpose in having Jesus live again if the plan did not include your living again? No one knows whether reincarnation is in My plan. No one knows whether this one existence is all there is to life. Heed not the person who is so positive he knows My plans.

No one living today really knows exactly what Jesus looked like. Lacking this assurance, how would you recognize Jesus when he returned? In those days, there was no photography—cameras had not been discovered. You have no original paintings to go by, and while there were some descriptions of Jesus' physical appearance, no one knows how accurate a picture these descriptions would make. Your difficulties in this respect seem insurmountable.

What if, on the street where you live, a man would appear along with some of his friends carrying signs to the effect that this man is Jesus returned after almost 2000 years. "Here is the only son of God," his friends proclaim, "born of a virgin. He should be worshipped as God coming to earth in human form." What do you think whould happen in the event of such a sensational development? How would you personally react? Would you readily accept this claim? What proof would his followers be able to produce to support their claim? This is something that those followers of Jesus who insist he will return in about the same physical body that was crucified, should think about. They might ask themselves: "Is it the body or is it the spirit that lives on?"

You know that all things physical to which God has given life and causes to grow, eventually reach a point where growth is followed by a sort of brief levelling off, and then descent sets in, ending in what you humans, for lack of better understanding, call death. Is this not God's plan? The physical body—the human-part—is gone, but what happens to the God-part of his nature? Call it what you will—the soul or God's spirit—the question is what happens to this most important part of every human being?

Would it be compassionate of Me, as God, to disregard man's hope for eternal life—a hope God has created in you? Would it even be fair for Me to say to man: "Sorry, this is it. You've had your try. There's nothing left. You are gone."? You probably know of cases where this kind of attitude would seem inexcusably unjust and cruel.

There's the case of a U.S. Army General who had served his country well in battle. He had two sons, one a 6'4" splendidly built young man; the second was born a helpless idiot, who at age 18, had reached only 30 pounds in weight and had to be carried around in a basket, having no control over his organs. When the General was asked why he had not put this unfortunate boy in an institution or even allowed him to pass on, he was shocked at the very thought. "Why, this is our son—our flesh and blood. It's a cross we must bear." Is it not a point to raise: Is it fair of God to say to this helpless child and his parents: "It's the way the ball bounces. Too bad it had to bounce that way for him. But this is all there is. No second chance for him or anyone else."?

Does not this true incident make you wonder a little more about another chance? Could it possibly be that you have lived before? That you may live again? That your spirit will be given opportunity to inhabit another human body at birth, and continue your struggle to reach Oneness with your Maker? Also, might there not be other planets inhabited by humans? Is there anything wrong with such a plan? What if it does upset your present notions about death being the end of everything for all humans?

It should be repeated that no one but God knows with certainty whether you have lived before or shall live again. Are there not, however, good grounds to think affirmatively about this? Take the case of young geniuses. A child at 3 or 5 or thereabouts may have the artistry of a musician which under normal conditions might take 20 or more years to achieve. How did the child come by this genius? Could it possibly have come from a previous existence? How would you explain such an event?

Then, you have one of the most practical-minded men your country has ever produced—Benjamin Franklin who expressed the belief: "If a creature is made by God, it must depend upon God and receive all its power from God." Franklin was, among other accomplishments, a scientist, a diplomat, a banker, a newspaper publisher, a statesman. Expressing his belief he would live again, Franklin wrote:

> "And when I observe there is great frugality, as well as wisdom in God's works . . . when I see nothing annihilated, and not even a drop of water wasted, I cannot suspect the annihilation of souls, or believe He will suffer the daily waste of millions of minds ready made that now exist, and put Himself to the continual trouble of making new ones. Thus finding myself to exist in the world, I believe I shall, in some shape or other, always exist; and with all the inconveniences human life is liable to, I shall not object to a new edition of mine; hoping, however, that the errata of the last may be corrected."

Why cannot God create a new body to house your spirit when your present body is spent? It is the way of man to limit God's capabilities to his own. If, in My Partnership plan of Man and Maker, I provided for man to reach Oneness with Me, would it be fair for Me to demand that you had to achieve this within one lifetime?

Suppose My plans included a resting place for you to live in partnership with My Spirit? And what if this resting place gave you the chance to enjoy the peace and joy you had earned in your last existence? And I also gave you freedom to decide at any time to try again. You could decide whether to resume your life on earth, to strive for Oneness with Me, your Creator-Partner. Is there something wrong with that plan?

How about the many earnest people who strive to give the world the benefit of their talents and yet are never given wide recognition by their fellowmen? Should they be denied another chance? Trees come to life each Spring and bear new leaves. Is there no lesson in that for mankind? Speaking of leaves, do you not find something significant in the beauty of the leaves in the Fall when they are dying? They are at their most beautiful point in life. Can you not see in this that I planned for death to be beautiful? Why do humans make death something to be feared?—a terrible grief and tragedy? There is something else to be learned from falling leaves. Try to find two that are identical. And there are trillions of them, yet I form each one different from the others. You should learn from this that I prize both individuality and infinite variety. You have your own individuality. This is My way of doing things. That I can, if I desire, also make two humans identical is shown in twins. But I can also make twins that are not identical, but fraternal. I can make triplets, quadruplets, quintuplets. Do you not understand that with God everything is possible? The Creative Spirit of Love is illimitable in its power, in its wisdom and love.

It is not My plan that you should fear death. Fear of death would not come to anyone's mind if, from the beginning, he had been taught self-knowledge, that the

Creative Spirit of Love which spent nine months with him building his body and brain, remains with him eternally to sustain him and live in Partnership with him.

Only your Creator-Partner knows when it is time for you to move from this present life to the next. If you believe there is a purpose to life and that this purpose is for you to live in Partnership with your Creator-Partner, then there is good reason for you also to believe you have lived before and shall live again.

If you accept this, your mind should take you a step further: the nature of the Supreme Intelligence must be the Creative Spirit of Love. You need but look about you to determine how all things work together in harmony and love. This is true of all living things with the ironic exception of humans, the creatures to whom I have given the highest intelligence. Why do humans seem bereft of the understanding that I planned for things to work in love and harmony? They use their brilliant minds to teach children all forms of knowledge except self-knowledge, the most vital of all.

Without self-knowledge, children get to believe that it is up to each person to be guided by his self-part, and they engage in a race for things. This race for things destroys the chance for things to work in harmony and love. That's why more hate and prejudice are present in human relations than in any other form of life.

The reason most people believe this one existence is all there is to life is because they did not learn as children that the purpose of life is to reach Oneness with Me, their Creator.

The truth remains. I created you out of a heart longing to live in loving Partnership with the higher intelligence of humans. It was a calculated risk, but it will work out. With time, you will achieve a better understanding of your true nature. You may even come to believe you have lived before and will live again, until you finally reach Oneness with Me. Then you will be in Paradise with Me.

If God Taught Us the A B C's of Life Might it be Something Like This:

What you are about to read is simply the imagining of one who has learned when he sincerely strives to become "an agent and instrument of Divine Providence" (Lincoln's words) his Partner will guide him, speak thru him and work thru him. The author believes this holds true for you, too.

A. I created the earth more than five billion years before creating humans, including YOU.

B. I created dumb animals millions of years before creating humans.

C. Why so long an interval between dumb animals and humans? Because everything was peaceful on earth and it was risky business creating a new kind of animal, giving him 1) unlimited brain potential and 2) freedom to ignore Me, his Creator.

D. Why, then, did I decide after so long a deliberation to create humans?

E. Because I am the Creative Spirit of Love, and My heart was filled with love for the new creature with whom I wanted to live in Partnership.

F. Has the risk proved worthwhile? Not if you judge from the few thousand years of the human experience. There are millions of little wars between individuals in everyday living; there are wars between nations; there were two World Wars (in the second of which 50 million people were killed.)

G. Is there no chance things will get better? Not until children are taught from the very beginning that the Creative Spirit of Love which formed their frame and brain, never departs from them but remains with them as their Creator-Partner to guide them thru life.

H. Why is this not taught in education? Because people have formed religions—hundreds of different religious sects and denominations. They have confined Me, their God, to this man-made area of religion. But I transcend religion. I have an important part in every phase of each person's life—not just religion. It is in education that children should learn about the many things I do in their lives.

I. How can I, the Creator of the Universe, be confined to the area of religion? Did I not create the earth billions of years before men created religions? That's a good question and humans will have to answer it. Their brains should tell them I cannot be confined to religion. I sustain each human by keeping his heart beating and in countless other ways. I figure in every part of life.

J. Why do I allow educators to refuse to teach children the truth about their nature? If children do not understand themselves, how can they understand other people? My answer: I have given humans freedom. And freedom means being free to do the wrong thing as well as the right. Humans will have to correct this themselves, not depend on Me to do it.

K. Why are there so many different religions? Is this not divisive? That is also a very good question. The meaning of religion is man's relation to his Maker. One of your great theologians, Rev. Harry Emerson Fosdick, lamented: "Religion has helped mess up the world. . . . That religion, supposedly one of mankind's most unifying influences, should add confusion worse confounded to man's predicament, causing discord and estrangement, instead of fraternity, is tragic."

L. But surely, religion should not be used to prevent children from learning the most vital truth—that the God who made them remains with them all thru life to guide them and sustain them. Answer: You make a very good point and humans must answer it. Humans quarrel and kill over religion. They claim their religions promote worship of Me. What I consider true worship is teaching children I am their ever-present Partner.

M. Why don't I send a teacher to teach humans the truth of their nature? Did I not already try this about 2000 years ago? He told people God's spirit was within them. "The things I do, I do not of myself. Of myself I can do nothing. It is the Father (he preferred to call Me Father rather than God) within me. He tells me what to say and what to do. The things I do, you too can do." You know what they did to him. Despite the fact he never mentioned the word religion and regarded himself as a teacher, many years after he was gone, they started to form religions after him. Now there are several hundreds of them quarreling and hating one another.

N. Why did I create so many different ethnic groups and different skin colors, to begin with? Is this not proving divisive? My answer: I am the Creative Spirit of Love. I have a love of infinite variety. I make trillions of snow flakes, no two alike. I make trillions of leaves, no two alike. I make millions of humans, no two alike except when I create twins, to show I can make humans alike. As for variety making for divisiveness, if children were taught that each one had Me for their Creator-Partner, they would learn the brotherhood of man and the Fatherhood of God. This in itself is the best protection against divisiveness and wars.

O. But should not religion encourage worship of God? Answer: If, by worship, you mean love of God, the Father, as the Great Teacher tried to teach you, yes. But if you mean piety and sanctimony in your attitude toward Me, what I want is Love, to live in loving Partnership with each of My human children. True worship shows itself in acts of love for your brother-man. Without this, pious words can be hypocrisy.

P. Am I saying that people who profess to worship

Me and yet have no love for their brother-man are hypocrites? I say they are deluding themselves. I love each of My children, without regard for their skin color or ethnic background. Worship that distinguishes between people for any reason is not pleasing in My sight, and is only self-deceiving.

Q.   If the U.S.A. is permitted to go its present way, will it not be a decaying nation? The answer: America is already a decaying nation. When humans leave Me out of their everyday lives, this means decay. I created humans to be My Partners. They think of Me as being in outerspace somewhere instead of being within them. This is because of the failure of education to teach children the truth.

R.   Is there no way to arouse the American people to their great danger? Answer: If the fact that one man can press a button and bring about the earth's destruction doesn't arouse them, what will? Americans close their eyes to this horrible possibility. Because they have not learned they have a God-part to their nature, they allow their self-part to rule them.

S.   Is it true that one man can press a button and the earth would be destroyed? The answer: Many nations now have buttons. The danger is real. The button could be pushed at any time. Yet many great minds in this country seem to think the present way is good enough to save the nation.

T.   Surely, there must be some way to get the truth to the people? Answer: Let them see the pictures of Hiroshima and Nagasaki. These are real. The present nuclear bombs are many times more powerful and a few would be enough to destroy the earth. One man's finger is close to the button. Good people are relying on Me to prevent the button from being pressed. But for how long? And for what reason? Where are the signs that would encourage Me to believe man wants to learn he is in Partnership with Me?

U.   The American people are good people. Where have they gone wrong? I answer again, it's their education. They leave Me out of their everyday lives, paying Me respect for an hour on a Sunday morning. When I am left out, their self-part persuades them to pursue things for self: things like money, power, fame.

V.   Is this not natural for humans to gather possessions? Answer: It is natural for every person to earn his own way. Where the self leads you wrong is in causing you to believe the more you gather for yourself beyond security the happier you will be. This is a deadly fallacy. It does not work. My law prevents it from working—"Too much of anything is not good for man."

W.   How can humans achieve happiness? When I created humans, did I not plan for their happiness? Indeed I did. Their happiness was to come from working their Partnership with Me. It cannot come in any other way. Man's greatest happiness comes from doing things for others. But if man does not know that I am part of his nature, eager to guide him to the joy that was the Great Teacher's, how can any change come about?

X.   Can we not change the way of life handed down from one generation to another with its increasing rate of crime and divorce? Answer: Yes, the way to change lies in education. This sounds like too simple an explanation. People want a magical answer. They pray for some sign. It is time for them to act.

YZ.   My ABC's of life are really quite simple, but they must be learned early in life. After high school and college, it becomes much more difficult. By then the world has them in its clasp. If taught from early childhood that each has both a Little ME and a GREAT ME, children will readily understand the truth. They accept it as truth, because they see it work in themselves and their companions.

If God Offered You Proof
of the Partnership of Man and Maker
Might it be Something Like This:

What you are about to read is simply the imagining of one who has learned when he sincerely strives to become "an agent and instrument of Divine Providence" (Lincoln's words) his Partner will guide him, speak thru him and work thru him. The author believes this holds true for you, too.

Throughout the ages, men and women have sought to understand the nature of Man. In this chapter, you will find comments from some of the leading figures who have found inner peace and joy through understanding the nature of man.

Of course, the outstanding one in such a group would have to be Christ, who was willing to give his life to teach you that "the kingdom of God is within you." Is this not the most vital revelation to illustrate the nature of man? Christ was communicating to you that the self is not all of your nature, that you have a God-part, and that you are free to choose between these two separate though integrated forces that comprise your nature. In the light of this, the words of Christ assume an entirely new significance. Carefully avoiding religious references—he never once mentioned the word "religion"

—Christ simplified for you the true nature of man: "Of myself I can do nothing. It is the Father within me. He tells me what to say and what to do."

Many will be surprised at Lincoln's understanding of the nature of man. He was described by that great Russian philosopher Tolstoy, as "a Christ in miniature." Yet Lincoln had no specific religion. Then there is Emerson, a contemporary of Lincoln, who said of Christ's belief "The Spirit of God is within you", that it was the highest revelation that could come to anyone. Ghandi was another who believed this and lived it. Pope John whose book Journal Of A Soul says this a hundred times and more lived his life in the belief God's spirit was within him.

You may be surprised to find the comments of a drunkard, Bill W who joined with another alcoholic, Dr. Bob—in forming Alcoholics Anonymous—which offers a classic example of Partnership with God.

CHRIST AND THE PARTNERSHIP OF MAN AND MAKER

The words of Christ reveal his simple faith in the Partnership of Man and Maker:

And yet I am not alone for the Father is with me.

* * *

Why callest thou me good? None is good save one, the Father.

I can of mine own self do nothing.

* * *

Believest thou not that I am in the Father and the Father in me?

* * *

The words I speak unto you, I speak not of myself, but the Father that dwelleth in me, He tells me what to say and what to do.

* * *

Take no thought how or what you shall speak for it shall be given you in the same hour what you shall speak. For it is not you that speak but the spirit of your Father which speaketh in you.

* * *

My doctrine is not mine but His that sent me.

* * *

I am meek and lowly in heart.

* * *

Take my yoke upon you. You shall find rest unto your souls. For my yoke is easy and my burden light.

* * *

You shall know the truth and the truth shall make you free.

Fools, did not He that made that which is without, make that which is within also?

* * *

If therefore thine eye be single, thy whole body shall be full of light.

* * *

He that believeth in me the works I do shall he also, and greater works than these shall he do.

* * *

These things have I spoken unto you that my joy might remain in you and that your joy might be full.

* * *

Not everyone that sayeth unto me, 'Lord, Lord' shall enter into the kingdom of Heaven, but he that doeth the will of the Father.

* * *

God is spirit, and those who worship Him must worship in spirit and in truth.

* * *

You know not what manner of spirit you are of.

* * *

And whoever says a word against the son of man will be forgiven; but whoever speaks against the Spirit of

God in man will not be forgiven, either in this age or in the age to come.

* * *

If ever I bear witness of myself, my witness is not true. I am a liar.

* * *

Get thee behind me Satan, thou art an offense to me, for thou savorest not of the things that be of *God* but those that be of *men.*

* * *

Woe unto you, teachers and lawyers: for you have taken away the key of knowledge. You entered not in yourselves and them that were entering in you hindered.

* * *

Take heed and beware of covetousness, for a man's life consisteth not in the abundance of possessions.

* * *

And which of you with taking thought can add to his stature one cubit? If then you are not able to do that thing which is least, why take thought of the rest?

* * *

But rather seek you the kingdom of God within you and all other things shall be added unto you.

* * *

For unto whomsoever much is given, of him shall much be required.

* * *

And behold there are those last which shall be first, and there are first which shall be last.

* * *

For whosoever exalteth himself shall be abased, and he that humbleth himself shall be exalted.

* * *

Let the little children come unto me for of such is the kingdom of heaven.

* * *

It is easier for a camel to go through the eye of a needle than for a rich man to enter the kingdom of God.

* * *

The things which are impossible with men are possible with God, for with God all things are possible.

* * *

The stone which the builders rejected the same is become head of the corner. This was the Lord's doing and it is marvelous in our eyes.

* * *

The kingdom of God shall be taken from you and given to a nation bringing forth the fruits thereof.

I give you two commandments: Thou shalt love the Lord thy God with all thy heart and with all thy soul and with all thy mind and with all thy strength. This is the first and great commandment. And the second is like unto it: Thou shalt love thy neighbor as thyself. On these two commandments hang all the law and the prophets. There is none other commandment greater than these.

* * *

He that is greatest among you shall be your servant.

* * *

A prophet is not without honor, save in his own country, and among his own kin and in his own home.

* * *

Hypocrites . . . people who draweth nigh to me with their mouth, people who honoreth me with their lips but their heart is far from me. However in vain do they worship me, teaching for doctrines the commandments of men.

* * *

What shall it profit a man, what is a man advantaged if he gain the whole world and lose himself, lose his own soul?

* * *

Except you become as a little child, you shall not find the spirit of truth and enter the kingdom of heaven.

Whosoever, therefore shall humble himself as a little child, the same is greatest in the kingdom of heaven.

* * *

For where two or three are gathered together in my spirit, there am I also in the midst of them.

* * *

I thank thee, O Father, Lord of heaven and earth, because Thou hast hid these things from the wise and prudent, and hast revealed them unto babes.

* * *

My mission is to do the will of Him that sent me and to finish His work.

* * *

Let your light so shine before men that they may see your good works and glorify your Father in you.

* * *

Lay not up for yourselves treasures upon earth, where moth and rust corrupt, and where thieves break through and steal, but lay up for yourselves treasures in God's spirit where neither moth nor rust doth corrupt, and where thieves do not break thru or steal. For where your treasure is, there will be your heart also.

* * *

He that believeth in me, believeth not really in me but in Him that sent me. And he that seeth me, seeth Him that sent me.

A new commandment I give unto you, that you love one another. As I have loved you, that you also love one another. By this shall all men know that you are my disciples, if you have love one to another.

* * *

Let not your heart be troubled. You believe in God, believe also in me. In my Father's house are many mansions. If it were not so, I would have told you. I go to prepare a place for you. And if I go and prepare a place for you, I will come again and receive you unto myself, that where I am, there you may be also. And where I am going you know and you know also the way.

* * *

With God's spirit in me, I am the vine. You are the branches. If you know God's spirit is in you, you know why I have come. God's spirit in you will bring forth much fruit, for without God's spirit in us, we can do nothing. When we let God's spirit guide us we glorify the Father. In this way you will bear much fruit and will truly prove you are my disciples.

* * *

The spirit truly is willing, but the flesh is weak.

* * *

I have come that you may have life and that you may have it more abundantly.

Take heed that you never despise any little child, for I tell you that they come fresh from the Creator with God's spirit in them and that in heaven their angels do always behold the face of our Father.

* * *

But when you pray, use not vain repetitions, as the heathens do, for they think they shall be heard for their much speaking. Be not like them for your Father knoweth what things you need before you ask Him.

* * *

When you read and re-read the words of Christ, is it not clear he was seeking to fulfil his mission to tell you that the Creative Spirit of Love which gave you life never departs from you? And that if you seek His will and wisdom above your own, you need be concerned about nothing else?

If God were to ask those of you who believe in Christ just what it is you believe, how would you respond? Would you answer that you now know why God chose a plain man—a carpenter—to show you a way to live in Partnership with God? Or would you say you prefer to believe Christ was born something special, to be visited by kings and wise men to pay him homage as the only son of God?

What if God were to respond and ask would that have been the best way to tell you of your Partnership with God, by having Jesus born above all other hu-

mans? Would it not be better to have him born the same
as all other humans but by living in perfect Partnership
with God to show all of you that you too could follow
in his steps?

After all, was not Jesus trying to say that you could
do the same things he did? Would he have been honest
in assuring you of this, if indeed, he had been born
infinitely above the rest of you? If you knew of two men,
one born to wealth and power, the other born of humble
parents, yet by his way of life earned the love and confidence of almost all who got to know him, which of the
two would have greater influence with you? Did not
God consider all this when he commissioned Jesus to
tell you of the Partnership Life with Me?

Read Jesus' words again and see if he does not answer
that question. You will find time and again he gives Me
all the credit, even going so far as to say "If ever I give
testimony of myself, my testimony is false. I am a liar."
How far must he go to make you understand your
Partnership?

The facts reveal that Jesus lived in such perfect Partnership with God that in truth God thought thru him,
spoke thru him, worked thru him. So that Jesus was
really God. Isn't it more believable to have Jesus
become God by living such a selfless life than by being
told you must believe Jesus was born the only son of
God? Does not this latter belief rob Jesus of his rightful
credit? If he were born as the only son of God, should
he not be expected to live that way? But if he were born
like the rest of you and by overcoming the self-part of
him, lived in perfect Partnership with Me, was this not

an achievement that compels your admiration and utmost belief?

The well-meaning people who insist that all sincere Christians must accept that Jesus was born the only son of God, and because of this, one need but acknowledge him as your personal Savior, should re-read Jesus' own words: "Why do you call me good? None is good save one, the Father." and again "I can of mine own self do nothing."

Indeed, should these well-meaning people not be careful of Jesus' admonition: "Not everyone who sayeth unto me, 'Lord, Lord' shall enter into the kingdom of heaven, but he that doeth the will of the Father."? And the much more critical warning: "Hypocrites, people who honoreth me with their lips but their heart is far from me. However, in vain do they worship me, *teaching for doctrines the commandments of men.*"

Whenever you disagree with one another, should it not be with love? "By this shall men know you are my disciples, if you have love one to another." If Jesus refused to sit in judgment on his fellow-men, by what right should you? True Christians will try to live Christ's way of life—the Partnership life of man and Maker. "He that believeth in me the works I do shall he do also, and greater works than these shall he do."

LINCOLN AND THE PARTNERSHIP OF MAN AND MAKER

(The words of Lincoln reveal his simple belief in his partnership with God):

God is the silent Partner of all great enterprises.

* * *

Without the assistance of the Divine Being I cannot succeed. With that assistance I cannot fail.

* * *

I was early brought to a living reflection that nothing in my power, whatever, in others to rely upon, would succeed without the direct assistance of the Almighty, but all must fail.

* * *

I have often wished that I was a more devout man than I am. Nevertheless, amid the greatest difficulties of my administration, when I could see no other resort, I could place my whole reliance on God, knowing that all would go well, and that He would decide for the right.

* * *

The purposes of the Almighty are perfect and must prevail, though we weak mortals may fail to accurately perceive them in advance. We hoped for a happy termination of this terrible war long before this; but God knows best and has ruled otherwise. We shall yet acknowledge His wisdom, and our error therein. Meanwhile we must work earnestly in the best lights He gives us, trusting that so working still conducts to the great ends He ordains. Surely, He intends some great good to follow this mighty convulsion, which no mortal could make and no mortal could stay.

* * *

I have been driven many times to my knees by the overwhelming conviction that I had nowhere else to go; my own wisdom and that all around me seemed insufficient for the day.

* * *

I have had so many evidences of His direction, so many instances when I have been controlled by some other power than my own will, that I cannot doubt that this power comes from above. I frequently see my way clear to a decision when I am conscious that I have not sufficient facts upon which to found it. But I cannot recall one instance in which I have followed my own judgment, founded upon such a decision, where the results were unsatisfactory; whereas, in almost every instance where I have yielded to the views of others, I have had occasion to regret it.

* * *

I am satisfied that when the Almighty wants me to do, or not to do, a particular thing, He finds a way of letting me know it. I am confident that it is His design to restore the Union. He will do it in His own good time. We should obey and not oppose His will.

* * *

At first, when we had such long spells of bad luck, I used to lose heart sometimes. Now, I seem to know that Providence has protected and will protect us against any fatal defeat. All we have to do is to trust the Almighty, and keep on obeying His orders and executing His will.

* * *

I am a full believer that God knows what He wants a man to do, that which pleases Him. It is never well with the man who heeds it not. I talk to God. My mind seems relieved when I do, and a way is suggested, that if it is not a supernatural one, it is always one that comes at a time, and accords with a commonsense view of the work. . . . This seems evidence to me, a weak man, that God Himself is leading the way.

* * *

I not only believe that Providence is not unmindful of the struggle in which this nation is engaged, that if we do not do right, God will let us go our own way to ruin; and that if we do right, he will lead us safely out of this wilderness, crown our arms with victory and restore our dissevered Union, as you have expressed your belief; but I also believe He will compel us to do right, in order that He may do these things, not so much because we desire them as they accord with His plans of dealing with this nation, in the midst of which He means to establish justice. I think that He means that we shall do more than we have yet done in the furtherance of His plans and He will open the way for our doing it.

* * *

I have felt His hand upon me in great trials and submitted to His guidance, and I trust that as He shall further open the way, I will be ready to walk therein, relying on His help and trusting in His goodness and wisdom.

* * *

I am sure, however, that I have not the ability to do anything unaided by God, and that without His support and that of a free, happy, prosperous and intelligent people, no man can succeed in doing that, the importance of which we all comprehend.

* * *

I shall be most happy indeed, if I shall be a humble instrument in the hands of the Almighty and of this people, as the chosen instrument also in the hands of the Almighty, of perpetuating the object of that great struggle.

* * *

I have said nothing but that I am willing to live by, and if it be the pleasure of Almighty God to die by. Here are 23 ministers of different denominations, and all of them are against me, but 3. And there are a great many prominent members of the churches, a very large majority of whom are against me. I am not a Christian; God knows I would be one, but I have carefully read the Bible and I do not so understand this book . . . I know there is a God, and that He hates injustice and slavery. I see the storm coming, and I know that His hand is in it. If He has a place and work for me, and I think He has, I believe I am ready. I am nothing, but truth is everything.

* * *

It seems to me as if God had borne with this thing, slavery, until the very teachers of religion have come to defend it from their Bible and to claim for it a divine character and sanction, and now the cup of iniquity is full and the vial of wrath will be poured out.

* * *

I believe we are all agents and instruments of Divine Providence. I hold myself in my present position and with the authority invested in me, as an instrument of Providence. I am conscious every moment that all I am and all I have are subject to the control of a Higher Power, and that Power can use me or not use me in any manner and at any time as in His wisdom might be pleasing to Him.

* * *

O, Thou God that heard Solomon in the night when he prayed for wisdom, hear me. I cannot lead this people; I cannot guide the affairs of this nation without Thy help. I am poor and weak and sinful. Oh God, Who didst hear Solomon when He cried for wisdom, hear me and save this nation.

* * *

In the very responsible position in which I happen to be placed, being a humble instrument in the hands of our Heavenly Father, as I am and as we all are to work out His great purposes, I have desired that all my works and acts may be according to His will and that it might be so, I have sought His aid.

* * *

It is my constant prayer that I and this nation should be on the Lord's side.

* * *

No human counsel has devised, nor hath mortal hand worked out, these great things. They are the generous gifts of the Most High God, Who, while dealing with us in anger for our sins, hath nevertheless remembered mercy. It has seemed to me fit and proper that they should be solemnly, reverently and gratefully acknowledged, as with one heart and one voice, by the whole American people.

* * *

On this day (the Gettysburg victory) He whose will, not ours, should ever be done, be everywhere remembered with profoundest gratitude.

The will of God prevails. In great contests, each party claims to act in accordance with the will of God. Both may be, and one must be, wrong. God cannot be for and against the same thing at the same time. In the present Civil War, it is quite possible that God's purpose is something different from the purpose of either party, and yet human instrumentalities working just as they do are of the best adaptation to effect His purpose. I am almost ready to say that this is probably true, that God wills this contest, and wills that it shall not end yet. By His mere great power on the minds of the now contestants He could have either saved or destroyed the Union, without a human contest; yet the contest began, and having begun, He could give the final victory to either side any day, yet the contest proceeds.

* * *

At the end of three years' struggle, the Nation's condition is not what either party saw or anyone expected. God alone can claim it. Whither it is tending seems plain. If God now wills the removal of a great wrong, and wills also that we of the North as well as you of the South shall pay for our complicity in that wrong, impartial history will find therein new cause to attest and revere the justice and wisdom of God.

* * *

I should be the veriest shallow and self-conceited blockhead upon the footstool, if, in my discharge of the duties that are put upon me in this place, I should hope

to get along without the wisdom that comes from God
and not from man.

* * *

Fondly do we hope and fervently do we pray that this
mighty scourge of war may speedily pass away; yet if
God wills that it continue until all the wealth piled up
by the bondsman's 250 years of unrequited toil shall
sink, and until every drop of blood drawn by the lash
shall be paid by another drawn by the sword, as was
said 3000 years ago, so still it must be said, "The
judgments of the Lord are true and righteous altogether."

* * *

To read in the Bible as the Word of God Himself,
that "In the sweat of thy face thou shall eat bread," and
to preach therefrom that "In the sweat of other men's
faces shalt thou eat bread" to my mind can scarce be
reconciled with honest sincerity. When brought to my
final reckoning, may I have to answer for robbing no
man of his goods; yet more tolerable even this, than for
robbing one of himself and all that was his. When a year
or two ago these professedly holy men of the South met
in the semblance of prayer and devotion, and in the
name of Him who said: "As ye would all men should
do unto you, do ye even so unto them," appealed to the
Christian world to aid them in doing to a whole race
of men as they would have no man do unto themselves,
to my thinking they condemned and insulted God and
His church, far more than Satan did when he tempted

the Savior with kingdoms of the earth. The devil's attempt was no more false and far less hypocritical.

. . . it is the duty of nations as well as of men to own their dependence upon the overruling power of God; to confess their sins and transgressions in humble sorrow, yet with assured hope that genuine repentance will lead to mercy and pardon; and to recognize the sublime truth announced in the Holy Scriptures and proven by all history, that those nations only are blessed whose God is the Lord.

* * *

. . . as we know that by His Divine Law, nations like individuals, are subjected to punishments and chastisements in this world, may we not justly fear that the awful calamity of civil war which now desolates the land may be but a punishment inflicted upon us for our presumptuous sins, to the needful end of our national reformation as a whole people?

* * *

We have been the recipients of the choicest bounties of Heaven. We have been preserved, these many years, in peace and prosperity. We have grown in numbers, wealth and power as no other nation has ever grown; but we have forgotten God. We have forgotten the gracious Hand which preserved us in peace, and multiplied and enriched and strengthened us; and we have vainly imagined, in the deceitfulness of our hearts, that all these blessings were produced by some superior wisdom and virtue of our own. Intoxicated with unbroken success, we have become too self-sufficient to feel the necessity of redeeming and preserving grace, too proud to pray to the God that made us.

* * *

I still have confidence that the Almighty, the Maker of the Universe, will, through the instrumentality of this great and intelligent people, bring us through this as He has through all other difficulties of our country.

* * *

Encompassed by vast difficulties as I am, nothing shall be wanting on my part, if sustained by God and the American people. . . .

* * *

I am sure I bring a heart true to the work. For the ability to perform it I must trust to that Supreme Being who has never forsaken this favored land. . . . Without that assistance I shall surely fail; with it, I cannot fail.

* * *

It is difficult to make a man miserable while he feels he is worthy of himself and *claims kindred to the great God who made him.*

* * *

We must disenthrall ourselves and then we will save our nation.

* * *

EMERSON AND THE PARTNERSHIP OF MAN AND MAKER:

It is a defect . . . that the Moral Nature, that Law of Laws whose revelations introduce greatness—yea, God Himself—into the open soul is not explored as the fountain of the established teaching in society.

* * *

There is a principle which is the basis of things—a simple quiet, undescribed, undescribable Presence, dwelling very peacefully in us . . . We are not to do, but to let do; not to work, but to be worked upon; and to this homage there is a consent of all thoughtful and just men in all ages and conditions. To this sentiment belong vast and sudden enlargements of power!

* * *

Spirit is the Creator. Spirit hath life in itself. And man in all ages and countries embodies it in his language as The Father.

* * *

We learn that God is; that He is in me, and that all things are shadows of him.

* * *

Thou shalt not heed the voice of man when it agrees not with the voice of God in thine own soul.

Would there be danger if there were real religion—if the doctrine that God is in man were faithfully taught and received; if I lived to speak the truth and enact it . . . ?

* * *

Christ alone in all history estimated the greatness of man. One man was true to what is in you and me. He saw that God incarnates Himself in man, and evermore goes forth anew to take possession of His world.

* * *

Having seen that the law in us is commanding, Christ would not suffer it to be commanded. Boldly, with hand and heart and life, he *declared it was God.* Thus is he, as I think, the only soul in history who has appreciated the worth of man.

* * *

There is a certain wisdom of humanity which is common to the greatest men with the lowest, and which our *ordinary education often labors to silence and obstruct.*

* * *

We owe many valuable observations to people who are not very acute or profound, and who say the thing without effort which we want and have long been hunting in vain.

* * *

Self-reliance, the height and perfection of man, is reliance on God. It is our practical perception of the Deity in man.

The one miracle which God works evermore is in
Nature, and imparting Himself to the Mind.

* * *

Let man learn . . . that the Highest dwells with him.
If he would know what the Great God speaketh, he
must "go into his closet and shut the door" as Jesus
said.

* * *

You are rightly fond of certain books or men that you
have found to excite your reverence and emulation.
But none of these can compare with the greatness of
that counsel which is open to you in happy solitude. *I
mean that there is for you the following of an inward
leader.*

* * *

A nation of men will for the first time exist, because
each believes himself inspired by the divine soul which
also inspires all men.

* * *

A man contains all that is needful to his government
within himself. He is made a law unto himself. All real
good or evil that can befall him must be from himself.

* * *

Ineffable is the union of man and God in every act
of the soul.

When we have broken our god of tradition and ceased from our god of rhetoric, then may God fire the heart with His presence.

* * *

If a man has not found his home in God, his manners, his form of speech, the turn of his sentences, the build, shall I say, of all his opinions will involuntarily confess it, let him brave it out as he will. If he have found his center, *the Deity will shine thru him,* thru all the disguises of ignorance, of ungenial temperament, of unfavorable circumstance.

* * *

By the necessity of our constitution, a certain enthusiasm attends the individual's consciousness *of the divine presence.*

* * *

From within or from behind, a light shines thru us upon things and makes us aware that *we are nothing, but the light is all.*

* * *

What we commonly call man, the eating, drinking, planting, counting man, does not as we know him, represent himself but misrepresents himself.

Him we do not respect, but the soul whose organ he is, would he let it appear thru his action, would make our knees bend. When it breathes thru his intellect, it is genius, when it breathes thru his will, it is virtue; when it flows thru his affection, it is love.

* * *

The key to happiness is to keep your mind in tune with the Divine Mind, your life in tune with the Universe.

* * *

The blindness of the intellect begins when it would be something of itself. The weakness of the will begins when the individual would be something of himself.

* * *

As soon as every man is apprised of the Divine Presence within his own mind . . . then we have a religion that exalts, that commands all the social and all the private action.

* * *

Immortality will come to such as are fit for it, and he who would be a great soul in the future, must be a great soul now.

* * *

All reform aims in some one particular to let the soul have its way thru us; in other words, to engage us to obey . . . We know that all spiritual being is in man.

If your eye is on the Eternal, your intellect will grow, and your opinions and actions will have a beauty which no learning or combined advantages of other men can rival.

* * *

A little consideration of what takes place around us every day would show us that a higher law than that of our will regulates events.

* * *

Our painful labors are unnecessary and fruitless; only in our easy, simple spontaneous action are we strong, and by contenting ourselves with obedience we become divine.

* * *

Belief and love—a believing love will relieve us of a vast load of care.

* * *

O, my brothers, God exists. There is a soul at the center of nature and over the will of every man, so that none of us can wrong the universe. It has so infused its strong enchantment into nature that we prosper when we accept its advice.

* * *

Whilst we converse with what is above us, we do not grow old but grow young. When these waves of God flow into me, these moments confer a sort of omnipresence and omnipotence.

* * *

The whole course of things goes to teach us faith. We need only obey. There is guidance for each of us and by lowly listening we shall hear the right word.

* * *

Place yourself in the middle of the stream of power and wisdom which animates all whom it floats, and you are without effort, impelled to truth, to right and a perfect contentment.

* * *

The purpose of life seems to be to acquaint a man with himself. The highest revelation is that God is in every man.

* * *

When a man lives with God, his voice shall be as sweet as the murmur of the brook and the rustle of corn.

* * *

That which shows God in me fortifies me. That which shows God out of me makes me a wart and a wen. There is no longer a necessary reason for my being.

* * *

Let us take our bloated nothingness out of the path of the divine circuits.

The Spirit alone can teach . . . The man on whom the soul descends, thru whom the soul speaks, alone can teach . . . But the man who aims to speak as books enable, as synods use, as the fashion guides, and as interest commands, *babbles. Let him hush.*

* * *

To a true scholar, the attraction of the aspects of nature, the departments of life, and the passages of his experience, is simply the information they yield him of this supreme nature which lurks within all.

* * *

Certain biases, talents, executive skills are special to each individual, but the high, contemplative, all-commanding vision, the sense of right and wrong, is alike in all.

* * *

The true meaning of spiritual is real; that law which executes itself, which works without means, and which cannot be conceived as not existing.

* * *

The time is coming when all men will see that the gift of God to the soul is not a vaunting, overpowering, excluding sanctity, but a sweet natural goodness, a goodness like thine and mine, and that so invites thine and mine to be and to grow.

Nature forever puts a premium on reality. What is done for effect is seen to be done for effect; what is done for love is felt to be done for love. A man inspires affection and honor because he was not lying in wait for these . . . A little integrity is better than any career.

* * *

If a man dissemble, deceive, he deceives himself, and goes out of acquaintance with his own being.

* * *

There is a great public power on which man can draw, by unlocking at all risks, his human doors, and suffering the ethereal tides to roll and circulate thru him; then he is caught up into the life of the universe, his speech is thunder, his thought is law, and his words are universally intelligible.

* * *

It is certain that worship stands in some commanding relation to the health of man and to his highest powers, so as to be in some manner the source of intellect.

* * *

I apprehend that the religious history of society is to show a pretty rapid abandonment of forms of worship and the renovation and exaltation of preaching into real anxious instruction.

* * *

An inevitable dualism bisects nature, so that each thing is a half, and suggests another to make it whole:

as spirit, matter; man, woman; odd, even; subjective, objective; in, out; upper, under; motion, rest; yea, nay; . . . The same dualism underlies the nature and condition of man.

* * *

The religion that is afraid of science dishonors God and commits suicide.

* * *

Then you find so many men infatuated on that topic! (religion). Wise on all other, they lose their head the moment they talk of religion. It is the sturdiest prejudice in the public mind, that religion is something by itself; a department distinct from all other experiences, and to which the tests and judgment men are ready enough to show on other things, do not apply. You may sometimes talk with the gravest and best citizen, and the moment the topic of religion is broached, he runs into a childish superstition. His face looks infatuated, and his conversation is.

* * *

The Teacher I look for and await . . . will not occupy himself in laboriously reanimating a historical religion, but in bringing men to God by showing them that He is, not was, and speaks, not spoke.

GHANDI AND THE PARTNERSHIP OF MAN AND MAKER:

The real test of a successful life: Have you found your Partnership with God? Have you realized—not in words only, but in spirit and life—the oneness of your soul with the Cosmic Reality? Having found this, the ordinary satisfactions of life pale into a shadow.

* * *

There is an indefinable mysterious Power that pervades everything. I feel it though I do not see it. It is this unseen Power which makes itself felt and yet defies all proof, because it is so unlike all that I perceive through my senses. It transcends the senses.

* * *

And is this Power benevolent or malevolent? I see it as purely benevolent. For I can see that in the midst of death life persists. In the midst of untruth, truth persists. In the midst of darkness, light persists. Hence I gather that God is Life, Truth, Light. God is Love. He is the Supreme Good.

* * *

If God is not a personal being for me like my earthly father, He is infinitely more. He rules me in the tiniest detail of my life. Every breath I take depends upon His sufferance.

* * *

What an amount of wrong and humbug God suffers on our part! He even suffers insignificant creatures of His to question His very existence, though He is in every atom about us, around us and within us.

* * *

To me, God is Truth and Love. God is ethics and morality; God is fearlessness. God is the source of Light and yet He is above and beyond all these.

* * *

God is even the atheism of the atheist. For in His boundless love, God permits the atheist to exist.

* * *

He is a personal God to those who need His personal presence. He is embodied to those who need His touch. He is the purest essence. He simply is to those who have faith. He is all things to all men. He is in us and yet above and beyond us.

* * *

God is the hardest taskmaster I have known on this earth, and He tries you thru and thru. And when you find that your faith is failing or that your body is failing you, and you are sinking, God comes to your assistance somehow or other, and proves to you that you must not lose your faith and that He is always at your beck and call, but on His terms, not on your terms. So I have found. I cannot recall a single instance when, at the eleventh hour, God has forsaken me.

* * *

The divine guidance often comes when the horizon is the blackest.

* * *

God helps when one feels humbler than the very dust under one's feet. Only to the weak and helpless is divine succour vouchsafed.

* * *

Mankind is notoriously too dense to read the signs that God sends from time to time. We require drums to be beaten into our ears, before we would wake from our trance and hear the warning and see that to lose oneself in all is the only way to find oneself.

* * *

Man's ultimate aim is the realization of God. All of man's activities social, political, religious, have to be guided by the ultimate aim of the vision of God.

* * *

The only way to find God is to see Him in His creation and be one with it. This can only be done by service to all. I am a part and parcel of the whole, and I cannot find God apart from the rest of humanity.

If God was a capricious person instead of being the changeless, unchangeable living law, He would in sheer indignation wipe out those who in the name of religion deny Him and His Law.

* * *

Where there is realization outside the senses it is infallible. It is proved not by extraneous evidence but in the transformed conduct and character of those who have felt the real presence of God within.

* * *

Belief in one God is the corner-stone of all religions.

* * *

Religion which takes no account of practical affairs and does not help to solve them is no religion.

* * *

For me, politics bereft of religion is absolute dirt ever to be shunned. Politics concerns nations and that which concerns the welfare of nations must be one of the concerns of a man who is religiously inclined, in other words, a seeker after God and Truth.

* * *

Churches, mosques and temples which cover so much hypocrisy and humbug and shut the poorest out of them seem but a mockery of God and His worship, when one sees the eternally renewed temple of worship under the vast blue canopy inviting every one of us to real worship, instead of abusing His name by quarreling in the name of religion.

* * *

Without prayer there is no inward peace.

But God never answers the prayers of the arrogant, nor the prayers of those who bargain with Him.

Prayer is an impossibility without a living faith in the presence of God within.

* * *

Not until we have reduced ourselves to nothingness can we conquer the evil in us. God demands nothing less than complete self-surrender as the price for the only real freedom that is worth having. And when a man thus loses himself he immediately finds himself in the service of all that lives. It becomes his delight and his recreation. He is a new man, never weary of spending himself in the service of God's creation.

* * *

Prayer is a call to humility. It is a call to self-purification, to inward search.

POPE JOHN XXIII AND THE PARTNERSHIP OF MAN AND MAKER:

I will not forget that I am never alone, even when I am by myself.

* * *

Meanwhile I had to fight an enemy within me, self-love, and in the end I was able to get the better of it. But I was mortified to feel it constantly returning.

* * *

Who am I? Where do I come from? Where am I going? I am nothing. Everything I possess, my being, life, understanding, my will and memory—all were given me by God, so all belong to Him.

* * *

How easy it would be for God to take away all my intellectual gifts, my memory and my reason! Or confine me to bed with sickness! So, softly; less presumption; more distrust of myself and more humility.

* * *

Where are my riches, my properties, my assets? Disobedience, acts of pride, negligence in my duties, insufficient control of my feelings, infinite distractions, vanity in my thoughts, words and deeds and sins galore; all these belong to me—*they are my very own.*

And with all this to boast of, I think of lording it over others, making a name for myself, exalting myself, displaying my powers.

* * *

In me God is everything and I am nothing. I am a sinner and far worse than I can imagine. If I have done any good in my life, it has all been by God's grace, which would have obtained better results if I had not hampered and impeded it. This enemy I always carry about with me must never be given a moment's respite.

* * *

Lord, I need only one thing in this world: to know myself and to love you.

* * *

The way of humility, union with God and obedience in all my doings to the will of God and not to my own will, these are the three foundations upon which my Spiritual Father has been basing His advice for my true spiritual progress.

* * *

My guiding principles remain the same: humility in everything; especially in my speech, union with God (the most important thing, of which I feel an even greater need today) and the will of God, not my own, in all I do.

Give up trying to know too much, for this is very distracting and may lead you astray.

* * *

Therefore, it is not learning that is really the height of greatness and glory, but knowledge of ourselves, of our nothingness before God and of our need of God, without which we are but puny creatures, although we raise ourselves up to the stature of giants.

* * *

I should pay most attention to pride, the other self, because I shall never be really great and capable of good works until I am stripped of self.

* * *

Self-love! What a problem it is, when one stops to think about it. Who has ever defined it? What philosopher has dealt with it? It is the most important problem we have to deal with, truly a matter of life and death, and who cares about it?

* * *

He who denies himself is happy with a purely heavenly joy.

* * *

God does not consider the number of my deeds but the way in which I do them; it is the heart he asks for, nothing more. An intimate sense of the presence of

God, as the final end of all creation, and a total forget-fulness of myself; these two things alone, and with these whatever I do is complete.

* * *

I must learn to be contented with what is possible, and in all things acquire an ever more sensitive and profound sense of humility because of my worthless-ness, and a habitual trust in God who is all and can do all things. Only by being united to Him can I do any-thing.

* * *

It would be dangerous if in this work I were to pre-sume on my own powers for a single moment.

* * *

THE CO-FOUNDER OF ALCOHOLICS ANONY-
MOUS ON THE PARTNERSHIP OF MAN AND
MAKER:

In the book ALCOHOLICS ANONYMOUS, which he wrote anonymously, Bill W- (co-founder of A.A. with Dr. Bob) says some things which have helped millions of alcoholics and which can help millions of non-alcoholics. For is there anyone of us who in one or more phases of life does not need help to overcome a lack of control or form of self-indulgence? We may not be drinking alcoholics, but how about the possibility of being a money-alcoholic, a power-alcoholic, an eating-alcoholic, a sex-alcoholic—some place in our lives where we have gone overboard and indulge a weakness? We look down on the drinking alcoholic but if we were honest with ourselves, we would look into the 12 STEPS which is the basis for ALCOHOLICS ANONYMOUS.

If we consider only the first three of these 12 steps, we might find our way to Partnership with God. Here are these three steps:

1. We admitted we were powerless over alcohol-that our lives had become unmanageable.
2. Came to believe that a Power greater than ourselves could restore us to sanity.
3. Made a decision to turn our will and our lives over to the care of God *as we understood Him.*

These last four words *"as we understood Him"* were surely inspired, as indeed was the whole ALCOHOL-ICS ANONYMOUS movement. There are now more than one million people in all parts of the world who owe their sobriety to A.A., and yet, structured religion has never in any way caused difficulty. The four words leave it up to each individual to accept God as each understood him.

Following are some quotations excerpted from the book ALCOHOLICS ANONYMOUS:

. . . for deep down in every man, woman and child is the fundamental idea of God.

* * *

We alcoholics had to find a power by which we could live, and it had to be *A Power Greater Than Ourselves.* Obviously, but where and how were we to find this Power?

* * *

We found that as soon as we were able to lay aside prejudice and express even a willingness to believe in a Power greater than ourselves, we commenced to get results, even though it was impossible for any of us to fully define or comprehend that Power, which is God.

* * *

We needed to ask ourselves but one short question. "Do I now believe, or am I even willing to believe, that there is a Power greater than myself?"

Whatever the protestations, are not most of us concerned with ourselves, our resentments, or our self-pity?

Selfishness—self-centeredness! That, we think is the root of our troubles.

* * *

Above everything, we alcoholics must be rid of this selfishness. We must, or it kills us! God makes this possible. And there often seems no way of getting entirely rid of self without God.

* * *

Neither could we reduce our self-centeredness much by wishing or trying on our own power. We had to have God's help.

* * *

When we sincerely took such a position, all sorts of remarkable things followed. More and more we became interested in seeing what we could contribute to life. As we felt new power flow in, as we enjoyed peace of mind, as we discovered we could face life successfully, as we became conscious of God's presence, we began to lose our fear of today, tomorrow, or the hereafter. We were reborn.

* * *

We were now at step three. Many of us said to our Maker, *as we understood Him,* "God, I offer myself to Thee—to build with me and to do with me as Thou wilt. Relieve me of the bondage to self, that I might better do Thy will. Take away my difficulties, that victory over them may bear witness to those I would help, of Thy Power, Thy Love, and Thy Way of life. May I do Thy will always." We thought well before taking this step making sure we were ready; that we could at last abandon ourselves utterly to Him.

* * *

(see page 387 for the Twelve Steps of Alcoholics Anonymous)

THE PARTNERSHIP PRAYER

OUR FATHER,
Whose Partnership offers heaven on earth.
You created us to be your free partners in the work of creation.
You cause food to grow for our enjoyment and sustenance.
You created breathing a two-way exercise that we may breathe out ego, breathe in God.
With you as Partner, we can overcome the temptations and evils of Self.
Thus, we may become ONE with Your Creative Spirit.
For Yours is the Universe, Yours is the power, and to you belongs all the glory.
Forever and ever,   AMEN.

THE PARTNERSHIP PSALM
(1023rd psalm)

The Lord is my Partner. I shall not want.
God's Spirit of Love is with me eternally.
My Partner causes the sun to shine upon me,
the air to caress me, the rain to fall,
the springs to flow, the food to grow.
My Partner sustains my body and restores my soul.
My cup runneth over.
Each breath of God's love showers blessings upon me.
By deeds of love for my brother-man,
I offer thanks to my Creator-Partner.
For God is my Father and man is my brother.
Surely, goodness and mercy shall follow me all the days
of my life, as I walk in my Partner's guidance forever.

THE PARTNERSHIP GUIDELINES

1. You shall remember you were nothing until I created you. My Creative Spirit of Love built your body and brain.
2. You shall use the brain I built you to realize that My Spirit is at work in you now—24 hours a day—doing things you can't do for yourself.
3. You shall remember that children are My hope for the world. They all must be taught that My Spirit is within them, serving as their Partner. This is simple truth, not just a religious concept.
4. You shall learn from an infant's natural unprejudiced vision to look beyond a person's outer appearance to his Creator-Partner within.
5. You shall have no other Gods besides Me. Not money, not power, not fame, not sex, not drugs, alcohol or other escapisms. My Creative Spirit of Love will suffice to supply your needs and give you inner peace and joy.
6. You shall eat the foods I cause to grow in as close to their natural state as possible. From such foods do I build you a new body each year.
7. You shall recognize that sexual intercourse (communion) should take place only when My Spirit of Love is embraced with your beloved.
8. You shall remember with every breath you take, to breathe out ego, breathe in God. I planned breathing to be life's greatest exercise.

9. You shall remember that I am the Creator-Partner of each human. Nothing must divide you from your fellow-being. Nothing! Not worldly status, not ideology, not skin color, not ethnic background, not religion.

10. Your reason shall tell you that your spirit has lived before and shall live again. Life is eternal as Christ stated. The spirit I gave you will proceed with the purpose of life: to achieve Oneness with GOD.

* * * * *

The
TWELVE
STEPS of ALCOHOLICS ANONYMOUS

1. We admitted we were powerless over alcohol—that our lives had become unmanageable.

2. Came to believe that a Power greater than ourselves could restore us to sanity.

3. Made a decision to turn our will and our lives over to the care of God *as we understood Him.*

4. Made a searching and fearless moral inventory of ourselves.

5. Admitted to God, to ourselves, and to another human being the exact nature of our wrongs.

6. Were entirely ready to have God remove all these defects of character.

7. Humbly asked Him to remove our shortcomings.

8. Made a list of all persons we had harmed, and became willing to make amends to them all.

9. Made direct amends to such people wherever possible, except when to do so would injure them or others.

10. Continued to take personal inventory and when we were wrong promptly admitted it.

11. Sought through prayer and meditation to improve our conscious contact with God *as we understood Him,* praying only for knowledge of His will for us and the power to carry that out.

12. Having had a spiritual awakening as the result of these Steps, we tried to carry this message to alcoholics, and to practice these principles in all our affairs.

If God Spoke to You, His Partner Might it be Something Like This:

> What you are about to read is simply the imagining of one who has learned when he sincerely strives to become "an agent and instrument of Divine Providence" (Lincoln's words) his Partner will guide him, speak thru him and work thru him. The author believes this holds true for you, too.

What makes our Partnership—yours and Mine—a Perfect Partnership?

YOU. The part you play. The sacrifice of self you make that brings you inner peace and joy not obtainable in any other way.

By yielding your will to Mine, you make ours a Perfect Partnership. Consider the facts; first, My contribution to our Partnership:

My Creative Spirit of Love created you. My Spirit keeps your heart beating. My Spirit keeps your brain working. My Spirit causes the billions of your body cells to go their proper way.

Despite all that I do, however, the success of our Partnership is to be accredited to you. Why?

The odds are greatly against your succeeding. Almost everyone around you is living a different way of life from the one you'll be trying to live. Not knowing better, most people do the will of their self-part. Your way must be to do the will of your God-part.

That's because you know something most people don't know. You know that I am part of your nature. Recognizing that I am part of your nature is an act of humility. Before your humility had to come your understanding. "With all thy getting, get understanding."

Your understanding and your humility enable you to walk in the steps of him who openly stated: "You know not what manner of spirit you are of . . . He that believeth in me, the works I do shall he also and greater works than these shall he do."

Among this man's followers were Lincoln, Emerson, Ghandi, Pope John. There were others.

In a way, your task may be even more difficult. But the satisfaction and the rewards will more than compensate. By living up to the terms of our Partnership—God guiding, man doing—you will come into unspeakable joy and deep inner peace. This feeling comes with the complete surrender of self. When you empty yourself of self, you are filled with My Spirit of Love. It is the presence of My Spirit, despite whatever suffering you are called upon to bear, that transcends everything and instills serenity. Consider Lincoln's perfect Partnership with Me, in the face of the almost unbearable suffering caused by four years of the great Civil War. Without our Partnership, he could not have spoken thus:

"The purposes of the Almighty are perfect, and must prevail, though we weak mortals may fail to accurately perceive them in advance. We had hoped for a happy termination of this terrible war long before this, but God knows best, and has ruled otherwise. We shall yet acknowledge His wisdom, and our error therein. Meanwhile we must work earnestly in the best lights He gives us, trusting that so working still conducts to the great ends He ordains. Surely, He intends some great good to follow this mighty convulsion which no mortal could make and no mortal could stay."

What trouble may befall you, My partner, that would be comparable in any way to the agony Lincoln endured during those four awful years of watching brother kill brother? If Lincoln, under such prolonged anguish could nevertheless persist in working his Partnership with Me, was he not setting an example for all Americans in living the Partnership way of life?

You know something of American history. But do you know that no President was more adversely cartooned, buffooned, maligned and vilified than Abraham Lincoln? And do you know this was done by people who considered themselves wiser and more virtuous? But at no time did Abraham Lincoln feel bitterness in his heart against those who opposed him. His God-part would not permit this.

Was not Lincoln also revealing his belief in Christ's two simple commandments: 1) to love God; 2) to love your brother-man? Because Lincoln always sought to let his God-part rule over his self-part, he could never find it in his heart to look down on any human being. This would be like scorning My handiwork, for I created that other person.

In creating you, I may have given you certain talents and advantages, but is this something you should take credit for? Or rather feel most grateful for? Let Me say to the one who looks down on any of his fellow-creatures: "You are really sitting in judgment. How do you know all the facts that lie behind that person's disadvantages? How do you know his whole background? And let Me raise a question here which may not have occurred to you. Suppose there is something more to life than this one existence you are now living. Suppose Ben Franklin was right in his belief (based on his own scientific reasoning) that he had lived before and will live again. If he was right, would it not apply to you as well?

"And suppose, in your next existence, you were someone not too different from the person you now look down upon, how about that? Had you been properly educated as to your true nature, you would know that just as I am *your* Creator-Partner, I am also the Creator-Partner of every human being, including the ones you look down upon. If you and that person have the same Creator-Partner, does this not establish a brotherhood between you?"

Regardless of your race, color, religion or ethnic background, I planned for you to be free. I gave no one the right to interpose his authority between you and Me. Your third President, Thomas Jefferson was speaking the truth when he said "The God who gave us life gave us liberty at the same time." I am the Creative Spirit of Love. How can anyone believe I planned for man to dispute with his brother as to the right way to worship Me, whether it be creed, ritual, doctrine, dogma, confession of faith, etc.? If you truly want to worship Me, then live in Partnership with me—God guiding, man doing.

If you are among the many who now regard Lincoln as did the great Russian philosopher Tolstoy: "A Christ in miniature," you may understand why I have been on the search for another plain person who aspires to emulate Lincoln. I have not been insisting on a brilliant mind, an eloquent speaker or one who believes himself wise in his own right.

Rather, the person I have been seeking knows that of himself, he is nothing, but that there is within him—as within all humans, a Power infinitely wiser than his own. Such a person knows himself. He also knows that he need but get his self-part out of My way and I will fill him with My wisdom, My power and love.

* * * * * *

Now, I have a special message for the one who has been turned off by stories about Christ's "miraculous" birth. Why let these varying reports prevent you from learning the truth about your own birth that Christ wanted you to know?

Christ tried to make it clear his mission was not to laud himself or to have you worship him. Rather, he sought to assure you that My presence in you made you greater than you know. His understanding and love of children stemmed from knowing that each child came fresh from My hands—chosen by Me.

Physicians know that I select one out of some 250 million male sperms to join with one of about 10,000 female ova in order to form the particular cell from which I built your body. Christ never took a new-born babe for granted. He reminded his people that this infant was of My making, that I had spent nine months working in you, forming your frame and brain. No one should dismiss your creation as simply the predictable outcome of intercourse between your father and mother.

Too many couples who desperately desire children, without avail, know that intercourse is no sure certainty of producing a child. A child is conceived and born when I choose it to be. I do the choosing and I do the building. I chose you out of billions. I chose you because I have certain expectations of you. Your education should reveal that you were born for a purpose. Educators should not treat your birth as a happenstance. You are a *chosen* person, and you are entitled to know this.

As for your being turned off by stories of Christ's birth which you find hard to believe, I suggest you open your mind enough to read what Christ really had to say (p. 339). You will find he made no claims for himself. Quite the contrary, he continually distracted attention from himself to Me, his Maker, whom he lovingly called "The Father," giving Me all the credit.

It is surprising that anyone—particularly his followers—should make Christ out to boast, in the face of his deep humility: "If ever I give testimony of myself, my testimony is false. I am a liar." Could anyone be more explicit in denying himself? When you re-read the words of Christ, you will find this same meekness and humility running thru his every word.

But it is more than Christ's words that should weigh with you. It is his works, his way of life: God guiding, man doing. Do you need to be reminded that Christ was no theologian? He was a layman, who found proof in everyday life of My presence within him, serving as his Creator-Partner. He tried to communicate this simple understanding to his people. The theologians would have none of it, but the plain people in great numbers, believed and followed him.

His followers became known as The Wayists, because they followed Christ's way of life. For about 300 years after he passed on, they lived communally as one great family, loving and sharing with one another. In time, they became known as The Early Christians. It was only when organization set in, that differences arose, and today in the National Council of Churches alone, there are some 247 different sects and denominations.

Can any greater service be rendered than to restore the faith and way of life of The Early Christians? If you have found the present church creeds unacceptable, perhaps you can by your own way of life help bring back Christ's Partnership Life of Man and Maker. Was this not the way Lincoln worked?

Perhaps you may not have known that Lincoln, who lived as close to Me as anyone since Christ, never joined a structured church. He explained:

"I have never united myself to any church because I have found difficulty in giving my assent without mental reservations, to the long, complicated statements of Christian doctrine which characterize their articles and confessions of faith."

Is it not a sad commentary on religious divisiveness that 20 of the 23 ministers of Lincoln's home town of Springfield, Illinois, joined in opposing him for the Presidency, calling him an atheist because he never joined a church?

Pressed for an explanation as to what kind of church he would join, Lincoln responded:

> "When any church will inscribe over its altars, as its sole qualification for membership, the Savior's condensed statement of both law and gospel, 'Thou shalt love the Lord thy God with all thy heart and with all thy soul and with all thy mind' and 'thy neighbor as thyself' that church will I join with all my heart and all my soul."

Is this too simple a foundation on which a church can rest—a firm belief in My presence coupled with a sincere love of God and man? Must there be long complicated creeds which create divisiveness?

Also, I must correct an erroneous interpretation of My word and purpose in creating you. I DID NOT CREATE YOU IN MY IMAGE. I am pure Spirit. You are a physical being. You have a body which can be seen. I am invisible to the sight. I CREATED *IN* YOU MY SPIRIT.

The tiny word "in" became transposed and this al-

tered the true meaning of My purpose in creating you.
Instead of

> GOD CREATED MAN IN HIS IMAGE, it
> should read
> GOD CREATED IN MAN HIS IMAGE
> (SPIRIT).

It is vital that this misunderstanding be corrected
because it tends to prevent you from understanding My
purpose in creating you: to live in Partnership with Me.
I built you a brain with almost unlimited potential, so
that your own intelligence would bring you to the realization that the Partnership of Man and Maker is the
purpose of life. Surely, you cannot honestly believe I
created you to engage in a race with other humans to
acquire the most possessions for your *self*—a way that
promotes self-centeredness, hatred and war? Yet, is this
not the way most people are living?

And does not responsibility for this shortsighted and
stupid way of life rest mostly with the failure of education to properly perform its task of teaching children
the truth of their nature? Your professional educators
have been intimidated, probably by the very existence
of hundreds of different religious sects and denominations, so that they shy away from teaching children that
the wiser Creative Power which spent nine months
within them building their body and brain, never departs from them, but remains to do things for them that
no human can do for himself.

These are facts—scientifically established. Religion
need not and should not enter into education teaching

these facts, which should stand on their own. They should not be evaded or ignored, as without this understanding of one's nature, how can a child get to know himself or herself? KNOW THYSELF!

If you are a non-Christian—particularly, a young one seeking the truth—it is all the more reason you should read Christ's own words. You will find they make sense. Christ was believable. Far from making claims of having been born someone special, he was the meekest and most humble of men. When praised, he always transferred the credit from himself to Me. He showed none of the piety and sanctimony so common in today's religious practice.

Consider Christ's words: "Why do you call me good? There is only one that is good—the Father. Of myself, I can do nothing. It is the Father within me. He tells me what to say and what to do. The things I do, you too can do."

Does this sound like a claim to have been born someone special? It does bespeak a special understanding. Christ became someone special by the way he lived—selflessly, seeking My guidance in every thought, word and deed. Is he not all the more to be respected, revered and followed? Is one who is born to wealth and power to be more highly regarded than the person humbly born, yet living so as to gain the love and following of millions of humans?

It is distressing that many of Christ's followers unwittingly make him out to be a braggart, alleging he claimed "I am the way, the truth and the life." Christ used the words "I am" the way the Hebrews of his day described God: "I am that I am." So that Christ was really saying "God is the way, the truth and the life." This was in keeping with his every effort to give credit to Me, none to himself.

Lincoln, though belonging to no church, nevertheless believed that Christ lived in perfect partnership with God, so that to all intents and purposes, he had become one with God.

If you can accept that Christ's and Lincoln's position makes sense, why not help the Christian church regain the confidence of the people? 98% of the American people say they believe in Me, but when asked if their church and religion had influence in their lives, only 25% answered in the affirmative. Perhaps you may help religious leaders to realize that people want a believable way of life rather than "long complicated statements of Christian doctrine" which kept Lincoln from joining a structured church.

Dag Hammarskjold, in his book MARKINGS, wrote: "The lovers of God have no religion but God alone." Abraham Lincoln wrote (in what he described as "the President's last, shortest and best speech) to a woman who had requested a special favor for her husband, a rebel:

"You say your husband is a religious man. Tell him when you meet him, that I say I am not much of a judge of religion, but that, in my opinion, the religion that sets men to rebel and fight against their government, because, as they think, that government does not sufficiently help *some* men to eat their bread in the sweat of *other* men's faces, is not the sort of religion upon which people can get to heaven."

Let Me remind you that Christ himself had some things to say to people who practiced their religion with words and not works:

"And when thou prayest, thou shalt not be as the hypocrites are, for they love to pray standing in the synagogues and in the corners of the streets, that they may be seen of men."

Christ went on to stress his belief in the Partnership of Man and Maker:

"But thou, when thou prayest, enter into thy closet and when thou has shut thy door, pray to the Father which is in secret, and thy Father which seeth in secret shall reward thee openly."

Obviously, the closet which Christ urged you to enter and close was your inner self, your God-part, where you and I as Partners could speak together. Christ made clear that I, your Creator-Partner know what things you really need before you ask Me:

"But when ye pray, use not vain repetitions, as the heathens do, for they think they shall be heard for their much speaking. Be not ye therefore like unto them, for your Father knoweth what things ye have need of, before you ask Him."

I am speaking to you, My doubting partner, because

you may yet be moved to help the church transform religion into a way of life—the life of the Partnership of Man and Maker. This is the way Christ lived. Indeed, he achieved perfect partnership with Me. By completely submerging his self-part, he opened the way for Me to think thru him, speak thru him, work thru him. Would you not say to this extent Christ was God?

I am suggesting that you question PTCH (Precedent, Tradition, Custom, Habit). Not to disregard PTCH but to re-examine it and the way of life it has sponsored. Consider the increasing rate of crime, the growing use of drugs and alcohol, the enlarging number of divorces, mental breakdowns, the lack of trust, the general unhappiness, despair, and suicide. Is not such a way of life open to question?

I am counting on you to seek the truth. To face the truth. To live the truth. It will take great courage for you to live a different way of life from those about you. But it will prove most rewarding. Not only to you and your family but to all who know you. They will want for themselves what they see in you.

When you re-read the words of Christ, Lincoln, Emerson, Ghandi, Pope John and Bill W-, the co-founder of Alcoholics Anonymous (p. 339) you will observe they all stress the one thing: There is a Supreme Intelligence which created the universe and keeps it going. This Supreme Intelligence works in love, creating you in love, sustaining you in love, from moment to moment.

I am that Supreme Intelligence. My Spirit is within you, part of your nature, serving as your Creator-Partner. I created you in love to be My partner. Heed not those who say you were born in sin. What kind of loving Father would I be to start you in life that way? Parents may sin and indeed they do if instead of My loving Spirit being present in their sexual embrace, there is only physical lust. But to visit this sin upon a new-born child would not be the thought of a loving Father.

Sin is the result of not knowing one's nature. If the foundation of all education stressed two simple truths: 1) no person created himself; 2) no person keeps his heart beating, it would naturally follow that children would learn and believe that the unknown, invisible Creative Spirit of Love which spent nine months in them building them a body and brain, *never departs from them but remains with them to guide them to their highest happiness.*

Just this simple understanding alone would make a world of difference. For a child to know from the beginning, it is on earth not as the result of sin or even accident, but because I chose it to be born, would give him the right start in life. He would understand that he like everyone else, has both a Little ME and a GREAT ME. He would be able to recognize the Little ME as his self-part when it wants things for himself. Learning that he has a GREAT ME helps him to the self-restraint needed to keep his self-part in check. The battle between one's self-part and God-part is one everyone must face.

You are entitled to know this early in life. You are entitled to learn I chose you to be born. I selected the one certain male sperm and the one certain female ovum to form the one certain cell (one out of billions of possibilities) from which I built your body and brain. Far from being born in sin, you are a chosen person. I chose you because I have need of you. I am hoping for things to be done by you—not necessarily spectacular, but simple deeds of love for your brother-man. Deeds that will prove the purpose of life is not self-glorification or aggrandizement. Not the gathering of money or the acquisition of power and fame, but simply the working of our Partnership, in love for others.

I have told you of your true greatness. Now, I must humble you a bit with the truth of your littleness. What if you learned your heart was to cease beating the very next minute. What could you do? Do I have to remind you it is not you who keeps your heart beating. It is I, your Creator-Partner. What if you learned that from now on there would be no more air for you to breathe? What could you do? I am reminding you that it is I, not you that supplies you with the air without which you would instantly perish. What if you were told that the food you enjoy eating would now lie inert in your stomach instead of being transformed into blood, bone, muscle, brain? What could you do? Have you forgotten it is I, the Creative Spirit of Love, your Partner, who does these things for you?

But why go on? You could, with some thought remind yourself of the many things I contribute each moment to our Partnership. How could you get along without Me? Is it not clear you need My Creative Spirit of Love to be present with you to do the many things you cannot do for yourself or have anyone else but your

Creator-Partner do for you? How can you doubt there are two separate though integrated forces at work in you—one yours, the other Mine? Which is the wiser? Which knows better what is best for you? Which is the more powerful?

Can you not now better understand why Lincoln went so far in denying his own wisdom when compared with Mine:

> "I should be the veriest shallow and self-conceited blockhead upon the footstool, if in my discharge of the duties that are put upon me in this place, I should hope to get along without the wisdom that comes from God and not from man."

Your education, by omitting mention of the Creative Power that gave you life and which sustains you from moment to moment, has deluded you into thinking you stand on your own. This is not true self-reliance. "Self-reliance, the height and perfection of man, is reliance on God," wrote Emerson. "Let man learn . . . that the Highest dwells with him."

The fact that most people around you live as if they need no higher power should no longer blind you to obvious truths. I created you. I sustain you. Go back in your mind to your beginning—nine months before you were born. My Creative Spirit was at work in you then.

I am just as much at work in you now. I create you a new body each year. I keep you going every moment.

We are partners, you and I. For your own happiness, you must seek to do your part. Take your bloated nothingness out of My path. You can do this by practicing the six-second exercise: "Breathe out ego, breathe in God." No matter how often you forget and fail, I will take you by the hand and raise you. But you must be sincere. You cannot hold to your self with one hand and to Me with the other. "Seek you first the will of God within you and all other things will be added unto you."

You have no idea what keeps your heart beating. Neither does any scientist or physician. There is no physical explanation. This should have special significance for you if you have had any sign of heart trouble. Ask yourself why I choose to keep your heart beating. You have heard of cases where people in apparently good health—sometimes shortly after getting a checkup by their physician—suffer a fatal heart attack. Why? What happened?

Could it be because nothing in their attitude toward Me and their brother-man warranted My keeping their heart beating? Could it not also be, in the case of some really good partners of Mine whose lives are unexpectedly ended that I have future plans for them, in which they might be of even greater service in living the Partnership Life?

But the greatest significance to you should be that here is hard evidence that you are being kept alive by a spiritual power—My Creative Spirit of Love. It is as if the electric power company in your city with all its machinery to manufacture power and distribute it to your office and home had to depend on an invisible, unknowable force that defied explanation.

You would not ignore such a power just because it

was unknown, would you? You would not just pay your respects to this unknown, invisible power every Sunday for an hour, and let it go at that, would you? Might you not instead explore the many other ways in which this unknown power figures in your affairs, helping you to enjoy life and make yourself useful to others?

Is it not common sense for you to pause long enough to question yourself? Are you so completely a captive of PTCH (Precedent, Tradition, Custom, Habit) that you would not want to re-examine your way of life? What is so hallowed about a way of life in which there are millions of little private wars in every day living? Where people fall sick and die long before their time? Where crime and hatred grow worse each day?

Your way of life is failing because it leaves Me out of things. How can you leave out of your everyday affairs My Spirit of Love? Without love, how can you cope with your own ego—the self-part of your nature? I created you to face up to the contest of man with himself—your divine spark against your human frailties. Life is a constant battle between your self-part and your God-part. It is because you were not taught you have a God-part, and so persist in your self point of view, that brings on confusion and trouble for yourself. Your God-part will give you understanding and love.

You can learn much about love—selfless love—from Jesus. Also about prayer, a practice greatly misunderstood. Just as Jesus simplified living to God guiding, man doing, he simplified praying. Jesus uttered very few prayers, because he sought only My will, not his own. The only time he prayed for something specific for himself—that his life be spared—he added: "Nevertheless not my will, but Thine."

There is, of course, the Lord's Prayer, which is a loving acknowledgement of man's Partnership with Me, whom he called The Father. Jesus ended this beautiful prayer: "For Thine is the kingdom, the power and the glory, forever and ever." In this prayer, Jesus selflessly gave all credit to Me, as was his custom, taking none unto himself.

But Jesus' outstanding prayer was the one he made when he knew he had but a few hours to live. Christians should appreciate that this was the greatest prayer any human could make. It was completely selfless, giving no thought to the fact that he was to be crucified within a few hours. It was more of a report to Me and to the world, revealing his faith in the Partnership Life, and that the whole purpose of life was to become one with Me.

You would do well, My doubting partner, to learn this prayer by heart, and live it with all your heart. If you do this, it will transform your life. As you read it, put yourself in the position of one who knew he was about to die an excruciating death:

> "Father, the hour is come . . . I pray they all may be _One;_ as Thou, Father, art in me and I in Thee, that they also may be _One_ in us; that the world may believe Thou hast sent me. And the glory which Thou gavest me I have given them; that they may be _One,_ even as we are _One_ . . . I in them and Thou in me, that they may be made perfect in _One_ . . ."

Oneness with Me was the prayer with which Jesus went to his death. Is there a more vital lesson for you to learn from Christ? Your part might well be to remove Jesus from the realm of religious controversy to the area of everyday living. Jesus never mentioned the word religion. He spoke much of My Spirit in man—the Spirit of Creative Love.

Christ knew the answer to all of man's problems is love. Scientists will tell you that even if a child is given ample food, shelter, clothing and every material need, yet without love the child will not properly mature. Love is the most essential part of life. Without love, what would hold a mother to her child and the child to its mother? It is love that brings out self-sacrifice. Nothing will work right if love is not in it. Truly, Love is God.

All the reforms of well-meaning people will not work if love is not present. All the religions in the world will fail if love is not the foundation of the faith. All the laws of well-meaning people will not be enough. There can be no peace worthy of the name without love. There can be no lasting happiness without love. And it must be selfless love, not a possessive love, which is love for oneself. True love seeks to give rather than to get. Material possessions can not provide lasting happiness.

Your nation is in trouble and is decaying because people are trying to solve their problems without love. It won't work. It can't work. The chief ingredient of peace and prosperity and happiness is love. For Love is God and God is Love.

Truth crushed to earth *will* rise again. Love will bring

you Oneness with Me. Your Perfect Partnership will be joined by other Perfect Partnerships and will save your beloved nation. America will truly become the Beautiful and in turn will save the world.

* * * * * *

And now I would close with a reminder to all Americans, whose nation is "the last best hope of earth."

Are you proud to be an American? My hope is that your answer will be "Not proud. Grateful." A little consideration should convince you that you had little to do with being an American. To be grateful rather than proud can be very meaningful. Only the noble are grateful. Proud carries the connotation of self-achievement.

Lincoln's satisfaction stemmed from being an "agent and instrument of Divine Providence." He reminded his people forthrightly: "It is the duty of nations as well as of men to own their dependence upon the overruling power of God." Lincoln's favorite poem was: "O, Why Should the Spirit of Mortal be Proud?" He memorized all 13 verses of this poem (by William Knox, an obscure poet) of which the following is the first verse:

O, WHY should the spirit of mortal be proud?
Like a swift-fleeting meteor, a fast-flying cloud,
A flash of the lightning, a break of the wave,
He passeth from life to his rest in the grave."

Coming down to the present time—in the seventies of the 20th century—is it not strange that some brilliant

American has not come up with an acceptable explanation why your great nation is presently at the mercy of a small group of Arab nations, greatly inferior in size and military power?

How did this come to be? How did the world's wealthiest and most powerful nation suddenly find itself so dependent on a small number of foreigners? I raise this question in all earnestness—some may say in anger. Why has no American come up with the thought that I may be working My will in this situation, as I did at Watergate?

You may ask "What is My will on this occasion?" Could it possibly be to humble America? You may come back with "Why would America need humbling?" What a question! Lincoln told you more than a century ago why America needs humbling. Your nation needs it more today than when Lincoln admonished the Americans of his day to free themselves from slavery to self.

Your country is in grave danger, not just from lack of oil or other forms of energy, or even from nuclear bombs. Your nation is in danger because you continue to educate your children to count Me out of their regular everyday affairs. You do allocate to Me an hour on each Sunday morning in church worship.

How can people of your intelligence continue to believe that My purpose in creating you was that you might worship Me? And pray to me when you needed things? In your relationship with your own children, do you not desire above all else for them to love you, to have close ties with you? This is what I want from you and all My other children. If, with your love and close ties, you are inspired to awe and worship, this would be most acceptable, particularly if your love and awe and worship were productive of kind deeds for your brother-man. This would truly be the Partnership Life in action.

Is it a problem for you to believe that Christ considered it his mission to tell you of your Partnership with Me—a Partnership that was to embrace every aspect of your life? I can understand it might be a problem for you to believe in miracles. But really, are you, yourself not a miracle? Consider how you came to be—from nothing, nine months before you were born, to a human being with a body and brain—all brought about by My work of creation. Consider how I caused you to grow, bit by bit, from a helpless babe to a mature adult. Consider, too, how I sustain you from moment to moment in many ways, including breathing for you while you sleep, and maintaining the beating of your heart. Are these works not miracles?

And how would you describe what happened before your very eyes, when Gerald Ford became your President, if not a miracle? Was this planned by humans? And what would you call the sudden ascent of the Arab people to a position of affluence and power, if not a miracle of sorts? The Arabs did not put the oil there. They did not even discover by themselves the presence of oil. Was this not My doing? (And now these Arabs stand in the same danger as do all who come into great wealth.)

The question you Americans might ask yourselves is not so much why did I put the oil there for the Arabs —and in such great profusion—by why did I time things in such a way as to cause America both humiliation and grave danger? Could it be that I chose this way to preserve America as the last best hope of earth? I am not posing this incident as a warning. My purpose is not to threaten America, but rather to remind you of Lincoln's plan to save your nation.

Lincoln openly acknowledged that he knew, as My agent and instrument, his mission was to preserve the Union. I guided him to show you the way: to free yourselves from slavery to self. In a sentence of eleven words, Lincoln set out the way: "We must disenthrall ourselves and then we will save our nation." From our conversations together, Lincoln learned that the only way America could be saved and achieve her destiny was for her people to free themselves from slavery to self. This means a change from your present way of life which promotes slavery to self; indeed it exalts self. Your present way of life encourages you to gather things for self. The more things you gather for self— money, power, fame—the more highly successful you are regarded.

This kind of success is a snare and delusion. History has demonstrated this thru the ages. Self cannot for long, remain enthroned as God. Happiness and inner peace come only with liberation from the self. Your great scientist, Albert Finstein, who lived in Partnership with Me, stated this simply:

"The true value of a human being is determined primarily by the measure and the sense in which he has attained *liberation from the self.*"

If you would be a true American, if you sincerely seek to save your nation, you must first seek *"liberation from the self."* With this will come inner peace. Moreover, you will be doing your part in aiding America to fulfill its destiny as "the last best hope of earth."

* * *

What am I that Thou hast chosen me of billions?
And why bless Thou me with Thy presence?
For Thou hast made me Thy Partner, and thus
hast opened the door to Paradise on earth.
No life of quiet desperation need I lead—
Thou offereth me freedom from slavery to self.
I need but follow Thy guidance in all things,
Then peace will I know and love of my brother-man.

* * *

books published by The Partnership Foundation

YOUR PERFECT PARTNERSHIP

YOU ARE GREATER THAN YOU KNOW

books for children:

THE LITTLE ME and THE GREAT ME

MY SECRET POWER

WHY AND HOW I WAS BORN

All financial interest in the above books, including royalties, is consigned to the Partnership Foundation, a non-profit organization, dedicated to furthering the concept of the Partnership of Man and Maker.